SEEING INTO THE FUTURE

SEEING INTO THE FUTURE

A Short History of Prediction

MARTIN VAN CREVELD

REAKTION BOOKS

For Erich and Anneke Vad

Published by Reaktion Books Ltd
Unit 32, Waterside
44–48 Wharf Road
London N1 7UX, UK
www.reaktionbooks.co.uk

First published 2020
Copyright © Martin van Creveld 2020

Printed and bound in India
by Replika Press Pvt. Ltd

A catalogue record for this book is available from the British Library

ISBN 978 1 78914 229 7

CONTENTS

INTRODUCTION

Do you want to make God laugh? Tell him your plans.

WOODY ALLEN

The idea of doing this book was born somewhere in mid-2017. Its parent was *Homo Deus*, the second of three volumes written by my former student, the famous Yuval Noah Harari. As I went along, a single thought kept entering my mind: how can he, as well as many others who have engaged on a similar endeavour, know what the future will bring? How about Ray Kurzweil, Stephen Hawking, H. G. Wells, Jules Verne? And how about Nostradamus, Hildegard of Bingen, the Roman augurs, the Greek Pythia, the Hebrew prophets, the 'Chaldean' astrologers? What were their underlying assumptions, what kind of reasoning did they apply, and what methods did they use? The more I thought about these questions, the more difficult they appeared. If I dared tackle them, then this was precisely because I saw them as a terrific challenge.

The role that the willingness and ability to look into the future plays in human life, both individual and collective, can hardly be exaggerated. Call it anticipation, call it vision, call it foresight, call it forecasting or call it prediction: without it, human life as we know it is utterly impossible. Goals cannot be established, nor efforts towards realizing them launched; nor the consequences of reaching, or not reaching, those goals be considered. Neither can threats and dangers be identified and either met head on or avoided. All this is as true today as it was when we first became human. Presumably it will remain true as long as human we remain. Briefly, but for foresight and the attempt to exercise it, much – perhaps most – of what we understand as thought would be impossible. 'Blind we walk, till the unseen flame has trapped our footsteps,' said the chorus in Sophocles' Antigone.[1]

Some philosophers and scientists go further still. To them, the ability to anticipate the future, meaning something that does not yet exist, and to act accordingly does not belong to us humans alone. Instead they see it as an essential, perhaps *the* essential, characteristic of that mysterious and hard-to-define phenomenon, 'life'.[2] After all, ours is the age of so-called posthumanism. And one key pillar of posthumanism is a renewed emphasis on our evolutionary ancestors and the things we have in common with them; this specifically includes the belief that our brains are nothing more than 'linearly scaled-up' versions of primate ones,[3] which in turn are nothing more than 'linearly scaled-up' versions of vertebrate ones. And so on and on, all the way back to the 'protoplasmal primordial atomic globules' of Gilbert and Sullivan fame. As a result, all sorts of qualities that until recently used to be considered exclusively human are now seen as being shared, at least to some extent, by many other animals as well. So with empathy, so with altruism, so with reason. And so, surprising as it may sound, with morality and what many believe to be morality's origin, religious feeling. Some vague form of the last-named, the greatest living expert on bonobos has been telling us, can be found among those animals.[4]

And as with those qualities, so with foresight. Starting at least as long ago as ancient Greece, all over the world folklore credits various animals with the ability to foresee important events, including the weather, sinking ships, earthquakes and other dangers that may threaten their lives to one extent or another. Scientific opinion on whether such is in fact the case remains divided.[5] However, the ability of some animals, notably squirrels and magpies, to exercise foresight by caching food and retrieving it later on has been well established. Experiments conducted by ichthyologists show that fishes are also able to look into the future. At least, to some extent, under some circumstances and for some purposes. Certain kinds of fishes, somehow aware that the seaside ponds in which they live are about to dry up, leap to nearby ones (how they know about those ponds and how to reach them is another mystery, but one that does not concern us here). Others wait their turn to do this or that, thus presumably showing that they have some idea that such a thing as the future exists and of what it will bring.[6]

Still the question remains. Hats off to Paul the Octopus, who, living in his tank at Oberhausen, Germany, and no doubt looking deep into the future, correctly predicted the outcome of so many football matches. But does it really make sense to attribute foresight to – and put ourselves on the level of – a mollusc, which strictly speaking does not even have a brain? And how about those simplest forms of life, germs and viruses? Do they too have visions concerning the shape of things to come and adjust their behaviour accordingly? Or are they simply blobs of protein that react to the stimuli to which they are subjected, such as heat, pressure, moisture, acidity and the like? True, every single vertebrate animal that has been tested was found to have the ability to link some signals to the events they portend. The animals in question could also foresee the consequences of their own actions a few minutes, or at least seconds, ahead.[7] But an ape that sets out to discover what will happen in the future in the way shamans or prophets, astrologers or futurologists make it their business to do, remains to be seen.

For years now, tens of thousands of scientists around the world have been doing all sorts of things to brains, both human and non-human, in an effort to show that they are 'nothing more' than electrochemical machines. And tens of thousands of computer engineers, coming from the opposite direction, have been trying to build machines that can 'think' as well as, or better than, humans do. Not entirely without success, as the introduction of chess- and Go-playing and trivia quiz-answering programs, as well as other marvels of artificial intelligence, show.

But there seem to be limits. All computers without exception do what they do because their programmers, ere they pressed the button and sat back to enjoy the show, fed them with such and such instructions to follow. They are activated by the instructions that have been fed into them in the past, not by what they expect to happen or want to happen in the future. They have a memory, but they do not have within themselves a vision or an objective they can first adopt and then pursue. They are incapable of seeking or expecting, or anticipating or intending, or looking forward to, anything. They are pushed from behind, not pulled or attracted or drawn from, and towards, the front. In brief, with them it is always the beginning that explains the end; not the end that explains the beginning. All they 'know' is that if x then y must follow. Whatever some authors may say, computers lack the very thing that this book is all about: meaning, foresight and the willingness to exercise it. Nor does it look as if this situation is going to change anytime soon. Building a computer that can do any, let alone all, of these things remains almost unimaginably far beyond our grasp. It is not even clear that, for all the decades-long efforts of the above-mentioned scientists and engineers, we have come one inch closer to doing so. Unless or until an extraterrestrial civilization is discovered, in our ability and willingness to look into the future the way we do we seem to be alone.

Thomas Hobbes, the great seventeenth-century philosopher and political scientist, suggested that our urge to look into the future is rooted in 'perpetual fear'. Fear, that is, 'of death, or poverty, or another calamity'. Of this fear, man, he says, 'has no repose, nor pause of his anxiety, but in sleep'. And often not even then. It 'gnaws' at him daily just as the eagle gnawed at Prometheus' liver, opening his mind to every kind of superstition.[8] For example, statesmen and senior officers must try to foresee, as best they can, whether a war is coming and, if so, when and what it will be like. Stockbrokers would give the moon in return for reliable knowledge as to where the market is going and when it will change direction. Farmers would dearly like to know whether the coming season will be wet or dry (a task, incidentally, that so far has proven too hard for even the most expert meteorologists). Public health officials must try and work out whether, so and so many years hence, there will be more or fewer patients who need hospitalization. And practically all of us – except, perhaps, patients in hospital and prisoners in their cells – would like to know what tomorrow's weather will be like so as to dress and behave accordingly.

For Jean-Jacques Rousseau, foresight was either 'the source of all the wisdom or the wretchedness of mankind'.[9] Right he was, of course. But that is only part of the answer. Our human wish to look into the future goes much deeper than utility alone. It is also, perhaps primarily, a question of satisfying our curiosity for its own sake. Of stretching our necks in order to peer over the wall and see what is on the other side. Of experiencing, as many science-fiction writers have put it, the thrill of being confronted with something new, different and unexpected. Something that will cause our heart to beat faster, our eyes to widen, our lungs to gasp for air, our mouth to fall open, our throat to narrow until we can barely speak, and our legs to feel as if they are melting away. Many of the reactions are somewhat similar to those inspired by hope, love, awe and a few other things. But they are not the same. Looking into the future, in other words, is not just a means. It is that – without some measure of it, we could not exist. But it is also an end in itself. Exercising it, we can attain as much fulfilment and as much joy as by anything else we do in life.

Yet even that may not reach the bottom of the matter. Putting the posthumanist perspective aside for the moment, we may well conclude that the ability to experience the lure of the future is one of the defining characteristics of our species. No less so, say, than morality, or the ability to distinguish good from evil (the Book of

Genesis and the Bible in general). No less so than reverence for one's elders and betters (Confucius). No less so than the capacity for rational thought (Plato and Aristotle); a belief in God (St Augustine); a sense of humour and the ability to laugh (Rabelais); a sense of selfhood, or consciousness, or free will (Descartes); working and producing for a living (Marx and Engels); the ability to create and appreciate beauty (Nietzsche); and the ability to feel guilt, shame and regret (Freud). Which is to say that, by tracing the methods that have been devised in an attempt to understand what the future may bring, we are at the same time looking at man's nature.

In this volume I do not intend to wax philosophical in trying to understand what the future is – an extremely difficult problem that, following centuries and perhaps millennia of thought, has not yet received an adequate answer. Nor, in the main, am I going to examine how good or bad the methods of looking into it are and how they may be improved. Both of these tasks, but the latter in particular, have been attempted a thousand times by a thousand different experts from a thousand different fields. Neither am I going to pile up examples of forecasts that have or have not come true. That too has been done a thousand times, often in ways that were either too complimentary or grossly unfair to the people involved.[10]

Instead, I shall adopt the historical approach. What I hope to do is find out, as far as possible, when, where, why and how some choice methods – choice they will have to be, for their total number must run into the thousands, perhaps more – originated. To this are added the principles and beliefs in which they were grounded; the ways in which they related to others of their kind; why the obstacles standing in their path are as formidable as they are; and whether our ability to look into the future has improved over the centuries. As much to satisfy my curiosity as to round off the study, I have included a section on what the world might have looked like if the methods in question had succeeded in doing what they were meant to do: namely, achieve certainty and abolish its opposite, uncertainty, once and for all.

Above all, I hope to draw readers' attention to methods of looking into the future other than, and different from, the ones most of us are familiar with and tend to take for granted. And thus to provide them with a kind of perspective, and perhaps a corrective, that can be attained only with the aid of a 'deep' comparison; such as very few people seem to have and even fewer, if any, have tried to provide them with.

Before getting to grips with the topic at hand, two very important reservations need to be made. First, in what follows I do not intend to discuss the kind of future that is so close at hand and so firmly rooted in the laws of physics that, unless a miracle takes place, it is perfectly certain to come about. Long before the true nature of fire was understood, no one doubted that, if we put our hand into it, we shall get burnt. Long before Newton discovered gravity, it was known that, if we leapt from a roof, we would fall to the ground. If we stood in the way of a cannonball that was speeding in our direction, we would be hit; and if we saw lightning, chances are that thunder would not take very long to follow. To look into this kind of future, no particular way of thought, no particular method, is required – just a little experience of the sort anyone who is over a few years old must have if he or she is to survive the next 24 hours.

Second, my intention is to examine the reasoning behind some of the principal methods that, throughout history, have been used for looking into the future. Not the ways in which those who used them sought to cheat their audiences in an effort to convince them that the methods in question, and they themselves, were genuine. And not the ways in which some clients, to obtain the predictions they wanted or needed, sought to influence or control the predictors. In other words, there is no attempt to discuss, let alone expose, fraudsters and fraud on one hand and the difficulty of telling truth to power on the other.

I do not mean to say that those problems did not exist. God knows they did and do so still. Starting at least as far back as the Egyptian Middle Kingdom, which began around 2050 BCE, many prophecies were first dusted and then backdated by hundreds of years. Next, efforts were made to tailor them to prevailing circumstances so as to give them the ring of authenticity.[11] Much later, the same fate overtook many of the books of the Old Testament, including that of Isaiah – whose chronology is so dubious that modern scholars decided to attribute it to two or even three different prophets who lived at different times – Daniel, and several of the rest. One of the most intriguing cases is that of Deuteronomy (Deuteronomy 18:22). Not only was the date in which it was written pushed back by several centuries, but it explicitly raises the question of how to distinguish 'genuine' prophets from 'false' ones.

Partly no doubt to prevent fraud, King Sennacherib of Assyria, who reigned from 705 to 681 BCE, advised his heir Esarhaddon to divide his astrologers into 'three or four' groups. By preventing them from communicating with each other, he said, you can always obtain the results you are seeking.[12] Later, one of Esarhaddon's own officials sent him a letter, reminding the king that an approaching lunar eclipse meant that a flood was coming. Whereupon he suggested that he, the official, would 'cut through a dike, here in Babylonia, in the middle of the night [so that] no one will know about it'![13] Countless others have used similar tricks and are still doing so day by day. As these examples show, there are times when the future is deemed too important to be left to futurologists, causing the latter to be kept on a tight leash or perhaps even silenced. At others it is prophets and forecasters of every kind who try to persuade their employers and clients to trust them. Either way, it is a question of some people leading others by the nose.

As Ptolemy in his defence of astrology says, though, the same difficulties surround any other field of human endeavour.[14] As long as the world has existed, there have always been con men and con women. Relying on the most outrageous premises, they promise their followers every kind of benefit, starting with instant wealth and leading through good health towards the supreme goal, salvation. Surely, though, that does not mean we cannot or should not investigate the history of medicine, e(con)omics or theology. The fact that, early in the nineteenth century, the famous 'Turk' misled many people into believing that he was a machine able to play chess does not mean that tracing the history of artificial intelligence is not a worthwhile enterprise. And the fact that, at the turn of the twentieth century, a German-bred horse named Clever Hans was discovered to get his answers to arithmetical questions from cues his owner (unintentionally, it should be said) provided him with does not mean that we should now stop trying to understand how horses think.[15]

Furthermore, fraudulent practices are deliberately tailored to fit people's beliefs. For that very reason, such practices may very well shed light on those beliefs. More so, in some cases, than genuine ones. That is why, in researching this volume, I have devoted little effort to separate the two kinds. To think about our wish to look into the future, the methods we have devised for doing so, and the way those methods relate both to each other and to civilization at large is to enter into the very essence of our humanity. It is this fact that endows the present volume with any importance it may have.

PART I:
A MYSTERIOUS
JOURNEY

1

A VILLAIN OF A MAGICIAN

I t hardly requires saying that shamanism, the 'method' for looking into the future that is the topic of the present chapter, is derived from the term 'shaman'. Originating in the Tungus language of Siberia, *samân* means 'a person who is excited, moved, or raised'. One modern author has related it to an ancient Indian word meaning 'to heal oneself'. It may also be linked to the Sanskrit word *saman*, 'song'.[1]

The first Westerners who incorporated the idea into their vocabulary and tried to explain what shamanism was were explorers who visited Siberia during the last decades of the seventeenth century and the first of the eighteenth. Some of them, notably the German physician Daniel Messerschmidt, worked for Peter the Great and his successors. Messerschmidt and others were charged with describing the geography and ethnography of the barely known regions in question and bringing back information concerning any useful and rare things they might contain. Other early explorers were missionaries or prisoners of war.

The way Westerners understood shamanism has changed over time. Five main stages can be distinguished. Prior to the emergence of secularization from about 1700 on, Siberian shamans and their colleagues in other parts of the world were often regarded as emissaries of the Devil, dangerous both to themselves and to others – 'a villain of a magician who calls demons,' as Avvakum Petrovich, the Russian priest who was the first to use the term publicly, wrote.[2] Some even went so far as to join 'shaman' to 'Satan'.

Enlightenment travellers and the scholars who, back home, drew on their accounts took the opposite view. Convinced that they had reason on their side, they saw shamans not as the Devil's creatures who were up to anything outlandish and sinister but simply as preposterous impostors. That accounts for the terms under which they were known in various languages: *giocolare* in Italian, *jongleur* in French, *Gaukler* in German and 'wizard' in English. Catherine the Great, no less, went to the trouble of penning a comedy in which she took this point of view. By doing so, she wrote, she had delivered 'a huge blow' against superstition. At the same time she reinforced her right to expand her enlightened rule into the vast, but unknown and backwards territories to the east.[3] Some even proposed that shamans be punished for making false claims.

But that was just the beginning. Nineteenth-century colonial administrators and anthropologists took shamanism for the product of minds 'half devil and half child', as Rudyard Kipling put it. They considered such practices 'repugnant' to humanity and common sense and did their best to suppress them. The rest they regarded with amused tolerance and, on occasion, tried to take advantage of as one of the ways to control the gullible natives, as they saw them. Next, around the turn of the century there emerged a growing tendency to look at shamans from the inside, so to speak. The objective was to bridge the cultural gap so as to understand the way they reasoned and the role they played in their societies.

The advent, from about 1970 on, of multiculturalism, diversity and 'New Age' ideas caused this tendency to gain momentum. More and more often, shamans, instead of being described as relics, good or bad, of a bygone age, came to be admiringly cast as sages, healers, teachers, leaders and even artists, all rolled into one. Such as were closer to 'nature', and therefore more authentic and more righteous, than Westerners with their science and technology had been for a long, long time past. And such as were deeply familiar with the social and psychological needs of those who believed in them and took their advice, which encompassed every detail of the world in which they lived: the weather and the climate, animals, plants, food and medical herbs, poisons and minerals of every sort. Their practices, far from being rooted in mere superstition, foreshadowed many modern medical and, even more so, psychological ideas. As such they were worth studying in depth and, when the occasion presented itself, adapting to modern life.[4]

The classic account of shamanism was written in 1951 by the Romanian cultural historian Mircea Eliade. He defined it as 'a technique of religious ecstasy'.[5] Considered in this broader sense, shamanism was not confined to the region in which the term originated, that is, northeast Asia (Siberia, China and Korea). Instead it is, or was, widespread all over the world. That is especially true of societies made up of hunter-gatherers, horti-culturalists and pastoralists – tribes without rulers, as I have called them in another book,[6] of which there are still a few left in remote and undeveloped areas such as the Upper Amazon. In Latin America it is known as 'mestizo shamanism'.[7]

But shamanism has also been imported into modern cities, especially developing ones in Latin America and South, East and West Africa, where many people remain relatively ill-educated and have been torn out of their native environments and left without a clear social network to provide direction or assistance. Some have large numbers of followers, and some allow them-selves to be rewarded accordingly. Some of those practitioners are ignorant of any link between themselves and the customs of earlier societies. Probably many more are aware of such links, however. They deliberately and explicitly make use of them so as to produce what is often a rather strange mixture of animist, Christian and even Jewish elements.

Shamanism being a spiritual practice first and foremost, it tends to leave few material traces behind. Nevertheless, some modern archaeologists claim they have been able to track it back all the way to the Palaeolithic, some 30,000 years ago.[8] True or not, certainly it far antedates the rise of organized religion, with its hierarchy of priests and followers. No known society, not even one as simple and lacking in institutions as that of Andamanese islanders in the Indian Ocean, is without it.[9] There is also some reason to believe that it is the oldest form of government, or perhaps one should speak of proto-government, on Earth.

The ability to communicate with spirits might be a gift made by the spirits themselves. But undoubtedly it also conferred some real benefits on those who had it or were believed to have it. The details varied from one society to the next; generally, though, shamans credited themselves, and were credited by others, with the ability to control the weather, cast and counter spells, cure the sick (or, to the contrary, cause illness in people and cattle) and other similar feats. Coming on top of the ability to look into the future, such feats could readily be translated into economic and political power.

Most shamans appear to have been men. However, in many societies there were also women among them. Remote rural areas in pre-Revolutionary Russia were familiar with the figure of the *klikusha*, plural *klikushi*, 'shrieking woman'. Modern feminists claim that it was male oppression that caused them to go off the rails and display all kinds of symptoms akin to madness. Traditionally, though, they were understood as being possessed by the spirits and credited with some ability to predict the future.[10]

In some of the simplest, least structured and most egalitarian societies, notably those of the Amazonian forest, shamans were self-selected. The implication was that anyone could find a way to communicate with the spirits, acquire powers and, if he or she was able to gather followers or believers, gain recognition as a shaman. On occasion this was taken to the point where anyone who had a dream was said to have a little bit of the shamanic spirit in them, specifically including the ability to look into the future.[11] In other societies the quality ran in families. In others still, shamans selected their own successors more or less as they pleased.

To become a shaman, it was almost always necessary to undergo a prolonged and complex period of training during which the novice absorbed the relevant myths and learnt the necessary incantations. In some societies the process was punctuated by tests requiring him or her to, for example, spend some time living in complete darkness or suffering pain and hunger. The climax was an initiation ceremony during which they discovered their personal guiding spirit and concluded the alliance with it that would govern their lives from that point. Normally, to be chosen was considered an honour, and the apprenticeship was willingly entered upon. But there were also occasions when youngsters became shamans against their will, either because the spirits commanded them to or because they had been summoned by their elders. Appearing in public, both apprentices and fully fledged shamans often carried special insignia and wore special clothing, amulets and other signifying items. There might, however, also be ceremonial occasions when they wore nothing at all.

Considered as a method for cracking open the future and providing guidance as to what it might bring, shamanism rested on the assumption, spoken or tacit, that doing so is very difficult and requires special qualities as well as expertise. That is why it could be accomplished only by extraordinary people acting under extraordinary influences and possessed of extraordinary powers that clearly distinguished them from the rest. And this only with the aid of the spirits that inhabit every tree, waterfall, rock and peak; invisible they may be, but there is no doubting their ubiquity, potency and ability to influence fate.

Contacting the spirits implied leaving the 'normal' world so as to enter into what is commonly known as an altered state of consciousness. An ASC may be defined as 'any mental state . . . which can be recognized subjectively by the individual himself (or by an objective observer of the individual) as representing a sufficient deviation in subjective experience of psychological functioning from certain general norms for that individual during alert, waking consciousness'.[12] Well-known examples are intoxication, ecstasy, trance, hypnosis, and epilepsy or similar conditions. Some students of the various forms of human mental life include dreaming in the list, as I myself have done in the present volume. What all forms of ASC have in common is that they seem to turn those who are caught up in them into different persons. Also, that they temporarily decrease the relevant person's awareness of his or her surroundings. Simultaneously they enhance their ability to perceive a variety of other things, or so it is believed.

As far as available information, both that provided by shamans themselves and that which originates in those who observed them, allows, all of these conditions bear certain similarities to a shaman's mental state. But none is exactly identical with it. Recently there has been an explosion of interest in using MRI tests in order to see whether shamanic rituals and ASC in general can alter the pattern of electric activity inside the brain that is supposed to constitute thought, and if so, in what ways. By using such methods, one team found that the areas of the brain whose activity departed most from 'normal' during ASC were the posterior cingulate cortex (PCC), the dorsal anterior cingulate cortex (DACC) and the insula.[13] Not that these facts, even if they can be verified, tell us much about the subjective experience in question.

The methods used to make the switch to an ASC varied from one culture to another.[14] In Siberia they included spending time in a steam room, from which the shaman, his blood pressure having gone up, would emerge in a state of high excitement and covered with sweat. Everywhere, one of the most common means was music, especially singing, rattling and sustained drumming, which were and often still are capable of having a hypnotic effect. Either the shaman himself played, or the music was sounded for him by others. Other methods were dancing, prayer, solitude, long vigils, fasting, vomiting (by way of purification), self-flagellation, and breathing exercises designed either to accelerate the metabolism or to slow it down. Sexual abstinence (or, less often, its opposite, engaging in sacred sex) and consuming strong alcoholic drinks were also used. All or parts of the ceremony might be carried out in full view of others. In some cultures, though, the relevant rituals were performed indoors and in the dark.

As part of the transition from one state of mind to another some shamans used special canes that were believed to have magic qualities and with which they tapped the ground. Others stripped naked, though whether doing so was a method for entering an ASC or one of the latter's effects is not always easy to say. Finally, there was the consumption of certain substances supposed to be associated with the spirits. Some scholars believe that the use of such substances stood at the origin of religion, and at least one has tried to show that Jesus himself was a shaman and that he and his followers consumed hallucinogenic mushrooms in order to transcend the limits of the here and the now.[15] In fact the use of hallucinogens by shamans and their followers had been documented in many places around the world. In some cultures the relevant ceremonies also comprised the bloody sacrifice of an animal, such as a sheep or a goat.

In each of these cases, the objective was to make the shaman, or rather his soul (since his body remained in place), abandon its normal surroundings and embark on a mysterious voyage. As a rule, the first thing the shaman had to do was to get past some kind of obstacle. This might be a high mountain pass, or a dark forest inhabited by all kinds of wild beasts, or an ice-cold stream. Often, doing so was not without some risk. Those who took a wrong turn might forget whence they had come, as, in Greek mythology, those who had drunk from the underworld river Lethe also did. Or else they might go mad, or even die.

Often, too, the exact nature of the experience was hard to put into words or convey to others in a way they could understand.

The crossing having been accomplished, the shaman would enter into a different domain, realm or reality – one in which, among other things, the difference between present, past and future is eliminated, turning the last-named into an open book. The domains themselves varied from one culture to another. For Plato, whose theories bear more traces of shamanism than most people realize, they were the place where souls, in between one incarnation and another, could see past, present and future.[16] Among the Inuit of the Yukon Territory it was the 'White Country', a mysterious place where anything was possible. Whether it got its name from the 'fact' that everything there was white or, later, from the indigenous people's belief in the miraculous powers of the white man, it is no longer possible to determine.[17] Among the Aboriginal Australians it was Dreamtime, understood as the place from which came the laws of existence. And in some other societies it was simply the place where the spirits dwelled.

Some of the spirits in question inhabited and represented certain geographical features – as, in Nepal, 'the master spirit of the forest' or 'the spirit of the crossroads' did.[18] Some appeared to speak to the shaman, who listened to them and did as they told him. In other places they entered him and spoke through his mouth or body; ventriloquism, it turns out, has always been a useful technique for prophets, real and fake, to master.

Queries concerning the future that were submitted to shamans tended to be concrete and closely related to day-to-day life; rarely was there any attempt to look far into the future or envisage a world radically different from the present one. Will I (or a member of my family or my livestock) fall ill? Will I die? Will I recover? Will I have children? Will this or that enterprise on which I am about to embark bear the intended fruit? To the question 'how do you know?', the shaman could reply, 'I, or my soul, have been there.' Meaning, the place, which is not really a place, where the answers to such questions became visible. To prove their claims, some shamans allowed their bodies to be pierced with sharp instruments, which were then withdrawn without any evident feeling of pain.

An important variant on this theme is presented by the seer Tiresias in ancient Greek myth. In his case, the mysterious country was neither geographically remote nor located in heaven, but that which is inhabited by the members of the opposite sex. Born a man, by some versions of the myth Tiresias underwent no fewer than six sex changes. In the process he gained the kind of foresight not available to ordinary mortals.[19] To enhance his powers further still, he was blind; just how he lost his sight was much disputed. Some claimed he had been punished by Athena (some sources say Artemis) for having seen her naked. Another story had it that he had seen two copulating snakes and beat them with a stick, incurring the wrath of Zeus' wife Hera. Yet another story had it that the punishment was due to his discovery that women enjoyed sex much more than men did.

The story of Tiresias continues to be popular both in literature and in film. The Greeks were well aware that people who are deprived of one of their senses sometimes respond by developing, even overdeveloping, the remaining ones.[20] It was precisely Tiresias' blindness that enabled him to mediate between this world and the underworld, humankind and the gods, male and female, past – for the past, too, was often considered a mystery – present and future. So great were his prophetic powers that people used to compare them to those of Apollo, whose priest he was.[21] By one tradition, set out in Sophocles' *Oedipus Rex*, it was Tiresias who predicted, quite correctly as it turned out, that Oedipus would slay his father and marry his mother. Oedipus' own subsequent fate, as presented by Sophocles in another play, *Oedipus at Kolonos*, is also significant. At the opening of the first scene the audience is confronted with a helpless, blind old man. To atone for his sins, he has just put out his own eyes. But soon it becomes plain that this man has greater insight than other mortals – so much so that, with a final, paradoxical turn of the screw, Sophocles has Oedipus lead his companions instead of being led by them.

The list of mythological blind seers does not end here.[22] Phormion, a fisherman from Erythrai in Asia Minor, lost his eyesight but was given the ability to dream prophetic dreams in return. Ophioneus, a Messenian seer, was blind from birth, regained his sight, but subsequently lost it again. Euenios of Apollonia on the Adriatic fell asleep while keeping watch over some sacred sheep. Wolves killed many of the animals, and the angry citizens of Apollonia condemned the unfortunate watchman to be blinded. But then infertility came upon the land. Having consulted oracles, the people realized that they had done wrong: the gods themselves had sent the wolves. The outcome was that the gods compensated Euenios by endowing him with the gift of prophecy. Polymestor, a dramatis personae in Euripides' play *Hecuba*, acquired prophetic powers after being assaulted and blinded by the captive Trojan women. Blind, he predicted that both King Agamemnon and his captive, Cassandra, would die at the hand of Queen Clytemnestra, as in fact they did.[23] All of these are mythological figures, not real ones. What they have in common, however, is that in their cases, being enveloped in outer darkness causes some kind of light to be kindled inside their souls. Now insight comes as a reward, now as a punishment. Either way it enables them to see things more clearly, and look ahead further, than ordinary people could.

Nor are blind shamans by any means limited either to antiquity or to mythology. In Japan, blind female seers known as *itako* were very much part of a traditional culture that goes back many centuries. Novices had to undergo a rigorous training course that could last as long as three years. It involved, among other things, hundreds of buckets of ice-cold water being poured on the body of a trainee over a few days. Later the entry into a different world was facilitated by strumming a *koto*, or zither. *Itako* continued to flourish until the second half of the nineteenth century, when the government, determined to modernize the country along Western lines, prohibited them and even had them arrested on sight as cheats. Not always with complete success, it appears, since a small number of *itako* – there are said to be just twenty of them, all over forty years old – may still be found practising their art. Controls having been relaxed after 1945, annual meetings are held at Mount Osore, a wild, remote volcanic area in northern Japan. There, believers gather to ask the *itako* to contact the spirits, or *kami*, so as to obtain their blessing as well as insight into the future.[24]

In Korea, too, *chambongs*, or blind male shamans, remain active to the present day. For some of them their lack of sight is congenital; for others, though, it is by their own will.[25] Demand for their services, one author says, originated in 'the popular concern with the uncertainty of the future. Having suffered from wave upon wave of foreign invasions, natural disasters, and contagious diseases, Koreans were naturally conditioned to be reflexly [*sic*] sensitive to things yet to come.'[26] Some of the rites in question have received the Korean government's official recognition as 'cultural treasures', to be fostered and preserved. And then there was the blind Bulgarian female seer Baba Vanga (1911–1996), who was said to have predicted the rise of IS, the events of 9/11 and the 2011 Fukushima disaster.[27] By her own testimony she lost her sight at an early age when a 'tornado' lifted her into the air, dropped her and filled her eyes with dust. Another place where the idea of the blind seer is often found is fantasy games of the kind many teenagers and some adults like to play. One source lists no fewer than seventy games in which such figures appear,[28] credited with being able to see not only spirits but 'subspace and hyperspace' as well.

Finally, it is important to emphasize that looking into the future and finding out what it may bring is but one of several functions that shamans, ancient and modern, real and fictional, have exercised. The details vary from one society to the next and even among individual shamans in the same society. The principal functions in question are casting spells and protecting against them. Others are divinatory justice – that is, finding out who is to blame for certain misfortunes, such as accidents, illnesses or deaths – and, above all, healing. In fact, success in healing the sick is often seen both as an outcome of shamanic powers and as proof that the person in question does in fact have such powers. What all these abilities have in common is that they were perceived as being beyond those vouchsafed to ordinary men and women. This is why, in dealing with them, they called for somewhat similar methods.

2

IN THE NAME OF THE LORD

Shamanism is hardly the only method in which ASC has been, and very often still is, enlisted in the cause of trying to look into the future. Another is prophecy. A line between shamanism and prophecy is hard to draw. In many ways, prophecy of the kind many of us are familiar with from the Old Testament in particular is little but a form of shamanism that has gained the approval of a monotheistic religion. And the other way around.

The modern English word 'prophet' comes from the Greek *prophetes*, meaning a person, male or female, who, granted divine inspiration, 'speaks before' (*pro*, before, and *phētēs*, speaker). What distinguished prophets was that they believed themselves, and were believed by others, to have the ability, among other things, to look into the future and see what it would bring. Like shamans, to do so they sometimes went on voyages to mysterious places or countries where all kinds of strange things could be seen and experienced. The Old Testament in particular tells us of many such episodes. 'The spirit of the Lord shall carry thee [Elijah] whither I know not' (1 Kings 18:12). 'A spirit lifted me up, and took me away' (Ezekiel 3:14). 'The spirit lifted me up between the earth and the heaven' (Ezekiel 8:3). Like shamans, they moved from an ordinary existence into an extraordinary one where the normal rules of life and nature did not apply.

So great was the change that it was easily mistaken for illness or madness.[1] Often it was both dangerous and painful: 'My bowels, my bowels!' Jeremiah called out. 'I am pained at my very heart; my heart maketh a noise in me; I cannot hold my peace' (Jeremiah

4:19). And again: 'Mine heart within me is broken because of the prophets; all my bones shake; I am like a drunken man whom wine has overcome, because of the Lord, and because of the words of his holiness' (23:9).[2] Deutero-Isaiah put it as follows: 'For a long time I have held my peace; I have kept still and restrained myself. Now I will cry out like a woman in labour; I will gasp and pant' (Isaiah 42:14).

The similarities may even extend to details. Delivering his prophecies, the first Isaiah stripped naked. Seeking to prove their links with the deities, many prophets engaged in healing and/or performed supernatural feats of endurance, as Elijah in particular did. The main difference was that, unlike shamans, they not only lived in literate societies but were often literate themselves. (Or else we would know next to nothing about what is, after all, the most interesting thing about them: the contents of their prophecies.) Indeed it has been claimed that the Hebrew (and Arabic) term for prophet, *nabi*, is derived from the Akkadian root *naba*, 'to read'.[3] Some prophets wrote down their own prophecies.[4]

Like shamans, the Israelite prophets owed their prophetic powers to the divine spirit (*ruach*, which depending on the context can also mean breath, or wind) that had entered and taken possession of them, not seldom to the accompaniment of musical instruments, as in the case of Elisha (2 Kings 3:15). A perfect description of the way a prophet was made is found in Deuteronomy 18:15–20:

> [Having reached the Land of Canaan] the Lord thy God will raise up unto thee a prophet from the midst of thee, of thy brethren, like unto Me; unto him ye shall hearken; according to all that thou desiredst of the Lord thy God in Horeb in the day of the assembly, saying, 'Let me not hear again the voice of the Lord by God, neither let me see this great fire any more, that I die not.' [Therefore] I will raise them up a prophet from among their own

brethren, like unto thee, and will put My words in his mouth; and he shall speak unto them all that I shall command him. And it shall come to pass, that whosoever will not hearken unto My words which he shall speak in my name, I will require it of him.

And the text goes on:

And if you say in thine heart, 'How shall we know the word which the Lord hath not spoken?' When a prophet speaks in the name of the Lord, if the thing follow not, nor come to pass, that is the thing which the Lord hath not spoken, but the prophet hath spoken it presumptuously: thou shalt not be afraid of him. (18:20–22)

Evidently, for a prophet to establish his or, on occasion, her credentials and be accepted as such was not always easy. Often, to do so he had to perform miracles. Ere his own people accepted him and listened to the message he brought, Moses had to 1) change a walking staff into a snake; 2) turn a hand from healthy to leprous, and back to healthy again; and 3) turn water into blood (Exodus 4:1–9). Said the widow after Elijah had revived her dead son: 'Now I know that you are a man of God and that the word of the Lord in your mouth is truth' (1 Kings 17:24).

Another method to achieve the same objective was to combat other prophets. Elijah first humiliated and then slaughtered no fewer than 450 prophets of the Canaanite god Baal, at Mount Carmel. King Ahab of Israel at one point had to choose between Zedekiah, who along with other prophets promised victory in a war against Aram, and Micaiah, the born pessimist who foresaw defeat and told Ahab that 'If you ever return safely, the Lord has not spoken through me' (1 Kings 22:28) (which was what happened). Somewhat later, Jeremiah engaged the prophet Hananiah in a public yoke-breaking match to see which one of them was

God's real appointee (Jeremiah 28:10). For as long as there were prophets claiming to speak in the name of the Lord, the problem of distinguishing 'real' from 'false' ones persisted. It does so still.

The prophet's place in society developed over time. The earliest ones, Moses and Samuel, doubled as powerful political leaders in their own right. The former, retaining his authority until the end, was later transformed into the most important prophet in the whole of Israelite/Jewish history; the one who, in other cultures, would have been called *pater patriae*. The latter at one point was compelled, much against his will, to anoint Saul as king over Israel. Even so he retained much of his authority, engaging in a bitter conflict with his former protégé, breaking with him and finally appointing David in his place (1 Samuel 9:16).

Once kings and kingship had become firmly established under David, prophets became much more widespread than they had been. On the other hand, they lost most if not all of the secular power they had once held. Some entered the royal service and became, in effect, court functionaries. Such a one was Nathan, who advised David on whether or not to erect a temple for the Lord and later played a key role in the succession of King Solomon.[5] Another was Gad, who several times advised David on how to expiate several of his sins (1 Samuel 22:5). Two others were Ahijah and Jehu ben Hanani. Following Solomon's death and the division of his realm in two, they worked for the kings of Israel, Jeroboam and Baasha, respectively.[6]

Others still, including all the better-known ones fortunate enough to have biblical books named after them, tended to drift into the opposition. Without exception, these men were trouble to themselves and troublesome to others. Had they lived today, no doubt some of them would have been assigned to psychiatric care. Not infrequently did they put on strange performances, as, for example, when Elisha had two bears tear apart 42 children who had dared comment on his bald head (2 Kings 2:23–4). Or when Hosea, to illustrate what he saw as the current relationship between the Lord and the people of Israel, married an unfaithful woman, Gomer, daughter of Diblaim, and went on to have children with her (Hosea 1:2).

Each in his own way, almost all denounced current practices as wicked in the eyes of the Lord and promised divine retribution to come. Not surprisingly, doing so could be a dangerous business, as Elijah, who had a death sentence passed over him by Queen Jezebel (1 Kings 19:1-2), as well as Micaiah and Jeremiah, both of whom spent time in prison (1 Kings 22:27); Jeremiah 37:15–16), found out. One prophet, Uriah (meaning 'light of God', and not the same as Uriah, Bathsheba's hapless husband) was actually executed. His body was 'cast into the grave of the common people' (Jeremiah 26:23). No wonder some prophets took up the role against their will, as Jonah famously did. Moses, early in his career, asked the Lord to find someone else to carry the burden, and Jeremiah cursed the moment He had chosen him to deliver His words, causing him to quarrel with everyone around. He, Jeremiah, had even tried to shut up, he says. But the Lord's words were stronger than he was, and he did not succeed (Exodus 4:3–7; Jeremiah 20:9).

Needless to say, the biblical prophets whose names are known formed only a small fraction of those who tried their hand at the practice. Among the anonymous ones, many did not act on their own but lived in bands. One such band was the one that Saul, the future king, joined at one point in his life.

> When he [Saul] had turned his back to go from Samuel, God gave him another heart . . . and when they [Saul and his servant] came thither to the hill, behold, a company of prophets met him; and the Spirit of God came upon him, and he prophesized among them. And it came to pass, when all that knew him beforetime saw that, behold he prophesized among the prophets, then the people said

one to another: What is this that is come unto the son of Kish? Is Saul also among the prophets? And one of the same place answered and said, 'But who is their father?' Therefore it became a proverb, Is Saul also among the prophets? And when he had made an end of prophesying, he came to the high place.' (1 Samuel 10:9–13)

Another band was the one formed by the above-mentioned prophets of Baal whom Elijah killed at Mount Carmel. They are also mentioned at other places in the Bible, which presents them as fanatics, drunk with religion. That apart, very little is known about their way of life. No specific predictions are associated with any of them, which is why they will not be considered further.

As one might expect, prophets often tailored their utterances to the immediate circumstances. Either they informed people of coming events or they warned them of what was to come. Many of their pronouncements were triggered by political or military crises. Go to Bethlehem, the Lord commanded Samuel, and you shall find the man whom I have chosen to be King of Israel (1 Samuel 16:1). You have sinned by taking Bathsheba for your wife and having her husband killed, the prophet Nathan told King David, and so the Lord is going to punish you by stirring up a rebellion against you and by killing the son you had with her (2 Kings 1:7–14). Jerusalem will not fall to the Assyrians, who were besieging it, Isaiah told the people of Judah; whereupon an angel of the Lord went out and did away with 185,000 Assyrian soldiers in a single night (2 Kings 19:35–6). There are many such examples. Some, like Ahab's war against Aram and the siege of Jerusalem, can be related to real events for which there is evidence in other sources. There is no point in listing them all.

Many of the most important prophecies were conditional. Not in the sense that the Jewish God tried to extort all kinds of material gifts in return for His support, as was the case in Mesopotamia and elsewhere, but in that He demanded moral and religious reform. Unless the people repented of their sins, worshipped Yahweh and paid heed to his laws, such and such a disaster would overtake them and their rulers. Said Hosea (8:1–9), whose often ferocious predictions date to the middle of the eighth century BCE:

> [The king of Assyria] shall come as an eagle against the house of the Lord, because they have transgressed my covenant, and trespassed against my law. Israel shall cry unto me, My God, we know thee. Israel hath cast off the thing that is good: the enemy shall pursue him. They have set up kings, but not by me: they have made princes, and I knew it not: of their silver and their gold have they made them idols, that they may be cut off. Thy calf, O Samaria, hath cast thee off; mine anger is kindled against them: how long will it be ere they attain to innocency? For from Israel was it also: the workman made it; therefore it is not God: but the calf of Samaria shall be broken in pieces.
>
> For they have sown the wind, and they shall reap the whirlwind: it hath no stalk: the bud shall yield no meal: if so be it yield, the strangers shall swallow it up. Israel is swallowed up: now shall they be among the Gentiles as a vessel wherein is no pleasure. For they are gone up to Assyria, a wild ass alone by himself.

And Jeremiah (15:5–9):

> For who shall have pity upon thee, O Jerusalem? Or who shall bemoan thee? Or who shall go aside to ask how thou doest?
>
> Thou hast forsaken me, saith the Lord, thou art gone backward: therefore will I stretch out my hand against thee, and destroy thee; I am weary with repenting. And I will fan them with a fan in the gates of the land; I

will bereave them of children, I will destroy my people since they return not from their ways. Their widows are increased to me above the sand of the seas: I have brought upon them against the mother of the young men a spoiler at noonday: I have caused him to fall upon it suddenly, and terrors upon the city. She that hath borne seven languisheth: she hath given up the ghost; her sun is gone down while it was yet day: she hath been ashamed and confounded: and the residue of them will I deliver to the sword before their enemies, saith the Lord.

For all that the language is poetic, this kind of prophecy refers to natural events of the kind that have taken place throughout history and could very well take place again. Some prophecies were specific in mentioning the king or the people – first the Assyrians, later the Babylonians – whom God would send to accomplish his will and inflict the disaster he had in mind. True, neither Hosea nor Jeremiah said when precisely the disasters they predicted would take place. In a year, perhaps, or in five, or in 25? However, their words, like those of most prophets, carried a sense of urgency. Clearly, time was not unlimited.

The disaster would not last for ever. Better times were coming. Often, however, it was far from clear whether they would do so in the real world in which all of us live. Or did the prophecy refer to the End of Days, a Jewish idea about which we shall have more to say later on? For example, was the destruction of Babylon, as prophesized in the Book of Daniel, meant as a real event that would take place in historical times to come? Or was it an apocalyptic one? In favour of the first interpretation is the fact that, for once, a date *is* mentioned – the end of the Babylonian captivity was to come after seventy years (Daniel 9:1–2). In the eyes of many modern scholars this is proof that it was actually written after the event to which it refers had taken place. Be this as it may, many other Hebrew prophets clearly had the End of

Days in mind. They portrayed it less as a time to come than as a time when time, and with it the future, would come to an end. At the End of Days peace, plenty and, above all, righteousness would prevail; the Davidic dynasty would be restored and the people of Israel, coming back from exile, united. Both Jews and gentiles would finally recognize that the Lord is the Lord one and indivisible, gather together in Zion, and serve Him as he should be.[7]

Many neighbouring peoples were also familiar with ecstatic prophets, including such as long antedated the known Hebrew ones. Most were male, but some were female, as the Israelites Miriam and Deborah also were. All claimed to speak in the name of the Mesopotamian deities Dagan (the biblical Dagon) and Annunitum.[8] They and their prophecies are known to us from letters inscribed on clay tablets found in the lands north and east of Palestine. Excavations at Mari, an ancient city on the Euphrates in today's Syria, have brought to light thousands of texts, some of them accompanied by a lock of hair or a piece of cloth from the author's garment for purposes of identification. Most are of an administrative and judicial nature. By present count, though, 27 are clearly concerned with the future and seek to tell the addressee about the things it might bring, such as revolts, assassinations, injunctions against going on certain campaigns or entering into certain alliances, and the like. Some are accompanied by warnings concerning the consequences that might follow if their instructions are not acted upon.

One such letter was sent to Zimri-Lim, King of Mari, shortly before 1757 BCE. It reads as follows:

> Am I not Adad the lord of Kalassu who reared him between my thighs and restored him to the throne of his father's house? . . . Now since I restored him to the throne of his father's house, I should receive from him a hereditary property [for a temple]. If he does not give it,

I am the lord of the throne, territory and city; and what I gave I will take away. If on the other hand he grants my request, I will give him throne upon throne, house upon house, territory upon territory; even the land from east to west I will give him.

And another:

> Thus (says) the *apilum* [lit. 'the answerer (of questions)'] of Shamash [the sun god]. Thus says Shamash, lord of the country: 'Please send immediately to me in Sippar, in order that prosperity continue [lit. 'for life'], the throne intended for my splendid residence, as well as your daughter whom I already have requested of you . . . as concerns Hammurabi, king of Kurda, he has spoken criminally against you. But when he attacks, you will be victorious; thereafter you are to relieve the land of its indebtedness. I grant you the whole land. When you take the city, you are to declare amnesty from debts.[9]

In the event the prophecy proved false, for it was Hammurabi who defeated and presumably executed Zimri-Lim; not the other way around.

Under subsequent rulers of the Mesopotamian lands, including the above-mentioned Sennacherib and Esarhaddon, the tradition continued. In 670 BCE the latter received a letter addressed to him by one of his officials. It reported, perhaps verbatim, a prophecy of a slave girl from Harran, a city in present-day Turkey, far from the Assyrian capital of Nineveh. At the time it was well known for the veracity of the prophecies that issued from it. One such had predicted that Esarhaddon's forthcoming campaign in Egypt would be successful, which indeed turned out to be the case. 'This is the word of Nusku [the god of light and fire],' the girl, seized by an ecstatic fit, is alleged to have cried out. 'The kingship is for Sasi [another son of Senacherib]! I will destroy the name and seed of Sennacherib.' The background was formed by an attempted coup. In the ensuing struggle Esarhaddon, who had already survived another coup in which his father was assassinated, came out on top. Understandably, though, the experience seems to have left its mark on him, making him more distrustful and suspicious than previously. Repeatedly he tried to elicit additional prophecies concerning his future.[10] As to the girl, one can imagine what happened to her after she had uttered these words. Or, on second thoughts, better not.

Still remaining with non-Israelite prophets in the Middle East, the Pentateuch tells the story of Balaam, son of Beor, a court prophet serving King Balak of Moab. An eighth-century BCE inscription found at Deir Alla, in today's Kingdom of Jordan, mentions a person with the same name and patronym. Accepting the biblical chronology, the two Balaams are separated by several centuries. How they are linked, if they are, is not clear. The Balaam of the inscription must have had some reputation, for when he started weeping and fasting, people took notice. Taken to task, he explained that the gods, having consulted together, were about to envelop the world in darkness.[11] The Balaam mentioned in the Book of Numbers was summoned by his sovereign to curse the people of Israel, who had trespassed on his lands. Instead of doing so, Balaam, having met an angel who gave him new marching orders, ended up by blessing them instead. Filled with the spirit of the Lord, among other things, he prophesized the coming of a king who would conquer Edom and Moab (Numbers 24:14–19); whereupon he was allowed to go home. However, the king's faith in him remained undiminished, for later he summoned Balaam again.

Further west, in Greece, Socrates claimed to have a daemon – best translated as a divine, or higher, kind of soul – that guided him throughout his life. It was the daemon, Plutarch says, that led him to predict that the planned Athenian invasion of Syracuse would fail.[12] For Socrates' disciple Plato, the ability to look into the future was rooted in 'divine madness', a form of what we today would call an ASC. A gift of Apollo, it was clearly differentiated from not only ordinary madness but ritual madness, poetic madness and erotic madness as well.[13] Those it affected stood apart from the ordinary herd, causing them to be regarded with a mixture of awe and respect. But it could also be rewarded by a death sentence, as happened to Socrates himself. Centuries later, Cicero in his *On Divination* (44 BCE) has his brother Quintus say, 'The human soul has an inherent power of presaging or of foreknowing infused into it from without, and made a part of it by the will of God.' There are people, Quintus explains,

> whose souls, spurning their bodies, take wings and fly
> abroad – inflamed and aroused by a sort of passion –
> these men, I say, certainly see the things which they
> foretell in their prophecies. Such souls do not cling to
> the body and are kindled by many different influences.
> For example, some are aroused by certain vocal tones, as
> by Phrygian songs. Many [are occasioned] by groves and
> forests, and many others by rivers and seas.[14]

And the vapours that enveloped the Pythia, of course.

Jeremiah's lament apart, in the whole of literature, no passage explains what being a prophet felt like better than the following. The text is part of a lost play whose authorship is disputed and a small part of which is quoted by Cicero.[15] The speaker is Queen Hecuba of Troy, wife of King Priam. She is addressing her daughter, the prophetess Cassandra:

> But why those flaming eyes, that sudden rage?
> And wither fled that sober modesty,
> Till now so maidenly and yet so wise?

To which Cassandra answers:

> Oh mother, noblest of thy noble sex!
> I have been sent to utter prophecies:
> Against my will Apollo drives me mad
> To revelation make of future ills.
> O virgins! Comrades of my youthful hours,
> My mission shames my father, best of men.
> Mother dear! Great loathing for myself
> And grief for thee I feel. For thou has borne
> To Priam godly issue – saving me,
> 'Tis sad that unto thee the rest bring weal
> I woe; that they obey, but I oppose.

She goes on to describe the approaching destruction of Troy:

> It comes! It comes! A bloody torch, in fire
> Enwrapped, though hid from sight these many years!
> Bring aid my countrymen and quench its flames . . .
> Already, on the mighty deep is built
> A navy swift that hastes with swarms of woe
> Its ships are drawing nigh with swelling sails,
> And bands of savage men will fill our shores.

To return to the Jews, the first to suggest that the 'spirit of prophecy' had left Israel after the Persian conquest and would not return were the Books of the Maccabees, which were written during the second and first centuries BCE.[16] Some two centuries later, that idea was echoed by the Talmud.[17] To be sure, it did not happen all at once. Sources dating to the period of the Second Temple, such as the Dead Sea Scrolls and the works of Philo of Alexandria (25 BCE–50 CE) and Josephus (37–100 CE), testify that some people continued to believe in its existence.[18] As time went on, however, would-be divinely inspired Jewish prophets were normally met with some suspicion. They tended to find themselves outside the mainstream rabbinic tradition with its emphasis on books, learning and scholarship – as happened, for example, to David Ha-Reuveni in the sixteenth century CE and to Shabbatai Tzvi a hundred or so years after him.

Prophets charged by the Lord with looking into the future did, however, continue to figure in the Christian tradition. Jesus himself uttered quite some prophecies, the best-known one being that Jerusalem would be laid waste (Luke 21:20–22), as indeed it was, some 37 years later. Early Christian centres such as Jerusalem, Caesarea (Acts 21:8–9), Antioch (Acts 11:27–8) and Corinth (1 Corinthians 12:10) all had their prophets and/or prophetesses.[19] At some time shortly before 100 CE the unknown author of 1 John urged his followers to 'Test the spirits, whether they are of God, because many false prophets are gone out into the world' (1 John 4:1). John himself, of course, came up with the most famous 'End of Days' prophecy of all. It promised, first, a long period of war, confusion and trouble, including the appearance of the four living creatures, the beast with seven heads, the war of Gog and Magog, and much more. This was to be followed, ultimately, by the end of suffering and death, the building of the New Jerusalem, the healing of the nations and peoples, the ending of the curse of sin and the announcement of Christ's Second Coming.

Probably the most famous prophet in history was Muhammad. Born about 560 CE, Muhammad practised his trade as a merchant. At the time the angel Gabriel contacted him and launched his career as the last of the great prophets (*rasul* in Arabic), he was about forty years old. Like so many others, initially he was reluctant to answer the call; however, half convinced and half compelled by Allah's command, from that point until his death, which took place in 632 CE, he never ceased telling his disciples what the future might bring. Two factors helped establish his credibility in the eyes of his followers. First, he always led an impeccable life according to his lights and those of his contemporaries. Second, he performed a number of miracles, including a water-creating miracle and a bread-multiplication miracle (both clearly modelled after similar stories in the Old and New Testaments). Above all, on one occasion he split the Moon so that one of its parts appeared in front of a mountain and the other behind it; how that miracle could be explained, and just what it meant, is being debated to the present day.[20]

One modern list, compiled by way of an MA thesis at Cairo's Al-Azhar University, mentions 'at least 160 known and confirmed prophecies of Prophet Muhammed which were fulfilled in his lifetime and the first generation after him'.[21] The following comprises a handful of the most important ones:

Preceding the Battle of Badr, the first and decisive confrontation with pagan Meccans in the second year of migration from Mecca in 623 CE, Prophet Muhammed foretold the precise spot every pagan Meccan soldier would fall. Those who witnessed the battle saw the prophecy come true with their own eyes.

The Prophet informed his daughter, Fatima, that she would be the first member of his family to die after him. There are two prophecies in one: Fatima will outlive her father; Fatima will be the first member of his household to die after him. Both were fulfilled.

The Prophet foretold the first maritime battle to be undertaken by Muslims would be witnessed by Umm Haram, the first woman to participate in a naval expedition. He also prophesized the first assault on Constantinople.

Prophet Muhammed prophesized an imposter claiming to speak in the name of God would be killed at the hands of a righteous man in Muhammed's lifetime [Al-Aswad al-Ansi, an imposter prophet in Yemen, was killed in the Prophet's lifetime by Fayruz al-Daylami].

After Jesus' death, Christianity never had anything like him again. However, minor prophets and prophetesses abounded. A typical description of an early medieval one is provided by Gregory of Tours (538–594):

About this time [the year 585], a woman resident in the town of Paris made the following pronouncement to the townsfolk: 'You must know that the whole of this town is about to be destroyed by a conflagration. You had better evacuate it.' They mostly laughed at her, saying that she had had her fortune told, or that she had dreamed it, or that she had been possessed by the noon-time demon. 'None of what you say is true,' she answered. 'What I tell you is what is really going to happen. I saw in a vision a man coming out of Saint Vincent's church, radiant with light, holding a wax candle in his hand and setting fire to the merchants' houses one after another.' Three nights after she had given this warning, just as twilight was falling, a worthy citizen lit a light, went into his storehouse to fetch some oil and other things which he needed, and then came out again, leaving the light behind quite near to the cask of oil. The house was the first one inside the city gate, which was left open in the daytime. It caught fire from the light and was burnt to ashes. The flames spread to the other houses. Soon the town gaol was alight; but Saint Germanus appeared to the prisoners, broke the great wooden beam and the chains by which they were held fast, undid the prison gateway and made it possible for those who had been locked up to escape. [The conflagration burnt most of the town, except for the churches and the houses belonging to them.][22]

By this time the Catholic Church in particular had long since organized itself into a formal structure, complete with officials who jealously guarded their monopoly as defenders of the faith. As a result, its attitude to prophets of every kind became more ambiguous; after all, one could never know whether or not they had 'really' been sent by God. Still, there was never a complete ban on prophecy. Important medieval Christian figures who were credited with prophetic powers included the eleventh-century Swiss monk Hepidanus (much later, his prophecies were scrutinized and found to have forespelled the rise of Napoleon).[23] Others were the Italian monk and theologian Joachim of Fiore (c. 1135–1202), his contemporary the French chronicler Rigord of Saint-Denis, the Austrian monk Johann Friede (1204–1257) and many others.[24]

The most authoritative, though not the only, source of prophetic powers were supposed to be visions sent directly by God. Often this happened while the prophet-to-be was lying sick in bed or even on the point of death (on the near-death experience, see below). The better-known a prophet, the more likely he or she was to be followed by hordes of hangers-on and imitators who claimed to have inherited his/her spirit and to speak in his/her name. Pseudo Joachims, Sibyls and Merlins abounded. They dug up old prophecies, faked new ones and might even see them as they came raining down from heaven. As had already been the case in antiquity, often the same prophecy, occasionally altered in certain details, was passed off as the work of different, more prestigious authors. The fact that plagiarism was not frowned upon but, to the contrary, regarded as a return to the good old sources helped.

One famous medieval prophetess was Marusha ('little Mary'), who is mentioned in some Norse sagas. Originally she was a housekeeper in the court of Prince Sviatoslav of Kiev. To him she bore a son who was destined to become Vladimir the Great. She herself was said to have reached the age of a hundred, lived in a cave and was sometimes brought to the palace so that she might predict the future. An even more famous medieval Christian prophetess was the Benedictine abbess Hildegard of Bingen.[25] Also known as the Sibyl of the Rhine, and said by contemporaries to have possessed powers greater than those of the biblical Miriam and Deborah, she was sought out by multitudes who came to listen to her prophecies. Hildegard was born to a noble family and at an early age was enclosed in the monastery of Disibodenberg. Later she asked for, and ultimately received, permission to move to the one of St Rupertsberg. In 1141, when she was 42 years old, God ordered her to make a record of what she saw and heard 'without leaving out anything'. Initially reluctant to do as she had been told, she fell physically ill. Only then did she start writing, 'in simple Latin', as she said.

Thirty-four years later she explained her 'method' to an admirer. It all went back to her childhood, she said, when God began sending her visions. She did not hear them with her outward ears, nor by the thoughts of her own heart, or by any combination of her five senses, but in her soul alone, and only while her outward eyes were open. That was why she never fell prey to ecstasy in the visions; she saw them while wide awake, day and night. 'The light which I see thus,' she added, 'is not spatial, but it is far, far brighter than a cloud which carries the sun. I can measure neither height, nor length, nor breadth in it.' She called it 'the reflection of the living Light'. Those who doubted her, she added, God would pierce with arrows from His quiver.[26] In providing this explanation, her intention seems to have been to ensure that people would attribute her prophetic powers to divine inspiration; anything else could have made life dangerous for her. In that she succeeded. When she died in 1179 her sisters claimed they saw two streams of light appear in the skies and cross over her room. In 2010, Pope Benedict XVI made her a saint.

At some time between 1397 and 1401 a soon to be famous Paris scholar, Jean Gerson, disturbed by the vast number of popular prophecies floating about, delivered a series of lectures on how to distinguish true prophets from false ones.[27] First of all, he said, it was necessary to put aside any visions originating in the minds of the sick or the mad – especially if they were female, who, owing to their greater natural heat, were more likely to go in this direction than their male counterparts.[28] Next he focused on all sorts of behaviours that betrayed excessive fervour and self-humiliation, such as wallowing in dirt, wearing a hair shirt, fasting, self-flagellation and even virginity. Extreme devotion, Gerson warned, could easily turn into its opposite, heresy. Mystic truths, he admitted, had been experienced by thousands upon thousands of people and could not be denied. But any prophecies that disturbed the peace, either that of the Church or the secular one, had to be treated with suspicion.

From around the middle of the nineteenth century, the Renaissance began to be interpreted as marking a shift from the supernatural to the ordinary, and from there to the scientific. There is an element of truth in this idea; however, the Renaissance also witnessed the appearance of a large number of prophets, or, more precisely, prophetesses.[29] The dukes of Mantua, for example, recruited two women, Osanna Andreasi and Stefana de Quinzanis, who provided spiritual advice through their visions and prophecies.[30] In Spain around 1500, a 'prophetess' acquired the patronage of such high aristocrats as King Ferdinand of Aragon and the head of the Spanish Church, Cardinal Cisneros.[31]

While court prophetesses had a field day, we seldom hear of male prophets in this period. Perhaps that was because of the fear that they might turn into political threats in a way female ones rarely could. In 1516 Leo X, the Medici pope whose family had been expelled from Florence by the monk Savonarola in 1494 but restored to power in 1512, was presiding over the Fifth Lateran Council. Worried that a similar revolt might break out again, he had the Council issue a ban on prophesying. The possibility of the existence of 'true' prophets and that they might present themselves was left untouched. However, to be on the safe side the Council resolved that every claim of divine revelation had to be tested by a bishop or the Pope before it could be made public. As a result, the place of prophets, both female and male, was gradually taken by Jesuits, whose approach both to religion and to life in general owed little if anything to ecstasy.

Sixteenth-century Catholic countries had the Inquisition to look after prophets who caused too much trouble. Not so Protestant ones, where prophets continued to flourish. John Calvin, it is true, wholeheartedly approved of the prophets of the Old Testament. But when it came to prophecy in his own time he was much more sceptical. As he wrote, 'God does not at this day predict hidden events; but he would have us to be satisfied with the Gospel.'[32] By contrast, Martin Luther was highly interested in it and maintained that it still existed. There were, he believed, two kinds of prophets: those who spoke of earthly things, and those who claimed to speak in the name of God. With the former he had no quarrel – let those who have the gift make use of it, he wrote. But the latter had to be treated with some caution.[33] On occasion he himself went so far as to prophesize; after his death his followers published a collection of 120 of his prophecies. Most were derived from the Book of Daniel and dealt with the approaching end of the world. Luther's own coming, incidentally, was said to have been foretold by his predecessor, Jan Huss. In 1415, before he was burnt at the stake, Huss had prophesized that, a century later, the goose (in Czech, *huss* means goose) would be followed by a swan to whom people would be forced to listen.[34]

Perhaps because her claim to the throne was disputed, Elizabeth I disliked prophets and did her best to suppress them. Her successors followed the same policy, and it was not until the Civil War of 1642–51 that prophets re-emerged en masse. Particularly impressive was a woman named Eleanor Davies.[35] Well born and highly educated, she was one morning in 1625 awakened by an extraordinary voice that said: 'Nineteen years and a half to the Judgment, and you as the meek Virgin.' From that moment she never looked back. First, she presented the Archbishop of Canterbury with advice on international politics. He was unimpressed and returned it to her husband, who threw it into the fire. She retaliated by prophesizing that he would soon die, which he did some three weeks later. Emboldened, Lady Eleanor began circulating around the court of the recently crowned Charles I, whom she advised about the fertility of Queen Henriette (it took her five years to produce an heir). Acquiring a national reputation, her biggest success was correctly foretelling the death of the Duke of Buckingham, which took place in 1628.

At this point Lady Eleanor started issuing tracts implying that King Charles was a tyrant ruling over Babylon. She was soon arrested, fined £3,000 – an enormous sum, levied on her husband – and imprisoned for two years; the magistrates judged that she was dangerous because she had acquired the reputation of a 'cunning woman' among the common people. No sooner was she released from prison than she appeared in a church carrying a kettle full of tar, which she smeared on the hangings, calling it 'holy water'. This time she was ruled insane and committed to Bedlam, in London, where she was visited by sightseers. Lady Eleanor spent the rest of her life issuing tracts in which she identified members of the government as the Beast of the Apocalypse. When Charles I was executed in 1649 – another of her prophecies come true – her reputation revived. Unusually, she even acquired a male disciple. Her last tract predicted a second flood, to occur in 1656. However, she died in 1652, before she could see whether she had been right (she was not).

A contemporary of Lady Eleanor was Anna Trapnel (or Trapnell).[36] Apparently born in 1622, she had her first vision at the age of fifteen. In 1657–8 she spent ten months in bed, her hands clenched and her eyes shut, occasionally uttering 'prophecies' that she claimed had been sent to her directly by

God. Living on toast and beer, throughout this period she was attended by varying groups of disciples who testified to her authenticity and to the wonder of her prophecies. Later they were collected and published.

Invoking God, Trapnel claimed that He would punish Oliver Cromwell for his 'corruptions'. Like Lady Eleanor, she was arrested and about to be put on trial; however, the authorities, aware of her fame, were reluctant to convict her. Eventually she was released, and she continued writing, claiming to have predicted, among other things, the English victory over the Scots in 1650 and over the Dutch in 1653. Many Protestant writers saw prophecy as a feminine activity and men who engaged in it as somehow womanized. In the United States, Puritan ministers in Massachusetts even called themselves the 'breasts of God', at which the congregation sucked the milk of the Word. Wrote the New England minister Cotton Mather: 'Such Ministers are your Mothers too. Have they not Travailed in Birth for you, that a Christ may be seen formed in you? Are not their lips the breasts through which the sincere Milk of the Word has passed unto you, for your Nourishment?'[37]

Meanwhile, on the Continent, confirming the maxim that hard times cause people to turn towards the irrational, the last great outbreak of prophecy took place during the Thirty Years War (1618–48).[38] Anyone who delves into the literature of the period will soon be inundated by hundreds of references to it. Either it is mentioned in the works of contemporaries, or else it comes in the form of pamphlets issued by the prophets themselves and/or their followers. Many prophets demanded that the people repent so as to escape due divine punishment; others, though, referred to specific events which they claimed they saw coming. The most interesting single prophet was probably Johann Warner Buckendorf, a Saxon farmer who enlisted in the Swedish army. So successful was he with his prophecies that he made a military career acting as a sort of divine representative on the staff. He even won the confidence of the Swedish commander Lennart Torstensson, who valued him for his political and strategic advice.

During the second half of the seventeenth century, the re-imposition of order caused the influence of divinely inspired prophecy in the West to decline. The advent of the scientific revolution and the subsequent move towards secularization helped; no longer was every historical event necessarily understood as part of God's design. Some scholars believe that another factor in this may have been the rise of the first newspapers, which took the place of prophecies in the popular understanding.[39] Seldom, if ever, did the remaining prophets pose a serious threat to the established socio-political order as they sometimes did in other countries, notably China and Islamic nations. Those who, claiming to be divinely inspired, seemed prepared to do so stood a better chance of being sent to an asylum than to prison.

However, as even the most superficial research will soon reveal, prophecy and prophecies have certainly not disappeared. The founder of the Mormon religion, Joseph Smith, is said to have uttered or written down dozens of prophecies. Some, such as those concerning the outbreak of the American Civil War, actually seemed to come true. Others, such as those predicting the destruction of New York and Boston by God's wrath, did not.[40] Over a century and a half later, Smith's successors as heads of the Mormon Church continue to be credited with prophetic powers.[41] Nor are the Mormons on their own in this respect. All over the world, lists of 'famous' and 'true' present-day prophets, along with the 'secrets' the Lord has entrusted them with and the miracles they have allegedly performed, continue to be published almost daily. At any given moment their number runs into the tens of thousands, perhaps more. Their methodologies, if that is the right word, vary enormously; one Greek woman, Athanasia Kriketou, even claims to be in touch with the Holy Spirit, which insists on writing prophetic messages on her breasts.[42] While not limited to any single country, many prophets are heads of American charismatic sects, such as the Neo-Pentecostal Church of Jesus Christ International, who are greatly honoured by their followers. Here and there, one of them has been exposed for not being a 'genuine' apostle; which, of course, implies the belief that such a thing as genuine prophecy still exists. The debate, which by now must have been going on for several millennia, is unlikely to be resolved.

3
ORACLES, PYTHIAS AND SIBYLS

Oracles were extremely popular in both ancient Greece and ancient Rome. At the beginning of Cicero's *On Divination* of 44 BCE we read: 'What colony has Greece sent into Aeolia, Ionia, Asia, Sicily, or Italy without an oracle from the Pythia or Dodona or Ammon? Or what war has been undertaken by Greece without the will of the gods?'[1] To which Celsus, a Greek philosopher who lived some two centuries later and who was an opponent of Christianity, added: 'How many cities were founded as a result of oracles . . . and as a result of oracles averted diseases and famine! And how many which neglected or forgot the oracles came to an evil destruction! And how many were sent forth for colonization and after complying with the things enjoined became prosperous!'[2] Some of the pronouncements were probably genuine in the sense that they originated near the time the enterprise they referred to was being planned. Many others, no doubt, were invented later on.

Much the most important oracle was the one at Delphi. At its centre stood, or rather sat, the Pythia. The word was used both for the local prophetess and generically for her colleagues elsewhere. Originally, perhaps, she was thought of as Apollo's bride. How precisely the Pythia was selected we do not know. Plutarch (*c.* 46–120 CE) says that, in his own day, the Pythia at Delphi was the daughter of a poor farmer; a woman of honest upbringing and respectable life, to be sure, but with little education or experience of the world.[3] Judging by this, perhaps character was considered more important than learning.

Still remaining at Delphi, at certain times there was not a single woman but several who took turns on different days of the week. The one whose watch it was would prepare by bathing, perhaps in the sacred spring called Castalia, which was also supposed to inspire poets. Next she established contact with the god by holding a laurel branch or by fumigating herself with laurel leaves. By another account, she chewed the leaves in question. Finally she sat down on a tripod in a dark, subterranean abode, the favourite location for all kinds of Orphic rites, those involving prophecy included. There she came under the influence of gases emanating from a split in the earth. They were said to have originated either in the carcass of a giant snake (the python) or in Apollo's breath. Modern scholars have often cast doubt on the truth of this story. However, there is no question that the region is geologically active. Recent studies have confirmed that some of the water found in nearby springs contains the gas ethylene. Inhaled at low concentrations, ethylene, which is sweet-smelling, produces a sensation of floating or disembodied euphoria as well as a reduced sense of inhibition. At higher concentrations a more violent reaction may occur, including delirium and frantic thrashing of the limbs. All this agrees rather well with what Plutarch has to say about the topic.[4]

Unlike shamans, the Pythia did not go on a mysterious journey. Instead she waited for Apollo to enter her body, sending her into a sort of trance while using her vocal organs as if they were the god's own. That is why the Delphic utterances were always couched in the first person and never in the third. Mostly, the pronouncements took the form of confused gibberish. Next, a special college of priests forming part of the temple complex interpreted the Pythia's words, often, but not always, putting them in the form of hexameters. Thus the task of looking into the future and finding out what it might bring was divided into two stages, each of which was the responsibility of a different person or persons. Needless to say, this procedure provided the priests with considerable freedom and power.

At times, things went wrong, as, for example, happened when one Pythia, entering her watch while feeling depressed and learning that the signs were unfavourable, appeared to be filled with a 'dumb and evil spirit'. She ended by rushing out of the temple, screaming and causing everyone to flee in terror. Later she returned to her senses, but died a few days after.[5] Generally, though, her powers were vast. As she herself said, she could 'count the grains of sand on the beach and measure the sea; [and] understand the speech of the dumb and hear the voiceless'.[6] Countless people visited her, either in person or by means of emissaries.

One of the Pythia's most famous pronouncements was delivered to the founder of Sparta, Lycurgus (*fl. c.* 820 BCE): 'Sparta will be ruined by money.' Others went to the lawgiver Solon – 'seat yourself now amidships, for you are the pilot of Athens. Grasp the helm fast in your hands; you have many allies in your city' – and to the Athenians on the eve of the Persian invasion: 'Await not in quiet the coming of the horses, the marching feet, the armed host upon the land. Slip away. Turn your back. You will meet in battle anyway. O holy Salamis, you will be the death of many a woman's son between the seedtime and the harvest of the grain.'[7] Note that, in this case as in many others, the pronouncement was ambiguous in that it did not say on whose side, the Persians or the Greeks, the dead would be more numerous; in other words, who would win and who would lose. Some pronouncements were supposed to look ahead by as much as five hundred years, as when one of the Pythias announced the Roman victory first over Carthage and then over King Philip V of Macedon.[8] To Plutarch, this provided 'manifest proof' that prediction could indeed provide foreknowledge.

Supplicants were expected to reward the oracle by conferring expensive presents on it. Judging by the descriptions of them in ancient sources, the priests who ran the sanctuary were particularly interested in gold and silver vessels. One golden lion, brought by Croesus, king of Lydia, was said to weigh 30 talents.[9] As time went on this resulted in the accumulation of great wealth. But things did not always proceed as decorously as they should. By one story, Alexander, later to be called the Great, once visited Delphi expecting to hear a prophecy that he would soon conquer the entire world.[10] However, the oracle surprised him by refusing a direct comment, asking him to come on another day instead, whereupon a furious Alexander – neither at that time nor later was self-control one of his outstanding qualities – dragged the Pythia by the hair out of her chamber until she screamed, 'You are invincible, my son!' No sooner had he heard these words, he dropped her, saying, 'Now I have my answer.'

Though the Delphic Pythia was the best-known of all, she was by no means the only one of her kind. Scattered all over the Mediterranean were the temples of eight others. Collectively they were known as sibyls, from the Greek *sibulla*, prophetess. The fifth-century BCE philosopher Heraclitus, who is the first ancient writer to mention them, is supposed to have said that, 'with frenzied mouth', 'unadorned and unperfumed', they 'utter things not to be laughed at, yet reach to a thousand years with [their] voice by aid of the god'.[11] Plato, no less, at one point commented that sibyls, 'by practicing heavenly inspired divination, have foretold many future things accurately'.[12] Most of the sibyls whose names we have were supposed to have lived so long ago that they may safely be regarded as purely mythological. Two, however, are known to have been historical figures.

To the nine Greek sibyls the Romans added a tenth, known as the Cumean or Tiburtine Sibyl. It was a sibyl credited with standing between life and death, and thus having a knowledge of both, who guided Aeneas into the underworld. The cave in which she lived, or was supposed to have lived, has been identified by modern archaeologists. By some sources, her successors continued to receive visitors and deliver oracles for hundreds of years after Aeneas' purported visit, though few details are known. An original Roman contribution to the field were the Sibylline Books. According to legend it was the city's fifth king, Tarquinius Priscus, who received them from the reigning sibyl during the sixth century BCE. Written in archaic Greek hexameters, they consisted of the half-understood sayings of various sibyls.[13] In 83 BCE the temple in which they were stored was burnt down. Upon this, the Senate ordered a new set to be assembled out of fragments collected from various places around the Mediterranean.[14] So seriously did the Romans take what the books had to say that, according to Plutarch, on one occasion, they overrode all tradition by carrying out a human sacrifice.[15]

As also happened with other people or methods that claimed to foresee the future, the trouble with the Sibylline Books was that they often contained dire predictions that could be, and sometimes were, interpreted as referring to the future of the powers that be, and thus could lead to political instability, revolts and so on. To avert this danger they were kept under tight control by a board of two (later ten, later still fifteen) specially appointed high officials, who were absolved of any other duty. No other Roman sacred object was guarded as carefully. Unauthorized disclosure of the books' contents was seen as akin to parricide, or else to a Vestal Virgin breaking her vow of chastity, and subject to as cruel a punishment.[16] In 380 CE, a consultation of the books led those responsible to the conclusion that the fall of the empire and the end of the world were close at hand. Perhaps that was why, twenty years later, they were burnt by Stilicho, the half-Vandal general who at that time was the most powerful man in the Roman Empire.

Yet the sibyls and their prophecies refused to fade away. After the Sibylline Books came the so-called Sibylline Oracles. A miscellaneous collection of pagan, Jewish and Christian writings apparently produced between about 150 BCE and 180 CE, at some point they were assembled into a single opus and given the name under which they became known. Among other things they predicted the coming of a saviour who, later on, could be identified with Jesus himself. That explains why prominent Christian writers, such as Theophilus of Antioch and Clement of Alexandria, both of whom lived during the second century CE, held them in high regard. So, two centuries later, did Augustine. Having discussed them at length, he concluded that the writers in question had said or written nothing against Christianity, and that they therefore deserved to be considered members in good standing of the City of God.[17]

Nor did things end at that point. Throughout the Middle Ages and the early modern age, countless 'sibylline' documents, many of them containing prophecies of all sorts, continued to circulate. Perhaps most familiar to the modern public are the Spanish *Cantos della Sibilla*. They form a collection of magnificent, if often melancholy, songs concerning the coming apocalypse and were performed in many different versions in different places. Later still, sibyls became a favourite subject of Renaissance artists. In particular, they were fascinated by one story which had the Emperor Augustus consult a sibyl as to whether he should allow himself to be worshipped as a god.[18] Arrayed around the centre of the ceiling of the Sistine Chapel are twelve figures who were said to have foreshadowed the coming of Christ. Seven are Hebrew prophets, all of them men, whereas the remaining five are sibyls of the classical world. Painting them, Michelangelo saw fit to give them strangely muscular, almost masculine, bodies.

In brief, literature, drama and even political discourse all evoked the sibyls and used them as they saw fit, for example during the debate as to whether Princess Elizabeth's sex should or should not stand in her way to becoming Queen of England and whether she ought to intervene in the French Civil Wars of 1562–98.[19] As late as 1801 a pseudo-historical Temple of the Sibyl, modelled after a similar structure in Tivoli (the site of the Tiburtine Sibyl), was erected in Puławy, Poland. To this day, many people and things are named after the sibyls, including books, movies and a television series. The name has even been applied to various computer programs, including a programming language, a 'bibliographic information retrieval program' and 'software for multiple genome comparison and visualization'.

4
A DREAM TO REMEMBER

The relationship between reality and dreams, as well as the things that can or cannot be learnt from the latter about the former, has probably been disputed for as long as human beings have been walking this earth. Aristotle in his *De insomniis* (On Dreams; *c.* 350 BCE) says that 'the faculty by which, in waking hours, we are subject to illusion when affected by disease, is identical with that which produces illusory effects in sleep.' In another one of his minor works, *De divinatione per somnum* (On Divination in Sleep), he says that dreams are the remnants of impressions received by a person while he or she is in a waking state. Such impressions can be as sharp and as vivid as those seen in a good mirror; however, he goes on, any similarity between them and the future is purely coincidental. To this rule there he admitted only two exceptions. The first are dreams that, originating in the dreamer's physiology, provide foreknowledge of his (or her, though Aristotle does not say so) health; the second, those that bring about their own fulfilment by causing the person to take a certain course of action.[1]

We know that most dreams coincide with rapid eye movement (REM) sleep. Some add that REM dreams tend to be hostile, whereas non-REM ones are pleasant and peaceful.[2] Since REM has been observed among the 'higher vertebrates', we can only assume that they, too, have dreams.[3] We know that the amygdala, twin almond-shaped sets of neurons located deep in the brain's medial temporal lobe which are believed to take a critical part in the formation of memory, as well as decision-making and emotional reactions, also play an important role in whatever process it is that makes us dream. Some have taken this as an indication that dreams help fix things in our memory. However, any kind of proof is lacking.

Armed with scanners, brain scientists have concluded that dreams are the result of electrical activity in the brain that is rather different from that which occurs while we are in a waking state. It is, however, anything but clear why and how that activity generates dreams in all their endless and often outlandish variety. The more so because they are often accompanied by sights, sounds, smells, tastes and a sense of touch that do not reach the dreamer by way of the senses, that is, from outside. Instead they are generated, as far as anyone can make out, by the dreaming brain itself.

In any case, brain scanners, however sophisticated, cannot detect anything as abstract as symbols and meaning. For example, I doubt whether any scanner has ever followed Freud in linking a coat in a woman's dream with a man without being programmed to do so first. Briefly, it is ignorance, not positive knowledge, that has made most neuroscientists agree with Aristotle. While learning more and more about dreams, they have given up on attempts to understand what they stand for and what may be learnt from them. It is as if the most prominent thing about dreams – their content – does not matter. This is unfortunate; after all, our first impression of a new day is often the dream we had while asleep; 'Then Pharaoh woke up; it had been a dream. In the morning his mind was troubled' (Genesis 41:7–8). For every person who takes an interest in brain-imaging technologies and the things they show, there are a hundred who want nothing so much as to have their dreams interpreted for them.

In the absence of a direct link to the dreaming brain, all we can do is look at what people remember, or say they remember, of the dreams they have had. Perhaps the earliest recorded dream is that of Gilgamesh, in the late third-millennium epic poem named after him: in the dream, Gilgamesh and his companion, Enkidu, were walking through a deep gorge when a huge mountain fell on top of them. Not a bit taken back, Enkidu interprets the dream. He explains that the mountain stands for the monstrous giant Humbaba, and that he and Gilgamesh will kill him (they do). Later in the poem, Enkidu dreams that he is going to die. This too comes about, and Gilgamesh mourns him.

From Mesopotamia the art of interpreting dreams spread to the Assyrians, Israelites, Greeks and Romans. Later, too, hardly a people could be found whose culture did not include dreams in their attempts to learn what the future might bring. Says God in the Book of Numbers: 'Hear my words: If there be a prophet among you, I the Lord will make myself known unto him in a vision, and will speak to him in a dream' (12:6). King Solomon had a dream, sent to him by the Lord, specifically so as to make him choose wisdom as the greatest good, whereupon we learn that this wish was in fact granted (1 Kings 2:5–15). The Israelites, in other words, saw dreams as a perfectly acceptable, indeed divinely mandated, method of looking into the future. In this dreams differed from some other methods, especially divination, which was prohibited on pain of death (Exodus 22:18).

As the story of Joseph shows, dreams were supposed to deliver their message not in plain form but with the aid of symbols. First he dreamt that he and his brothers were busy harvesting grain and that his brothers' sheaves bowed to his own. This was followed by a dream in which the Sun, the Moon and eleven stars were bowing to him (Genesis 37). Next he interpreted the dreams of three other people, the most important of which was the one Pharaoh had in which seven fat cows stood for seven good years and seven lean cows for seven bad ones (Genesis 41). Lists of such symbols, each with the thing or things they meant written alongside, are known from ninth-century BCE Assyria. What follows is an excerpt from a seventh-century BCE Assyrian dream book:

If [in his dream] he falls into a river [and] the river enters his mouth: he will become important.

If he sinks into a river and emerges (again): [this man will have] riches.

If he [sin]ks into a river in his clothes: the foundation of this man [is solid].

[If] he falls [into] a river and [drifts/swims] up-stream: he will ask (something) from a person (who is) not friendly to him and he will give (it) to him; in the pal[ace].

[If] he falls [into] a river and [drifts/swims] down-stream he will ask (something) from a person friendly to him and he will give (it) [to him.]

[If] he ... to a river, sinks and comes up (again): prison.
. . .

If he walks constantly in 'dark waters': a diff[icult] law-suit [ ], they will sum[mon him] to testify.

If he washes (himself) in a river: losses [ ].

If he sinks into a river and comes up (again): he will have w[orries].

If he crosses a river: he will experience confusion.

If he goes down to the river and comes up (again): he will stand up (in court) against his adversary. If he comes up from the river: good news.
. . .

If the 'throne' in his dream sleeps with a woman ...

If the 'throne' in his dream [kisses(?)] the lips of a woman ...

If the 'throne' in his dream [ ] the breasts [of a woman]

If the 'throne' in his dream, a woman [ ]s [her] br[easts]

If the 'throne' in his dream [sleeps(?)] with [ ]'[4]

Obviously sex was as important to the ancient dream-interpreters as it is to their present-day followers. The list goes on and on, endlessly and in excruciating detail. Almost every possible contingency is covered, from eating worms, which heralds a coming triumph, to meeting a horse, which means that the dreamer will have a rescuer.

The Greeks, too, had their dream books.[5] The first known one was written by Antiphon in the fifth century BCE. It was followed by many others. Most dreams were considered to be of the 'messenger' type, meaning that they were sent by the gods to serve as a warning concerning the future. Explanations as to just what they meant and where they got their prophetic power from abounded. Thucydides did not bother to write about any dreams his protagonists may have had. Polybius, the sober, businesslike second-century BCE historian, went so far as to say that doing so was a waste of time.[6]

Such explanations are, however, plentiful in the works of others. Herodotus tells innumerable stories of people, most of them prominent in public life, who had dreams that subsequently came true (in interpreting them, he seems to have made use of Assyrian material). For example, the Median prince Astyages dreamt that his daughter Mandane had growing out of her vulva a vine that covered the whole of Asia. Consulting the magi, he was told that her offspring would take his own place on the throne – which indeed was what happened in the end.[7]

Philip II of Macedon, father of Alexander the Great, dreamt that he had sealed the womb of his wife Olympias, which was interpreted to mean that she was pregnant and would have a son with a lion-like nature. King Tarquinius Superbus dreamt of a star that reversed its course and took a new one, which was interpreted to mean that Rome would one day rule the universe. Caesar, on the night before he was murdered, had a dream in which he was floating above the clouds and stretching his hand to Jupiter. And his wife Calpurnia had another, in which she saw the pediment of their house collapsing and her husband stabbed to death in her lap.[8] The humblest people had dreams and wanted to know what they meant for the future;

Aristophanes in *The Wasps* has a slave who is prepared to pay two obols for the privilege.[9]

Some dreams visited those who had them not once but twice. Not all dreams came true. In the *Iliad*, Zeus sends Agamemnon a false dream specifically to mislead him into the belief that victory in the Trojan War is imminent. And Herodotus relates how Xerxes of Persia at one point had a dream in which a mysterious luminiferous being appeared to him, encouraging him to go ahead and invade Greece. Unsure of himself, he took the trouble of having his uncle Artabanus don his, Xerxes', clothes and sleep in his bed. Only when Artabanus, following instructions, had the same dream as he did the king order preparations for the expedition to go ahead.[10] Whether this episode really took place may well be doubted; it does, however, shed some light on the way people thought.

Explanations abounded as to where sleep got its prophetic qualities from. Aeschylus observed that 'the sleeping mind is lightened with eyes.' His rough contemporary Pindar believed that dreams often sport 'a decision of joy or adversity to come'.[11] The early fourth-century BCE commander and writer Xenophon believed that in sleep, which is akin to death, a man's soul is most revealed in its divine aspect, and can look to the future, for it is not tied down so much by the flesh. The Hellenistic philosopher Iamblichus explained the prophetic power of dreams from the fact that the sleeping soul is no longer distracted by the management of the body and is thus free to contemplate realities, specifically including the future. Also, that the more a soul separates itself from a body, the more it becomes one with its original source, an omniscient intellectual or divine principle.[12] For Plutarch, dreams were the result of certain 'effluences'. Coming from outside, they entered the body through its pores and provided the dreamer with a vision of the future.[13]

Much later, the fourth-century CE Christian writer Athanasius put it as follows:

When the body is still, at rest and sleeping, a man is in
inner movement – he contemplates what is outside himself, he traverses foreign lands, he meets friends and
often through them [the dreams] divines and learns in
advance his daily actions.[14]

There is some similarity, here, to Freud's idea of the way sleep
causes the superego to lower its guard allowing what is usually
underneath to float to the surface, so to speak. So important were
dreams that people made deliberate attempts to bring them on,
for example by sleeping in the temples of the god whose advice
they were seeking, especially those dedicated to Asclepius, the
Greek god of medicine. Other methods, used less frequently,
were fasting, spending time in a sacred cave, or sleeping with
various objects, such as laurel wreaths under the pillow. The
second-century poet Juvenal says that in the Rome of his day
there were some Jewish women who, in return for a few pennies,
would readily sell you any dream you fancied.[15]

Inscriptions and dedications set up by their authors in grati-
tude for dreams that had come true have been found all over the
Mediterranean world. They were, Plato says, especially popular among 'women of all types [and] men who are sick or in
some danger or difficulty, or else have had a special stroke of
luck'.[16] Galen, surely one of the greatest physicians of all time,
was launched on his career when his father, Nicon, had a 'vivid
dream' in which he saw his son studying medicine in Pergamon.
Later, disagreeing with those who denied the validity of dreams,
Galen incorporated them into his teaching. On one hand he
claimed to have saved many people by applying a cure prescribed
by dreams they had. But he also provided examples of physicians
who, paying no heed to their patients' accounts of their dreams,
brought about their death.[17]

Much the best-known ancient expert on the interpretation
of dreams was Artemidorus. Originally from Ephesus, in western

Asia Minor, he flourished around the middle of the second century CE.[18] His masterpiece, the *Oneirokritikon*, or *Interpretation of Dreams*, is the only one of its kind that has survived in its entirety; since then it has been published in any number of editions and languages and has never been out of print.[19] He had, Artemidorus wrote, put many years of experience into his art, studying it as thoroughly as possible: reading, travelling and inquiring, not even shrinking from rubbing shoulders with the despised diviners of the marketplace whom others, assuming a holier-than-thou attitude, dismissed as beggars, charlatans or buffoons.

Dreams, Artemidorus wrote, were sent by the gods. However, they might take on different forms in accordance with the nature of the human soul that receives and expresses them – old or young, male or female, free or slave, prominent or obscure, and so on. Not all were either subject to interpretation or future-oriented. But some were, and it was in them that he was mainly interested. Predictive dreams fell into two kinds. On one hand were simple ones that came true almost immediately; on the other, those that, carrying their message in allegorical form, took longer to do so. The first kind was easy to interpret: for example, if a borrower dreamt of the lender coming to visit him, then obviously that was what would in fact happen soon enough. To reach that conclusion no special wisdom was required. Artemidorus himself focused on dreams of the second kind. As he wrote, 'the interpretation of dreams is nothing other than the juxtaposition of similarities' between the dream imagery and the prospective outcome.[20]

For example, 'the oak tree signifies a rich man because of its nutritional value, an old man because of its longevity, or time itself for the same reason.' Dreams of having sex with prostitutes in brothels indicated a little embarrassment as well as some expense. To dream of an ass (*onos*) predicted profit (*onasthai*). This kind of analogous reasoning enabled a judgement to be made as to whether a dream was favourable or not, even though the similarity was sometimes aural rather than visual. 'It is a basic principle that all imagery which is in accordance with nature, law, custom, occupation, names or time is good, but that whatever is contrary to them is bad and inauspicious.' Some dreams provided their own interpretation at the hands of a figure, such as a parent, teacher or other respected personage, who appeared to the dreamer and explained what the future had in store for him or her. The same dream, Artemidorus continues, could very well mean different things for a man and for a woman, for a pauper and for a prince. An ordinary citizen who dreamt of sleeping with his mother was one thing – he might, in fact, go ahead and do just that. For a demagogue, though, it might mean that his wish to govern his city would likely be fulfilled.

In no civilization did dreams play a greater role than in that of Islam. The Prophet Muhammad is said to have received 'true dreams' from God for six months before he was ordered to start reciting the Quran. His wife, Aisha, is recorded as saying that the 'commencement of the divine inspiration was in the form of good and righteous [true] dreams in his sleep. He never had a dream but that it came true like bright day of light.'[21] Scant wonder that, partly by drawing on older Mesopotamian and Greek traditions, partly by adding elements of their own, the Arabs built up a science of dream interpretation (*tâbír*) as extensive and as elaborate as any in history.[22] Like the Bible, both the Old and the New Testament, the Quran takes it for granted that dreams are sent by God and may serve either as encouragement or as warnings. Some dreams, however, were sent by the Devil. Hence the first step in any attempt at using them should consist of separating them and putting those originating in the Devil aside.

Muhammad himself used to open each morning by asking his companions about any dreams they might have had. Adding his own, he would preside over a sort of seminar in which these things were discussed and either accepted or rejected. His successors, the caliphs, continued the tradition. Thus Umar, the second caliph after Muhammad, was warned of his approaching end by dreaming of a white cock thrice pecking him with its beak, the manner of his death being verified in the number of stabs he received from the hand of his assassin. Piruz Al-Amin, son and heir of the famous eighth-century caliph Harun al-Rashid, derived his fear of the encroaching power of the Seljuks from a warning that reached him while he was asleep. The list could be continued for ever.

Such being the case, dream interpreters were in high demand. Some were amply rewarded, and some followed Joseph and reached high office. The art itself gave rise to numerous dream books. In them, the nature of sleep and dreams, the rules for their interpretation and the import of their various objects were discussed with analytical minuteness. One book alone, the *Kamil al tâbír*, or *Complete Dream Book*, by Abu al-Fazl Hussain Ibn Ibrahim bin Muhammad al-Tiflisi, contained 1,000 subjects of dreams, alphabetically arranged.

Arab experts differed from their modern successors in that they rejected all dreams that obviously proceeded from the mind's preoccupation with some engrossing idea – as, for example, when a lover sees the beloved person in his sleep, or a merchant dreams of his wares, a weaver of his loom, or a soldier of his weapons. That apart, dreams were divided into two kinds: those that told the true state of past and current affairs, and those that foretold the results of man's undertakings. The latter, again, were divided into those that offered encouragement and those that provided warnings. To obtain a good dream the dreamer had to be calm and sober but moderately filled with food. Perhaps to allow his heart to beat freely, he also had to make sure he was lying on his right side.

Interpreters for their part had to be good, pious, holy men; steadfast in prayer, constantly invoking divine assistance in directing them, and assiduous in all the duties of religion, especially in reading the Quran. They should also be masters of all sorts of other religious texts as well as divination. Dream interpretation sessions should start with a thorough enquiry into the identity of the dreamer, his circumstances, his state of mind, his religious faith and so on, all of which made a difference in respect to the way the dream should be interpreted. The dreams of rich men carried greater weight than those of the poor; the time – that is, whether the dream occurred at night or during the day – also mattered, as did the season of the year. A man who dreamt of sitting on an elephant, if it seemed to occur at night, would have to undertake an important affair, from which he would derive much benefit. But if the same seemed to happen by day it was believed that he would divorce his wife, and much trouble and grief would ensue. There was even a branch of dream interpretation that sought to recover forgotten dreams – to explore what we today would call the unconscious.

A dream in which a man found himself reading the Quran signified four things: safety from misfortune, wealth after poverty, success in achieving desired objects and a coming pilgrimage. He who dreamt of reading half the Quran was warned that half his life is past; accordingly, he should put his spiritual and worldly affairs in order. Hearing the Quran read by another in a dream was good and promised an increase of grace; however, to hear it read but not to understand it portended grief. Towards the end of the *Kamil al tâbír* there are a few 'remarkable dreams' introduced as examples of ones difficult to interpret. One man dreamt that he saw ten coffins come out of his house. There had been only ten inhabitants of the house, including himself; of those, nine had died of plague. He was awaiting his turn when a thief came into the house; falling from the roof into the court, the thief was killed. The number having been completed in this way, the dreamer escaped death. Another man dreamt that his right leg was made of ebony; the interpreters were unable to explain its meaning. It happened afterwards that the man bought an excellent slave, a Hindu. The interpreters said that the leg must have signified a servant; its being on the right, the excellence of that servant; and ebony, that he would be from India.

To this day, Islam remains the largest dream culture on the planet – so much so that even Al-Qaeda and Islamic State members claim to have received their inspiration to wage jihad from their dreams.[23] Osama bin Laden personally once claimed that he had dreamt of a team of his own men, dressed as pilots, winning a game of football or soccer against an American team. From this he concluded that the plot now known as 9/11 would succeed.[24]

Starting with Tertullian in the second century CE, many Christian writers were ambiguous about dreams.[25] Some, they agreed, were divinely inspired and pointed towards the future. But others had been sent by the Devil and were nothing more than delusional ravings. The most important authority of all, St Augustine, distinguished between 'corporeal' and 'spiritual' dreams. The former, he warned, could lead men into 'great errors'. The latter, though, were inspired by angels and could lead to equally great insights unavailable by any other method.[26]

At this point traditions diverged. The Byzantines had Achmet's *Oneirocriticon* (Treatise on the Interpretation of Dreams), a text written around 700 CE.[27] In the introduction, the author, apparently an unknown Greek who used 'Achmet' as a nom de plume, explains his intention: namely, to provide a short but handy account of dream symbols together with their interpretation. As one would expect, much of the material was in fact taken from pagan, mainly Greek, sources. But not before it was covered by a thick layer of Christian ideas about the Trinity, the Virgin Mary, angels and more.

Meanwhile, in the West, the most important authority was Gregory the Great, the Pope from 590 to 604 CE. He distinguished between dreams that had been sent by the Devil, those originating with God, and those that stood in the middle. On occasion, even those belonging to the first class could be trusted;

however, the three were not always easy to distinguish from each other. Hence, in drawing conclusions from them, extreme caution was advised.[28] Partly because of the rediscovery from about 1150 onwards of Aristotle, with his rather sceptical views about the question, a perfect consensus was never reached. Still, some of the most important medieval thinkers, such as Vincent of Beauvais (*c.* 1190–1264) and Albertus Magnus (*c.* 1200–1280), agreed that at least some dreams were trustworthy and provided reliable guidance concerning the future.[29]

At this time and others, so great was the belief in dreams that people sometimes deliberately dressed their hopes and wishes in them so as to make others believe that their predictions were worth taking seriously.[30] Here is a particularly crass example of the way it was done. In 1516 the Italian lawyer Mercurino di Gattinara, living in Brussels, where he had fallen on hard times, wrote a long letter of supplication. It was addressed to a sixteen-year-old prince, Charles of Burgundy, of whose realm Brussels was then a part.[31] In the letter Mercurino prophesized that the prince in question would become a universal ruler. The idea, he claimed, had reached him in a dream: a voice coming from up high told him that the origin of all earthly evil was in the 'plurality of princes' – a problem that Charles was destined to correct. Much of Mercurino's text was not original; instead it had been taken word by word from a late fifteenth-century treatise on the topic penned by another Italian scholar, Annio da Viterbo. As Charles was crowned first King of Spain and then Holy Roman Emperor under the name of Charles V, the 'dream' came true, though the problem of the 'plurality of princes' was never solved. Never mind. Mercurino had his reward when he was appointed the king's grand chancellor, a post he held until his death in 1530.

However much neuroscientists may scoff at the idea, interest in deciphering the meaning of dreams and what they may mean for the future both of the dreamer and of the world at large still persists among untold millions of people all over the world. Those who believe in religion still see dreams as messages from God. Many others refuse to believe that what they experience during sleep, which after all takes up one-third of their entire lives, is meaningless and has no links with their waking state. Psychologists still try to use dreams to gain a better understanding of their patients. In fact, the methods used by modern interpreters of dreams are quite similar to those the Arabs used to advocate. There has even been an attempt to link dreams to 'creative problem-solving'.[32] Starting in the 1950s, an Austrian series of books with titles such as *Altbekanntes Wiener Schusterbuben Traumbuch* (Traditional, Viennese Apprentice-Cobblers' Dreambook) and *Vollständiges Zigeunerinnen-Traumbuch* (Complete Female Gypsies' Dreambook) has sold millions of copies. In the former book, dreams of marriage mean severe illness; pain, a happy event; and a hangman, great honours. In the latter, oranges on a tree signify an unhappy love affair, a fur coat a gloomy future, birth an unhappy loss, and an ambulance, ingratitude.[33]

Today, anyone who surfs the Internet will quickly discover that future-oriented dreams are two a penny.[34] They will also find that a few of them, following the laws of chance, have in fact come true. Nor has advancing technology skipped the interpretation of dreams. People who want to record their dreams and understand their meaning can obtain software said to have been specially developed for the purpose. 'It is designed to help you discover a secret world where you can control everything. It presents a world that is very real, actually more real than conscious waking life. This world is exciting and you can learn how to make anything happen.'[35] One self-proclaimed specialist in the field, Gillian Holloway, claims to have collected a 'data base' of 22,000 dreams. It all started, she says, during childhood, when 'I recorded my dreams and found that the parallels to waking life were sometimes quite obvious. At other times I was delighted by the quirky, almost poetic way that dreams sought to buoy my confidence and hint at talents that would later surface.' Dreams, she says, are 'a barometer of internal pressure'. They hint at 'feelings, memories, values, and intentions'. 'On the threshold of big decisions and new relationships, our dreams tend to be particularly important and full of deep insights. When faced with a crossroads in your life, one of the most practical things you can do is pay close attention to the perspective offered by your dreams.'

What separates this particular dream interpreter from many of her predecessors is that she has only good news to deliver. For example, the 'tragedy' of a dream does not necessarily foretell 'a failure in your relationship, marriage, or a new career. The voyage you're embarking on isn't doomed but the overblown plans surrounding it are threatening to obscure the happiness you are entitled to feel.' Dreams about the imminent death of a relative can be 'terribly unnerving' – not because they are going to come true, but because of the 'hidden feeling of hostility' they may reveal. But stay calm, she advises: 'contrary to our worst fears, death in dreams is often a reflection of change, rather than an image of literal death.' 'Dreaming about the death of a parent need not be a portent of a coming event, nor the fulfilment of a wish as Freud would have it. It simply means that the end of an era has arrived, and a new parent–child relationship will be part of the future.' Worrying dreams, according to Holloway, such as those about forgetting one's children, 'tend not to be warnings of actual events'.[36]

One self-declared Jungian author has followed the above-mentioned Abu al-Fazl Hussain in compiling an alphabetically arranged dictionary of dreams.[37] An abortion in a dream stands for 'a decision to eradicate [something] in order to make way for something new', while an abyss means that you have come to the edge of your known reality and are being asked to confront the unknown in a courageous way. An accident 'could be a warning that where you are headed needs to be considered differently', and an acorn stands for 'a seed that can eventually grow into a mighty oak tree'. 'A baby', he writes, 'is likely to be expressing some new chapter in your life that is just beginning and has yet to unfold into full manifestation.' And so on.

To sum up, starting at least as far back as ancient Greece there have always been some scholars who, anticipating modern brain scientists, rejected any notion that dreams could have something real to say concerning the future (or anything else, for that matter). By far the most influential among them was Aristotle. Starting even further back, though, in ancient Mesopotamia, others believed in them and came up with various reasons why sleep could help throw a particularly good light on what they, the dreams, had to say. Dreams, it was thought, were neither chaotic nonsense nor symbolic expressions of whatever was going on inside the sleeping mind. Instead they were signals sent from on high. Mostly it was the gods or, in the case of the Israelites of the Old Testament, God who initiated them. Sometimes they did so at the prospective dreamer's own request, sometimes not. However, there were also a number of Christian and Islamic scholars who believed that some dreams originated with the Devil.

The idea that dreams are sent by God and have prophetic powers still retains a powerful influence in Islamic communities throughout the world. By contrast, such Westerners as believe in them are more likely to see them as emerging out of the dreamer's personality and inner life. The first interpretation, which held sway during most of history, is that dreams reflect the impact of the outside world on the dreamer's soul. The second, which made its appearance during the nineteenth century and was later advocated by Sigmund Freud above all, is that the dreamer projects his inner life on the outside world. Either way, we have seen that most dreamers put their trust in specialists – who have often formed a sort of guild of their own – but some dreamers choose to interpret their own dreams.

Dreams themselves are rooted in the altered state of consciousness known as sleep. However, specialists in the interpretation of dreams always approached the problem in a rational, calculated way that had nothing to do with ASC. Doing so, they often followed rules that could be mastered only by years of study. In the manner of both Artemidorus and modern psychoanalysts, very often they took into account not only the dream itself but the circumstances in which it had occurred and the personality of the dreamer.

What else is new?

5

CONSULTING THE DEAD

As far back as we can look, one important method for looking into the future has been to consult the dying and the dead. The basic assumption underlying necromancy (from the Greek *nekros*, dead, and *manteia*, divination) is that people belonging to those two groups are either approaching a certain threshold or have crossed it already; either way, they know more than the living do.

Genesis 49:1–2 has the patriarch Jacob, 147 years old and lying on his deathbed, speak up as follows: 'Gather yourselves together, that I may tell you what shall happen to you in days to come. Assemble and listen, O sons of Jacob, listen to Israel your father.' Actually the old patriarch's words must have come as a disappointment, for they are more like blessings than like forecasts and have almost nothing specific to say concerning the future of anyone present. However, the tradition of 'famous last words', many of them claiming to look into things to come, is alive and well. Any number of examples, real or invented, can be found on the Internet.[1]

The earliest known case of necromancy is found in the above-mentioned *Epic of Gilgamesh* of about 2100 BCE.[2] Here Nergal (who is also mentioned in the Bible, in 2 Kings 17:30), god of both the sun and the underworld, calls on the ghost of the dead Enkidu to rise from a hole in the ground 'like the wind' and speak to the grieving hero. From this point on, many encounters with the ghosts of the dead are found in Mesopotamian magical literature, covering over two millennia and reaching all the way to the Neo-Assyrian period (*c.* 900–600 BCE). One tablet dating to the period in question refers to a 'dead queen' who is renowned for her 'truthfulness'. She seems to be promising a prince, perhaps her son, that his descendants will 'rule over Assyria'.

The tablets also inform us that communicating with the deceased was considered dangerous. Improperly carried out at the hands of unqualified personnel, it could very well lead to the death of those who attempted it. Several neo-Babylonian letters now in the British Museum explain how it was done. First one must have a skull. Next one crushes mouldy wood and fresh leaves of Euphrates poplar in water, oil, beer and wine; to this are added crushed and sieved snake tallow, lion tallow, crab tallow, white honey, a frog, the hair of a dog, a cat and a fox, bristle of a chameleon, bristle of a red lizard, the left wing of a grasshopper, and marrow from the long bone of a goose. One mixes all this with wine, water, milk and *amhara* plant. These preparations having been completed, one smears the resulting ointment over one's eyes. Then it is time for the following incantation, repeated three times: 'I call [upon you], O skull of skulls: May he who is within the skull answer me!'

Though anyone who engaged in necromancy put their life in jeopardy, this fact did not prevent the practice from spreading from Mesopotamia all over the ancient Middle East.[3] As one text tells us, among the Hittite the procedure of making the dead speak opened by digging a pit and making sacrifices. Then came the incantation: 'The soul is great. The soul is great. Whose soul is great? The immortal soul is great. And what road does it travel? It travels the great road. It travels the invisible road.' Other peoples, including those of the cities of Ebla, Ugarit and the above-mentioned Mari (all in present-day Syria) were also familiar with the practice, as were the occupants of pre-Israelite Canaan.[4]

As so often, the one exception were the Israelites, whose holy book, the Pentateuch, expressly prohibits necromancy (Deuteronomy 18:11 and Leviticus 19:30). Whether that was because the rites in question were of foreign origin, or because they implied worshipping ancestors instead of Yahweh, or because they clashed with the laws of impurity as set forth in the Book of Leviticus – or simply because they were considered ineffective – is not entirely clear.[5] 'The dead know not any thing,' says the Book of Ecclesiastes (9:5). Isaiah 19:3 promises that 'the spirit of Egypt shall empty out in its midst, and I will thwart its counsel, and they shall turn to the idols and to the sorcerers and to the necromancers and to those who divine by the *jidoa* [knowledge] bone.' Resorting to necromancy, in other words, far from being regarded as a valid method of looking into the future, was understood as a sign of weakness and confusion. As such it could be of no use to those so foolish as to take it up.

Yet there is scattered evidence that some Israelites/Jews did engage in the practice.[6] The necromancer, the Talmud explains, 'takes the skull of a dead person after the flesh has decomposed. He offers incense to it, and asks of it the future, and it answers.'[7] Elsewhere it says that Caleb, one of the spies Moses sent to find out what the Land of Israel was like (Numbers 13:22), used the opportunity to visit Hebron and the patriarchs' graves. Later generations of rabbis, anxious to safeguard Caleb's reputation, did their best to prove that this did not mean he had gone to consult with them.[8] Then there is a story about a Roman by the name of Onkelos; possibly he was Aquila of Sinope (a city in present-day Turkey), a nephew of Emperor Hadrian who lived in the early second century. At one point Onkelos was considering whether to convert to Judaism. Desirous of learning more, he succeeded in raising several dead people, including Yeshu (Jesus). That done, the two had the following conversation:

'Who [asked Onkelos] is of importance in the coming world?' He [Jesus] answered him: 'The children of Israel are.' 'Do you [Onkelos further queried] advise me to cleave in/to them?' He [Jesus] answered: 'Seek what is good in/for them, do not seek what is evil for them. [That is because] whoever touches them [with intent to harm] is as if [he] is touching the pupil of his [God's] eye.' He [Onkelos] said to him [Jesus]: 'How will that man be judged?' He [Jesus] said to him [Onkelos]: 'In excrement [that is] boiling.' (Gittin 57a)

In the whole of literature, no more dramatic description of the way the dead were raised can be found than the one in 1 Samuel 28:7–20. So finely crafted is it that it is worth quoting in full:

Then [having seen the host of the Philistines, and grown afraid] said Saul unto his servants, Seek me a woman that hath a familiar spirit, that I may go to her, and enquire of her. And his servants said to him, Behold, there is a woman that hath a familiar spirit at Endor. And Saul disguised himself, and put on other raiment, and he went, and two men with him, and they came to the woman by night; and he said, I pray thee, divine unto me by the familiar spirit, and bring me him up, whom I shall name unto thee. And the woman said unto him, Behold, thou knowest what Saul hath done, how he hath cut off those that have familiar spirits, and the wizards, out of the land: wherefore then layest thou a snare for my life, to cause me to die? And Saul sware to her by the Lord, saying, As the Lord liveth, there shall be no punishment happen to thee for this thing. Then said the woman, Whom shall I bring up unto thee? And he said, Bring me up Samuel. And when the woman saw Samuel, she cried with a loud voice: and the woman spake to Saul, saying, Why hast thou deceived me? For thou art Saul. And the king said unto her, Be not afraid: for what sawest thou? And the woman said unto Saul, I saw gods ascending out of the earth. And he said unto her, What form is he of? And she said, An old man cometh up; and he is covered with a mantle. And Saul perceived that it was Samuel, and he stooped with his face to the ground, and bowed himself.

And Samuel said to Saul, why hast thou disquieted me, to bring me up? And Saul answered, I am sore distressed, for the Philistines make war against me, and God is departed from me, and answereth me no more, neither by prophets, nor by dreams: therefore I have called thee, that though mayest make known unto me what I shall do. Then said Samuel, Wherefore then doeth thou ask of me, seeing the Lord is departed from thee, and is become thine enemy? And the Lord hath done to him, as he spake by me: for the Lord hath rent the kingdom out of thine hand and given it to thy neighbour, even to David; because though obeyedst not the voice of the Lord, nor executeth his fierce wrath upon Amalek, therefore hath the Lord done this thing unto thee this day. Moreover the Lord will also deliver Israel with thee into the hand of the Philistines; and tomorrow shalt thou and thy sons be with me: the Lord also shall deliver the host of Israel into the hand of the Philistines.

Then Saul fell straightaway all along on the earth, and was sore afraid, because of the words of Samuel; and there was no strength in him, for he had eaten no bread all the day. Nor all the night.

But before he left, his servants, along with the woman, compelled him to do so (28:23).

The Greeks, and after them the Romans, always thought of the Middle East as the region whence 'diviners by the dead' (the first-century geographer Strabo) had come.[9] Perhaps that is why, in Aeschylus' play *The Persians*, Darius's ghost reveals the coming defeat at Plataea to his son Xerxes.[10] As necromancy made its way westward, many of its elements remained more or less as they had been, even as others were transformed. To take the earliest known Greek example of the practice, the hero of the *Odyssey*, on the advice of the witch Circe, decides to visit the underworld in order to learn whether he will ever get home again. First Odysseus and his men sail to the land of the Cimmerians, a miserable place enshrouded in 'one long melancholy night'. A trench is dug and a drink offering is made to the dead – first honey and milk, then wine, then water – over which barley is sprinkled. After praying to the dead, the above-mentioned Tiresias (whose prophetic powers have not deserted him even in death) appears. Odysseus has two sheep slaughtered and their blood poured into the trench. From every direction the souls of the dead approach, some of them well known to the hero. Among them is Tiresias, who tells Odysseus what he wants to know concerning what the future has in store for him.

A scholiast of the *Odyssey* explains how necromancy was supposed to work. 'For, they say, after the dissolution with the body, souls somehow retain a perception and knowledge of things here, a knowledge that is less corporeal and purer than that of the people who are composed from both body and soul.'[11] Shortly after Odysseus had visited the underworld, it was the turn of Aeneas to do so.[12] Using as his guide his deceased father Anchises, Aeneas is introduced to quite some future figures, among them his own son, Silvius (who according to legend later became king of Rome's parent city, Alba Longa), as well as Romulus, Scipio Africanus ('the lightning of war and the scourge of Libya'), Cato, the Gracchi brothers, and Caesar and Marcellus. Looking ahead about a millennium, no less, Aeneas is even told of the return of the Golden Age under Augustus. It is on this occasion that the famous prophecy concerning Rome's future rule over the world is pronounced:

Others, I doubt not, shall with softer mould beat out
the breathing bronze, coax from the marble features to

the life, plead cases with greater eloquence and with a pointer trace heaven's motions and predict the risings of the stars: You, Roman, be sure to rule the world (be these your arts), to crown peace with justice, to spare the vanquished and to crush the proud.[13]

Other references to necromancy abound. Plutarch says that the Spartan commander Pausanias, following his defeat of the Persians in 479 BCE, was overcome by hubris and summoned a 'free maiden' by the name of Cleonice ('Ringing Victory'), to serve him at night. However, as she came near there was some confusion, causing him to kill her. Thereupon her ghost started haunting him, telling him that hubris was 'a very bad thing for men'. Unable to get rid of her, Pausanias sailed to Heraclea Pontica, on the Black Sea, to visit the local *psychopompeion*, the place where the souls of the dead gather. Having arrived, he offered the usual propitiations and libations to call up the girl's soul. It did indeed appear to him and told him that, to be delivered from his troubles, he had to return home to Sparta. He made the journey, only to die immediately thereafter.[14]

Heraclea apart, the most important oracles where people went to consult with the dead were Lake Avernus in Campania (the one Aeneas visited), the Tainaron on Mani (the central 'finger' of the Peloponnese) and the Acheron in Epirus. All four have been excavated to one extent or another. The work done at the Acheron, as the most important of all, brought to light an entire temple complex, complete with the remnants of machinery for moving spectres and acoustically designed echo chambers to produce the appropriate sounds. Or so, at any rate, some of the archaeologists involved in the work believe.[15] Arriving at the site, visitors were made to wait a few days while being put on a strict diet. Only then would they be allowed to enter the main building, where, assisted by the staff and following a complex ritual, the spirits of the dead would reveal themselves and answer questions.

Other places commonly used for necromantic rites were tombs, battlefields, caves and the kind of lakes located inside volcanic craters in Italy and Spain. There were also professional *psychagogoi*, 'leaders of souls'. Hoping to attract customers, they went from one place to another. Among them were a group of *engastrimythoi*, literally 'stomach speakers'. Some necromancers were highly respected members of the community, whereas others were looked down upon as poor hucksters.

Following the *Odyssey* and the *Aeneid*, many other Greek and Roman literary works also describe necromancy in some detail.[16] Lucan in *Pharsalia* (*c.* 61–5 CE) has Pompey's son Sextus Pompeius paying a visit to a witch, Erichtho, in order to learn the outcome of the coming battle between his father and Julius Caesar. 'A body selected at length with pierced throat she [Erichtho] takes, and, a hook being inserted with funereal ropes, the stretched carcass is dragged over rocks, over stones, destined to live once again.' Next she prepares a lotion, made up of all sorts of loathsome materials, and uses it to anoint the corpse, causing the clotted blood to grow warm, the lungs to palpitate in the cold breast, new life to creep into the marrow, the sinews to stretch, the body 'to lift itself and stand erect as if the earth had spurned it', and the eyes to open. In a dreadful voice, one 'that penetrates to Tartarus' (hell) she demands to know about what the future will bring. Having learnt that the battle will be lost and Sextus and his kin killed, at length she allows the reanimated youth to expire again.[17]

Or take Heliodorus of Emesa's novel *Aethiopica*, which was probably written during the third century CE. Two travellers meet an old woman whose son has been killed in a battle between Persians and Egyptians. Following her without her knowledge, they learn that she has found his corpse and is planning to ask it about her other son. Having made sure, as she thinks, that she is not being observed, she begins by digging a pit and lighting a fire beside it. Heliodorus writes:

After positioning her son's body between the two, she took an earthenware bowl from a tripod that stood beside her and poured a libation of honey into the pit, likewise of milk from a second bowl, and lastly of wine from a third. Then she took a cake made out of fine wheat flour and shaped it into the effigy of a man, crowned it with bay and fennel and flung it into the pit. Finally she picked up a sword and, in an access of feverish ecstasy, invoked the moon by a series of grotesque and outlandish names, then drew the blade across her arm. She wiped the blood onto a sprig of bay and flicked it into the fire. There followed a number of other bizarre actions, after which she knelt over the body of her dead son and whispered certain incantations into his ear, until she woke the dead man and compelled him by her magic arts to stand upright.[18]

By using these 'base methods' she forces the corpse to tell her his brother's fate – only to learn that not only he but she herself will also perish in war. Not long thereafter, that is just what happens.

A somewhat similar story is told by Apuleius in his much better-known novel the *Metamorphoses*, or *The Golden Ass*, written in Latin in the second century. At one point an Egyptian, Zatchlas, 'a prophet of the first rank', is invited to 'reanimate a corpse from beyond the threshold of death' and 'bring back [its] spirit'. A substantial fee having been agreed upon, Zatchlas opens the proceedings by putting some magic herb on the mouth and chest of the corpse, then prays to the rising sun. Whereupon 'the chest lifted with breath, the veins pulsed with health, and the body was filled with life. The corpse sat up and spoke like a young man: "Tell me, why after drinking the draughts of Lethe and swimming the pools of the Styx do you call me back to the duties of this fleeting life? Stop now, I beg, stop and release me back to my rest."' Next, when some of those present doubt whether he can really provide any secret knowledge, the corpse, now standing up, promises to deliver 'crystal-clear proofs of my unsullied truth, and . . . reveal what no one else in fact could know or predict'. Which promise he proceeds to keep.[19]

Clearly one objective of such *pièces de résistance* was to make readers and audiences shudder with horror. That apart, public opinion about necromancy seems to have been divided. As Apuleius makes clear, there were always those who regarded practitioners as fraudsters out to bamboozle their foolish audiences. In Heliodorus' novel the old woman is actually punished – not for making false predictions, but because the practice is rather disgusting. But that was only one side of the coin. Neither the four above-mentioned oracles nor numerous less important ones where the dead were contacted could have existed over periods measured in hundreds of years if many people had not believed in them, journeyed to them and paid for the right to consult with them concerning the future. Nor, as institutions open to the public, could they have survived if persecution of them had been at all systematic.

Taking up where the Israelite/Jewish tradition had left off, early Christian writers opposed necromancy as they did other forms of sorcery. This was not because they did not believe in its reality, however. Necromancy, argued the church leader Caesarius of Arles (*c.* 468–542 CE), was the work of devils. However, devils could only operate with God's permission. Clearly, then, it had been instituted by God specifically in order to test Christian people much in the way that Job had been. Wariness was thus the order of the day.

Still, it was only in the twelfth century that generalized wariness turned into active concern. A modern historian explains the change as follows. Up to that point necromancy, along with sorcery in general, had been part of folk traditions. Left over from pagan times, it was practised mainly by lower-class people with the aid of primitive rituals. Passed from one generation to the next by word of mouth, it was not taken seriously enough to attract much opposition. Now, however, it began to be adopted by the highest social classes, including even elite clerics such as Gerald of Wales (c. 1146–c. 1223).[20] They used all their learning to engage in it, to the point where it threatened to enter the Church itself. Come the fourteenth century and every prince and every court took care to draw to its service entire shoals of sorcerers and necromancers of every kind, forcing successive popes to deal with them.[21]

In the bull *Super illius specula* (On His Watch; 1326), Pope John XXII commanded the Inquisition to use 'every means available' to persecute sorcerers in general and necromancers in particular. But it was to no avail; by the time of the Renaissance, necromancers were everywhere. In Christopher Marlowe's version of the story, the legendary Dr Faust was suspected of engaging in 'cursed necromancy',[22] though not for looking into the future but for raising Helen of Troy, 'the face that launched a thousand ships', and having her lips suck forth his soul. So were the French astrologer Nostradamus and his English colleague, the polymath John Dee. The latter at one point defended himself by claiming that he only conjured up good spirits, not bad ones. In the process, necromancy was incorporated into magic in general, thus losing much of its specificity as an instrument for predicting the future.

By the end of the eighteenth century, necromancy had become assimilated into the widespread contemporary 'Gothic' horror tales, complete with their ice-cold temperatures, vast cataracts and raging storms; lofty towers and pitch-dark nights; ghosts, goblins, vampires, serpents and madmen; low, tremulous, intermittent sounds such as moans, sighs or whispers; and gloomy buildings, incarceration, torture and tyranny. As, for example, in Karl Friedrich Kahlert's *The Necromancer* (trans. from German Ludwig Flammenburg, 1799), which combines all these elements and then some.[23] In this form it continues to haunt a certain genre of books, films and television shows right to the present day.[24]

That was hardly the end of the matter. The decades from 1850 to 1920 or so were the golden age of spiritualism.[25] Spreading from Britain to the u.s. and Europe, and from the ladies and gentlemen of the middle classes upwards, it fascinated countless people. Even the Church, locked in combat with positivism and materialism as it was, was prepared to adopt it to some extent. One of those who believed in it was Abraham Lincoln's wife, Mary Todd. Distracted by the death of two of her sons, she brought spiritualism into the White House, engaging mediums and organizing seances, at some of which the president was present. One account claims that it was she who, with the spirits behind her, persuaded her husband to abolish slavery. Another prominent advocate was Arthur Conan Doyle, creator of Sherlock Holmes, who also had a son who died. Having attended hundreds of seances, he wrote several volumes in defence of spiritualism and mediums, only to retract his support for them later on.[26]

Since Isaac Newton had proved that remote action, in the form of gravity, existed even though no one could see it, why could some other kind of invisible force not also exist? This way of thinking may explain why quite a few of those who experimented with spiritualism were natural scientists. The earliest is said to have been Augustus de Morgan (1806–1871), a pioneer logician and mathematician who developed relation algebra and still has a moon crater named after him. A least two were followers of James Clerk Maxwell, the greatest nineteenth-century expert on electromagnetism, whose equations remain in use even today. One of those followers was John William Strutt, Lord Rayleigh, Maxwell's successor as head of the world-famous Cavendish Laboratory at the University of Cambridge from 1879 to 1884. In 1904 he received the Nobel Prize in Physics, and from 1905 to 1909 he was president of the Royal Society.

A man of many interests, he tried to reconcile science with religion and actually served as President of the Society for Psychical Research.[27] Even more important was Oliver Lodge. Born in 1851 to a prosperous and highly intellectual family, Lodge studied physics at the University of London and in 1877 gained the title of Doctor of Science. Not knowing about the work of Heinrich Hertz, he independently discovered radio waves. To contemporaries he was 'a great leader both in physical and psychic science', in the words of Conan Doyle.[28] Today he is remembered chiefly for his invention of spark plugs.

As if to obey the summons, the years from 1870 to 1909 witnessed the discovery of one previously unknown form of radiation after another. The first step was taken by an English physician, Richard Caton, who showed that the brain itself was an electrical apparatus (as late as the 1930s, textbooks sometimes compared it to the control room of a large power plant).[29] As such it emitted waves that could be detected, recorded, classified and experimented with, thus opening the way to the subsequent invention of the encephalogram. Next, following hard on radio waves, came X-rays, alpha, beta and gamma rays, and finally cosmic rays. These last were first detected by a German scientist, Theodor Wulf. Perhaps because he had started life as a Jesuit priest, he too took a strong interest in spirituality. To Raleigh, Lodge, Thomas F. Varley (a close colleague of the famous William Thomson, Lord Kelvin)[30] and many of their contemporaries, the conclusion from these recent discoveries was obvious. By claiming that light consisted of particles, Newton had pointed entire generations of scientists in the wrong direction. In reality, it was made up of waves.

Waves of the kind we see at the beach presuppose the existence of water, and sound waves, that of air. Similarly, as Maxwell himself pointed out in an article he wrote for the 1878 edition of the *Encyclopaedia Britannica*, the 'undulatory theory of light' depended on some previously unknown material ('medium', to use his own term) capable of carrying electromagnetic waves. To this material he and his contemporaries gave the name 'aether'. The idea itself went back thousands of years: it was the name of an ancient Greek god and also, in Aristotle's words, the 'perfect' (that is, eternal and immutable) material of which the planets were made. In its modern form it was a strange phenomenon indeed. Omnipresent and filling up universal space, it was an elastic, inert 'material'. Yet the tiny movements of deformation caused by light waves aside, the particles of which it consisted could carry out no movements relative to one another. As a result, it could not be detected by any kind of physical instrument or experiment. But that was only one of aether's remarkable qualities. Light, it was known, is capable of being polarized – that is, made to vibrate in a single plane. However, transverse waves, by which are meant oscillations occurring perpendicular to the direction of energy transfer, are not possible in a fluid. Therefore, it was concluded, aether had to be a solid!

To resolve the dilemma, it was suggested that aether, apart from being luminiferous, had to be 'quasi-rigid' too. Before Einstein (on one of whose lectures these paragraphs draw[31]) proved that there was no need to assume its existence in such a form, almost all qualified scientists believed that the aether was real. From all this it was a relatively small step to the belief that there might also be other kinds of hitherto undiscovered radiation, attraction or influences passing through it. (Presumably, Varley was not the only scientist who carried a galvanometer in the hope of detecting them.) This in turn raised the possibility that certain people, known as mediums, were provided with special gifts – gifts that went beyond the laws of 'ordinary' science and enabled them to breathe the aether, and by so doing to sense whatever vibrations – another name for waves – the spirits of the dead might emanate. To complete the picture, it is worth noting that Lodge himself was also greatly influenced by the fact that he lost a son, Raymond, who was killed in the First

World War. Briefly, spiritualism, the discovery of various new kinds of electromagnetic waves and the invention of the non-existent aether proceeded in tandem. They complemented and reinforced each other.[32] Much like electricity, spiritual power had its uses. However, it was also dangerous and had to be handled with caution.

Supposing the aether was real, it was thought, some people might even be able to acquire special qualities by breathing it in, much as yogi did with ordinary air. Doing so, wrote Conan Doyle, they often emitted 'the peculiar hissing intakes with which the process begins and the deep expirations with which it ends'. He concluded that 'A fruitful field of study lies there for the science of the future.'[33] The techniques by which the dead revealed themselves varied. Sometimes they did so by speaking through a medium's mouth. In other cases it was a question of audible knocks, or else of automatic writing in the form of a glass or other small object which, without any visible object to push it around, moved from one letter to another on a board that had been prepared especially for the purpose.

Mediums came from all classes and all professions. Most claimed that they had become aware of their gifts from an early age. Many were women, who were regarded as especially sensitive to communication with the deceased. The term 'attuned', which was often used in this context, is itself derived from the branch of physics known as acoustics. Much later, women's heavy presence in spiritualism gave rise to an entire literature concerning the way it had helped them cope with the chains patriarchy had burdened them with,[34] though whether it did so by empowering them or by helping them deal with sexual frustrations, as many members of the medical profession claimed, is far from clear.[35] Some mediums of both sexes probably acted bona fide, but others were exposed as self-conscious frauds who used all kinds of methods to hoodwink their gullible adherents. A few, headed by the Scottish medium Daniel Dunglas

Home (1833–1886), acquired considerable fame and, with it, wealth. The Spiritualist Association of Great Britain (sagb), an organization founded in 1872, has its headquarters in London, where, in return for a fee, private thirty-minute sittings with a spiritual medium may be provided during opening hours.

Much like shamans and prophets, old and new, some mediums performed miraculous feats to prove their claims, for example by levitating, or making their body shrink or stretch so as to become shorter or longer than it was, or handling red-hot coals apparently without suffering injury. Like shamans and prophets, too, they sometimes claimed to have travelled to some other place; returning, they regaled their followers with news of things to come. Most of the questions they asked the dead, and the responses they received, did not involve major public events but concerned the life, both before and after death, of the people present, their relatives and their friends. That is why few of them have survived.

Procedures for raising the dead and consulting them are also commonplace in some non-Western cultures today. In Madagascar, the Merina people believe that the boundary between life and death is not so impermeable as to prevent the spirits of their ancestors from passing back and forth. There even exists a funerary custom, the *famadihana* or 'turning of the bones', held every seven years, when the corpses of the deceased are dug up. Amid feasting and rejoicing, people proceed to ask the dead for blessings and guidance. The Toraja of Indonesia are also said to see the borderline between life and death as permeable, more like gauze than like a wall. Making good on this belief, they dig up the corpses of the dead two years after they have been buried. Once suitably cleaned and decorated, the dead are expected to listen to questions from the living and answer them.[36]

It remains to discuss a further variant of necromancy: the near-death experience. This refers not to people who are on the point of death but to those that, having died already, somehow return to life very soon afterwards. Having performed this feat, they inform others of what they have gone through. More or less detailed accounts of near-death experiences may be found in all civilizations at all times.[37] They were rife during the Middle Ages, lost some of their popularity during the Reformation, and reappeared in connection with the spiritualist movement of the nineteenth century. From about 1970 on they resurged in full force and are now as numerous and as prominent as they have ever been.

Most of those who have been interviewed about their near-death experiences were ordinary people. But a few were celebrities, with Hollywood in particular acting as a fertile breeding ground for them; among the most important were Elvis Presley, Peter Sellers, George Lucas and Ronald Reagan.[38] The term itself was coined in 1975 by Raymond Moody, a forensic psychiatrist, in his best-seller *Life After Death*. Since then the controversy about the man, the book and the topic has never died down. This particular method of looking into the future has attracted the attention of some modern scientists who have looked into it and tried to draw conclusions as to its veracity. There have also been attempts to explain it on bio-neurological grounds. Some physicians believe it originates in a sudden flood of dimethyltryptamine (DMT), a naturally occurring brain chemical well known for its hallucinogenic power, which is apparently somehow linked to dreams and dreaming as well.[39]

As far as anyone can determine from reports about it, the near-death experience is not so very different from a shamanistic journey or that which takes place in a dream. Sometimes it leads to a feeling of ecstasy, sometimes to one of profound resignation and peace, and sometimes to the revelation of all kinds of interesting information – for example that death is but a doorway to a better life or that 'love is the essence of creation', or that the universe, only a tiny part of which can be known, is 'teeming with life'.[40] Many reports tell of situations in which their authors' souls seemed to levitate over their bodies, watching and taking in what was being done to them by relatives, priests, doctors or other people. Others tell of encounters with deceased people or supernatural beings, luminous or otherwise; a particular favourite being Jesus.

Most important for our purpose, many who have had near-death experiences claim that time seemed to become confused or lose all meaning. Though not all those who have been through such experiences report having had visions of the future, either of their own or of the world in general, some do.[41] On 5 February 2018 an unsigned list of alleged predictions made by people in such states was posted online under the title 'The Future and the Near-death Experience'. Events listed in the article include the First and Second World Wars, the 1929 Stock Market Crash, the fall of the Soviet Union and Communism, the discovery of the Dead Sea Scrolls, the Desert Storm war against Iraq in 1990, the 9/11 terrorist attacks and a great many others.[42]

While reliable figures are extremely hard to obtain, polls show that, in the UK, over half of people believe in life after death. Among teenagers, one in three believe that contacting the dead is possible.[43] So, according to a 2005 survey, do one-quarter of all Americans.[44] They include, to mention but one, the late singer Michael Jackson's sister LaToya, who enlisted the aid of a professional medium, one Henry Tyler, for the purpose.[45] Attempts to correlate belief in the spirit world with psychological problems of various kinds, as for example by seeking to find out whether 'neurotic' people are more likely to hold such beliefs, have not led to clear-cut conclusions.[46]

The Internet positively bristles with people giving advice on how to establish contact with spirits. Mediums apart, some suggest using white feathers ('considered a sign that our deceased loved ones are near'), or Ouija boards (a board printed with letters, numbers and other signs, to which a planchette, or movable indicator, points). There are '6 Ways to Communicate with Departed Loved Ones' and '10 Signs the Dead Are Communicating With You'. Henry Tyler's own net worth, incidentally, is believed to be in excess of $3 million, and he claims to have a list of 15,000 people waiting to consult him.

There are also many stories, real or fake, about brains that remained alive or were kept alive after their owner's death. Some of the most recent cases have been reported by scientists; one in particular that hit the headlines was that of a thirteen-year-old American boy named Trenton McKinley. Badly hit on the head during an accident, for several days the doctors considered him brain dead, meaning that electrical activity inside his brain had ceased. His parents had already given their permission to donate his organs when he suddenly started giving signs of life.[47]

Or take Dr Ami Citri, a neurobiologist who works for the Hebrew University of Jerusalem and has written articles with titles like 'A Reciprocal Tensin-3-Cten Switch Mediates EGF-Driven Mammary Cell Migration'. Using mice as test subjects, Citri claims to have discovered that 'memories, the retention of information over time, often for the purpose of influencing future action, leave a genetic mark on [their] brains, even after death.'[48] If the report is confirmed, the findings are extended to humans and ways are found to draw on the information in question, then no doubt necromancy will have a great future in front of it.

PART II:

BE SOBER AND

REASONABLE

6

SEARCHING THE HEAVENS

As the reader will have noticed, the methods surveyed so far – shamanism, prophecy, oracles, oneirology (the interpretation of dreams) and necromancy (communicating with the dead) – have something in common. Regardless of whether those involved in predicting were male or female, these methods were, indeed often are, based on the assumption that, to learn what the future may bring, it is first of all necessary to take leave of the 'ordinary' world and enter into a different one. It is not a question of deploying reason and logic as modern analysts, futurologists and forecasters do (or claim to do). To the contrary, it requires using various means to put reason and logic aside and to liberate oneself from them so as to enable other influences to come into play.

That, however, is but one side of the coin. Almost as far back into history as we can look, there also existed methods that did not make that assumption – meaning methods that required those who developed and relied on them to be in full possession of their senses. This was so that they could make detailed observations and then use them in order to formulate rules, and use those rules to draw conclusions concerning the future, among other things. These methods require the user to adopt the attitude not of the ecstatic but of the scientist, or at the very least the technician.

As far as we know, much the earliest and longest-lived of the methods in question is astrology – literally meaning the 'logic' or the 'word' of the stars. Long before writing was invented

– perhaps, judging by some marks found on Mesolithic bones and cave walls, as much as 25,000 years ago[1] – people must have spent time gazing at the heavens above. As they did so, it can hardly have escaped them that what took place there was, in many ways, regular and orderly. That fact having been understood, they must have wondered about any links that might exist between what they saw there and their own lives here on Earth.

The first place in which astrology is known to have been practised was Mesopotamia at some time after 3000 BCE. As different civilizations and empires rose and fell, those concerned passed their knowledge along. By the seventh century BCE, priests' knowledge was sufficiently good to allow them to predict both solar and lunar eclipses.[2] Hundreds of predictions referring to events here on Earth, made over the centuries and recorded on clay tablets, have survived. The following are some typical Assyrian astrological forecasts. They were made for the aforementioned Neo-Assyrian king Esarhaddon (r. 681–666 BCE) and his son Assurbanipal (r. 668–627 BCE):[3]

[If] on the fourteenth day the moon and sun are seen together: reliable speech, the land will become happy. The gods will remember Akkad favorably; joy among the troops; the king will become happy; the cattle of Akkad will lie in the steppe undisturbed.

Mars, the giver of decisions of the land Amurru, shone brightly in the Path of the [god] Ea (and) it revealed its sign concerning the strengthening of the ruler and his land.

[If] Venus reaches (her) secret place: favorable – she reaches the Lion.

[If] Venus does not reach the secret place and disappears: the land will suffer.

[If] Venus becomes visible in the West, reaches the secret place and disappears / the gods [will be] reconciled with Amurru.

> [If] Venus becomes visible in the west, does reach the secret place and [disappears . . .] the gods will be angry with Amurru.

One prediction dating to the early days of Esarhaddon ran as follows:

> Venus, brilliant one of (all) stars
> Appeared in the west in the path of Ea.
> In order to appease the gods she reached
> The hypsoma and[then] disappeared.
> Mars, who decides decision concerning Amurru
> Shows brightly in the past of Ea.
> He showed his charter
> For the strengthening of
> The King and his country
> As his sign . . .
> When I saw these
> Favorable omens,
> The sun appeared.
> I took courage in my heart
> And my feeling is confident.[4]

The material is often hard to interpret, the more so because many of the tablets are incomplete. As far as anyone can make out, though, predictions were based on oral or written records of past events, which were associated with heavenly phenomena similar to those being observed; and the association of ideas – sometimes involving no more than a play upon words – in connection with the phenomenon or phenomena observed. Unlike many of their successors, both of these techniques were value-free: in other words, they were unconnected either to people's behaviour here on Earth or to any divine rewards or punishments that might follow from that behaviour. Above all, they were based not on some kind of mystical experience but on fixed rules such as anyone, provided he or she was intelligent enough, could study, apply and pass to others.[5]

The names of several Assyrian astrologers are on record. They worked for the king, just as so many other officials did; possibly some of them submitted regular reports to him, though this is uncertain. From Babylon and Nineveh the art of astrology spread eastwards to China and westwards to Egypt. If the first-century historian Josephus is to be believed, the latter country received it from no other than the patriarch Abraham, who, having been born in Mesopotamia (Ur-Kaśdim) and moved to Palestine, spent some time living there.[6] From the Middle East astrology spread to Greece, which made a crucially important contribution in the form of the zodiac and the horoscope, and to Rome. Its Mesopotamian origin explains why the practice was known in Rome, sometimes with respect and sometimes without, as the 'Chaldean' science.[7]

One Jewish text, written in Palestinian Aramaic (the language Jesus spoke) around the time of his life and discovered almost two millennia later in a cave at Qumran, near the Dead Sea, runs as follows:

1. When [the Moon] rises its horns are equal, the world is in danger.

2. If you saw the moon upright towards the south and its other horn inclined towards the north, let it be a sign for you; be careful of evil; trouble will come from the north.

. . .

5. [If] its face was yellow/green on the north, high prices and famine will be in the world . . .

8. If (the moon) was red and eclipsed in Sivan, there will be confusion in the depth . . . of the sea: a command to be killed was issued against the donkeys and the non-domesticated animals.[8]

And so on, one rhyme following another, until number seventeen is reached. The first five omens could occur at any time of the year. The rest were tied to specific months. Most were negative and were to be understood as advance warnings of trouble to come; but a few were positive and announced glad tidings. Generally, the less expected an astronomical event, and the more helpless people felt in front of it, the more afraid of it they were and the greater the need to interpret it so as to bring out what it meant for the future.

Working independently on the other side of the world, the Maya too practised astrology. So much so, in fact, that Maya astronomy was really astrology. However, the principles on which it operated were, as one might expect, somewhat different. A year did not necessarily last 365 days but, depending on the purpose it served, could be 365, 360 or 260 days. Of the three, the last was the one on which most predictions were based. Months lasted either twenty or thirteen days. The Maya zodiac consisted of thirteen animal signs (13 × 20 = 260). Some of the signs can be identified, others not. For example, Venus was much feared at the time when, following its heliacal rising (when it becomes visible from Earth) it passed between Earth and the Sun. This was when its rays were supposed to slay various categories of persons or personified manifestations of nature, causing people to lock themselves in their homes by way of a precaution. Solar eclipses were also greatly feared.[9] Some present-day scholars believe that Maya rulers may have timed their campaigns according to astrological considerations, but this question is moot.

There were, however, always those who opposed astrology. For example, the second-century BCE sceptic philosopher Carneades argued that belief in astrology entailed relinquishing the idea of free will.[10] One early Christian author, Bardaisan (154–222 CE), devoted a special essay, the 'Book of the Law of Countries', to an attempt to resolve this issue.[11] There he divides the world and all that is in it into three kinds of things: those that are governed by fate alone, and can therefore be discovered by astrological methods; those that God has left to man's free will; and those, which he called 'nature', that lie in between. As we shall see, the problem of determinism and what to do with it refused to go away. It has remained one of the principal objections not just to astrology but to many other kinds of forecasting, right up to the present day.

After the fall of Rome, European astrology went into decline. Partly this was because the Fathers of the Church feared lest their flock be misled into believing that the stars, inexorably moving across the heavens, had power even over God. To St Augustine, as the most important among them, astrology was both theoretically false and practically useless – a product, he wrote, of the 'impious ravings' of those who practised it.[12] He and his successors also made occasional attempts to suppress it. And partly, perhaps, because of the general deterioration in literacy and education, which may have left experts capable of performing the often complicated calculations involved in short supply.

This caused leadership, if that is the term, in the field to pass to the Arabs.[13] Some of the most important medieval Islamic scholars, notably Al-Farabi, Avicenna (Ibn Sina), Al-Ghazali and Averroes (Ibn Rushd), opposed astrology, denouncing it as the province of superstition or fraud, or both. Religious authorities issued fatwas against it, and secular ones occasionally launched drives to suppress it, doing their best to ban it from the principal marketplaces and streets. But reality proved stronger than they were. Ordinary people, presumably motivated by the usual combination of hope and fear, kept asking astrologers for advice, while many more saw astrology as part of the wholeness of the universe and of wisdom (*hikmah*), to which it was linked.

As was the case in so many other fields, Arab astrologers started by translating ancient Greek works. To harmonize them with Islamic principles, they also added some original ones of their own. Probably the most important single contribution was made by Abu Ma'shar, whose life spanned the century from 787 to 886 CE. Like so many others, he based his understanding of the world, and especially the nature of the planets and the spheres that carried them, primarily on Aristotle. Like everyone else, he began by pointing to the obvious correspondence between the Sun and the seasons as well as the Moon, the tides and menstruation. By adding 'planetary conjunctions' and 'the indications of celestial bodies', he wrote, one could arrive at a coherent doctrine capable of providing predictions – one that, to the extent that it suggested suitable days for farmers to plough, sow and reap, navigators to set sail and doctors to design their treatments, was even subject to empirical confirmation.[14] That was one reason why he saw astrology as a master science: one that could, and indeed should, serve all the rest as their model.

Another key figure was the mathematician Al-Battani (c. 858– 929 CE). It was he who first supplemented the familiar signs of the zodiac, which go back to ancient Babylon and are based on the Earth's movement around the Sun, with so-called houses, which are based on its rotation around its own axis. Supposedly this enabled Al-Battani's colleagues to tell their clients not just what their most important qualities were but in which fields of life they would come to fruition. As so often, what predictions have survived tend to touch on the lives of the great. Thus the conjunction of Saturn and Jupiter, which was scheduled to take place in 1006–7 CE, was interpreted as heralding the end of the caliphate, a period of ruin, slaughter and famine, and perhaps even the waning of Muslim power in front of a non-Muslim civilization.[15]

By that time, the process whereby astrological knowledge moved from west to east was already beginning to go into reverse. Some four hundred years after Muhammad, it was the Arabs to whom the first European universities turned in order to reacquire the expertise they had lost. Abu Ma'shar's own work was translated into Latin not once but twice. Perhaps more important, no less a luminary than Gerbert of Aurillac, later to become Pope Sylvester II (999–1003), travelled to Spain specifically in order to obtain some astronomical – for which read astrological – works. In 1184 one astrologer, the Spanish ecclesiastic John of Toledo, gave rise to a panic by sending a letter to Pope Lucius III. In it he predicted that a terrible catastrophe would take place on 23 September 1186, when all the planets would unite under the sign of the scales (Libra). There would be wind and storms, drought and famine, pestilence and earthquake. The air would grow dark and a dreadful voice would be heard that would destroy the hearts of men. Coastal towns would be covered with sand and earth. The news caused the emperor in Constantinople to have the windows of his palace walled up. In England, the Archbishop of Canterbury proclaimed a national day of atonement. Not even the fact that, come the day, nothing special took place could entirely alleviate people's fears; instead the date kept being postponed and variants of the letter continued to circulate.

Other key thinkers who spent time and effort trying to link the revolutions in the heavens to events here on earth included Thomas Becket and Roger Bacon. During the twelfth century one work, the pseudo-Ptolemaic *Centiloquium* ('one hundred sayings'), was translated into Latin six times. More than 150 manuscripts of it have been identified so far.[16] In *Paradiso*, the third part of his *Divine Comedy*, Dante Alighieri alludes to astrology no fewer than 1,431 times. But it was by no means the literate classes alone who believed in astrology and allowed it to govern their lives to one extent or another. Rather, it made its effects felt among ordinary people too – just think of Chaucer's Wife of Bath. In *The Canterbury Tales*, her character and fate are described in terms of the planets that watched over her birth. As she explains:

I'm truly born of Venus, most certainly,
In all my feelings, but my heart belongs to Mars.

Venus gave me lecherousness and all the parts
I needed, but it was Mars that made me daring.
My astral ascendant was Taurus, with Mars sharing
The sky. Alas, alas! That love should be sinful.
I followed the path my stars placed me in,
I had no choice but to be what I have been.
I never was good at holding back: my chamber
Of Venus was open to any man who was able.
And yet, remember, I wear Mars on my face
And also in another private place.[17]

Using this text as his starting point, one modern astrologer sees 'a dialectic between Venus and Mars that works well to reveal her character and her conflicting attitudes toward life, especially men'.[18]

Some astrologers also worked as physicians. They tried to establish links between the signs of the zodiac and the four temperaments – sanguine, choleric, melancholic and phlegmatic – so as to determine who would live and who would die. Others drew parallels between six planets (Saturn, Jupiter, Mars, Sun, Venus, Mercury), and the Moon and the world's six main religious groups: Jews, Chaldeans, Egyptians, Christians, Muslims and followers of the Antichrist. At least one tried to guess which sexual position a male child born under the sign of Venus would prefer (it turned out to be the 'woman on top' position).[19] One, the polymath Girolamo Cardano, was said to have committed suicide so as to prove that his prediction that he would die at 76 years of age was indeed correct.[20] Another calculated that Islam, coming under the influence of Jupiter and Venus, was destined to last exactly 693 years and no more. As the appointed year of its demise arrived and passed, he could not help wondering what had happened.[21]

Astrology and astrologers incorporated every kind of material from cultures the world over – Greek, Arabic, Persian, Jewish and so on. Often linked with other methods of predicting the future, notably necromancy, astrology steadily gained both adherents and status. It probably reached the peak of its influence during the Renaissance. No self-respecting prince could afford to be without one or more astrologers. Pope Urban vii, Queen Elizabeth i and King Philip ii of Spain all maintained them and consulted them as a matter of course. University libraries reflected the interest in astrology, and there were many endowed chairs for those who practised it. Here it is worth noting that astrological terms still continue to permeate our everyday language. Conjunction, opposition forecast, aspect, lunatic, mercurial, bovine, saturnine, martial, jovial, ill-starred and 'lucky stars', even *mazal tov* (since the Mishnaic Hebrew word *mazal* means constellation): all show its impact.

Johannes Müller von Königsberg, aka Regiomontanus, a prominent German scholar of the period, called astrology 'the most faithful messenger of the immortal God' who had 'everywhere placed fiery stars, signs of future events'.[22] Martin Luther himself went on record as saying that, though astrologers might err, the art itself was not only permitted by God but firmly anchored in reason.[23] His most important follower, Philip Melanchthon, resorted to astrological methods in order to find out whether Luther was indeed God's appointed one. Following a little manipulation (even today, the exact date and hour of Luther's birth remain somewhat obscure) he ended up deciding that such was indeed the case.[24]

The factor that separates astrology from any of the methods discussed so far, but which makes it more like modern science, is that it is not based on any kind of altered state of consciousness. What counts are precise observation, fixed – if, as many would argue, entirely imaginary – rules and, from very early on, mathematical calculations. The last-named are indispensable for casting horoscopes (from Greek, meaning observation of the hours), a second-century CE innovation that has since become the mainstay of the field. Had it not been for knowing the date, sometimes even the hour, of a person's birth, where would modern astrologers and astrology be? It goes without saying that such methods are used, and can only be used, by perfectly sober people in full possession of their faculties so as to be able to perform the often complex mathematical calculations involved. Often they employed the most advanced equipment available, including clocks, various kinds of celestial globes, astrolabes (instruments for measuring the altitude of celestial objects), Mercator rings (a device consisting of three rings, used for various astronomical purposes) and volvelles (an advanced form of an astrolabe). As one modern practitioner explains, it is only by such means that the 'unique vibratory emanations of the sun and the sun's position in relation to other celestial bodies and constellations attending the birth of each person can be determined'.[25]

By linking astrology to well-established sciences such as surveying, cartography, navigation and optics, the instruments in question enhanced the status of astrologers specifically as opposed to magicians of every kind – to the point that, in the homes of the powerful and the rich, entire rooms were sometimes designed to reflect their owners' horoscopes, thus showing where those owners had come from and what they might still be expected to undergo and accomplish. So deeply rooted in mathematics was astrology that, far from being an inferior offshoot of astronomy as most people see it today, it often acted as the latter's parent.[26] From the time of Ptolemy in the second century to that of Johannes Kepler in the seventeenth, it was precisely the demand for horoscopes that caused scholars to put their efforts into detailed investigations of the heavens. Deliberately or not, by so doing they helped astronomy to emerge as the queen of the sciences and prevented those who practised it from starving.

At the heart of astrology is the idea that the Sun and the Moon (which, pay heed, used to be classified as planets until

Copernicus showed that they were not) have a great and even decisive impact on life here on Earth. And indeed so obvious is this fact that no one has ever denied it. The changing of the seasons, rain and drought, the shifting length of day and night, the length and direction of shadows and the movements of the tides are all governed by heavenly bodies. And so, as a glance at a field of sunflowers will suffice to show, are numerous aspects of plant and animal life.[27] Not for nothing did many religions regard the Sun as the great divinity from which all life flowed. And not for nothing did their priests devote their efforts to studying it and its impact on earthly life as best they could.

From antiquity on there have also been attempts to link the annual risings and settings of the fixed stars with the weather. Some of those attempts were associated with the greatest scientific names of the day, such as the philosopher Democritus and the astronomers Eudoxus of Cnidus, Meton of Athens, Callippus and, above all, Hipparchus. The achievements of the last-named are said to have included the first attempt to calculate the circumference of the Earth, resulting in a figure very close to the correct one. The results were recorded either in books or on specially cut stones. Known to the Greeks as *parapegmata*, they were intended for the use of ordinary people. About sixty such devices have been found. The earliest ones date to the fifth century BCE, but there is reason to think that they go back much further.[28] Even today, throughout the world many scientists, and physicians in particular, are hard at work trying to discover links between the season in which a person was born and his or her future health, intelligence and character.[29] Qualities which, it need hardly be added, will go a long way in determining his or her fate.

In the words of the Roman poet and astrologer Marcus Manlius, who plied his trade during the reign of Emperor Augustus:

So the whole earth lies divided between the stars, from which are to be drawn the rights proper to each; for they enjoy the same communication with one another as the signs between themselves, and as they [the signs] join together in hatred separate, at one time diametrically opposed, at another joined in a trigon [triangle] by different causes directed to various influences, so lands are related to lands, cities to cities, shores to shores, and kingdoms to kingdoms. So will each man have to avoid or choose a place for himself and, according to the stars, mutual trust is to be hoped for or dangers to be feared, as his gens [race, family] has come down from the highest heavens to earth.[30]

Briefly, as in the perfect heavens, so here on Earth, which, though less than perfect, was modelled upon them. It was this supposed correspondence that caused Renaissance scholars such as Pietro Pomponazzi to look at astrology as part of natural science.[31] As in natural science, too, astrologers do their best to make the correspondence as specific and as detailed as they can by taking into account the movements of the remaining planets, the fixed stars and the relationships among all of these. The more accurate the astrologer's calculations, the better positioned he or she is to look into the future.

Ptolemy, who surely must be ranked among the greatest astronomers of all time, in his *Tetrabiblos* readily admits that the planets and fixed stars, being further away, have less impact on things on Earth than the Sun and the Moon do. However, that does not mean that, when the time came to work out the details, they could or should be excluded. Modern research may have proved him right: the authors of one recent study have concluded that exploding stars, by sending out innumerable electrically charged particles that move at close to the speed of light, do affect the climate here on Earth.[32] No less a physicist than

Stephen Hawking has argued that it is the large-scale structure of the universe that determines local physical laws.[33] Either way, John Dee, the famous sixteenth-century English astrologer who advised Elizabeth I when she was still a princess, appears to have had reason on his side when he wrote: 'The true sizes, not only of the earth's globe but also of the planets and of all the fixed stars, should be known by the astrologer.'[34] Which is to say that, for correct results to be possible, everything that takes place in the heavens should be discovered, watched and taken into account.

Translations of the *Tetrabiblos*, some of them intended to provide guidance to practising astrologers, continue to be published even today. Other works that tell practitioners how to go about their business also abound. One modern astrologer warns us that *The Planets and Signs Do Not Control Our Lives*. Rather, they are just indicators of the natural laws in operation. They are moved by the same principles and forces as we are. They form a giant 'Cosmic Clock or extended calendar to which we can refer.'[35] Researching this book, I was surprised to find, in the library of my alma mater, a volume titled *Recent Advances in Natal Astrology*. Apparently meant to be taken perfectly seriously, it discusses, among the new discoveries that astrologers have to take into account, the recently discovered planets Neptune, Uranus and Pluto; any hypothetical planets that are still awaiting discovery; asteroids; and something called 'harmonic charts', which are based on multiples of three. These last, it turns out, were mainly the work of the British master astrologer John Addey (1920–1982). A 'monumental four-year survey of planetary motion effects', we are told, led him to the conclusion that 'stationary planets', defined as those which changed their direction of movement and went into retrograde within two days of the date of a person's birth, can dominate the entire chart.[36]

All this shows that neither astrology nor the kind of reasoning on which it is based are dead and done with. In the Western world alone, tens of millions of people are said to believe in it to an extent. By some reports, most young Americans think astrology is a science. If anything, their number is increasing.[37] If tax records are any guide, in France in 1991 there were more astrologers than Catholic priests.[38] The sums spent on searching out the secrets of the stars each year certainly run into the billions of dollars – which includes not just those sums paid for private consultations but those spent by the media, which, whatever their editors may think in private, keep publishing horoscopes and occasional interviews with astrologers as part of the fare they ladle out to their customers. There used to be a time when strangers meeting at a party introduced themselves by saying, I am sign so and so, what are you?

To this day, there are countries whose leaders consult astrologers on a more or less regular basis. A notorious case in point was President Ronald Reagan, who, if some of his aides are to be believed, was drawn into the business by his wife, Nancy.[39] Astrology even took a part in the preparations for Reagan's Reykjavík meeting in 1986 with the Soviet leader Michael Gorbachev. Gorbachev's successor, Boris Yeltsin, also had astrological data collected for him.[40] Rarely does one meet someone who does not know his or her astrological sign. Presumably that is one reason why searching the heavens has been subject to so many attacks that question its credibility.

7
CLEAR AND MANIFEST

O mens and portents are naturally occurring phenomena distinguished from the rest by their anomalous nature. Supposedly they were sent by the gods (in monotheistic societies, God himself), who used them to serve fair warning of coming events. Among the phenomena in question were comets, eclipses, earthquakes, violent storms and floods, as well as the birth of people or animals with deformities, and all kinds of apparitions. Without well-understood natural causes and obvious explanations, such novel, strange and rare occurrences left those who witnessed them with a sense of wonder and, on occasion, stupefaction. Yet few people considered them sufficiently unimportant to simply shrug them off. Instead, every effort was made to bring out what they might mean for the future. Where they differed from the signs used in divination was that, rather than being deliberately and often ceremoniously sought, they made themselves manifest unexpectedly and of their own accord.

The things that omens could foreshadow varied enormously. Among them were the births and deaths of important people; impending political and military events; all kinds of natural disasters waiting to happen; and much more. The following list, put together from various sources by a modern scholar, illustrates how these things were done in Mesopotamia between about 1800 and 600 BCE:

If moths are seen in a person's house, the owner of that house will become important.

If there is a mole to the right of his eyebrow, what his mind is set on he will not attain.

If a malformed newborn [lamb] has two heads and the second one is on its back, and its eyes look in different directions, the king's reign will end in exile.[1]

A somewhat different example of the way omens worked is provided by the *Iliad* (8.68–79). Here we find Zeus, incensed at the other gods' interference with the Trojan War, sitting alone on Mount Ida, which gave him a view both of the city of Troy and of the Greek ships arrayed along the seashore. From this comfortable position he hurled three successive thunderbolts, encouraging the Trojans, who pressed the Achaeans hard – so hard, in fact, that Zeus worried lest the latter might indeed be defeated, give up the siege and save Troy from the destruction that fate had ordered for it. He sent out an eagle, 'greatest of winged omens, gripping a fawn, the offspring of some swift doe, in its talons. It dropped the fawn by the glorious altar of Zeus, where the Greeks offered sacrifice to him from whom all omens come. Knowing the bird was sent by Zeus, they ran at the Trojans with a better will, their minds filled with thoughts of battle.'

Behind the belief in omens and portents was dread, the ever-present feeling that man was a helpless plaything in the hands of jealous, interfering and perfectly amoral gods. Zeus, we read in a fragment of the seventh-century BCE poet Semonides of Amorgos, 'controls the fulfilment of all that is, and disposes as he will. But insight does not belong to men; we live like beasts, always at the mercy of what the day may bring. Knowing nothing of the outcome that God will impose upon our acts.'[2] Or take the following lines, attributed to the poet Theognis at some time during the sixth century BCE:

No man . . . is responsible for his own ruin or his own success; of both these things the gods are the givers. No man

can perform an action and know whether its outcome will
be good or bad . . . Humanity in utter blindness follows
its futile usages. But the gods bring all to the fulfilment
that they have planned.[3]

Entering classical, Hellenistic and Roman times, we find that
opinions concerning the reality and predictive value of omens
and divination generally varied very much. At one extreme were
the Spartans. Always tending to be conservative, they took omens
very seriously and often allowed their military expeditions to be
cancelled or delayed by them.[4] Alexander at one point tried to
make his diviner-in-chief, Aristander, bless a coming battle, only
to be repeatedly rebuffed.[5] At the other extreme was the mid-
third-century BCE Roman commander Claudius Pulcher. On the
eve of a naval battle with the Carthaginians he discovered that
the sacred chickens aboard his ship refused to eat, whereupon
he had them thrown into the water, saying, 'If they won't eat,
at least let them drink.'[6] The outcome, incidentally, was a total
Roman defeat as almost all of Pulcher's ships were sunk. He was
recalled to Rome, had his office as consul taken away from him,
was tried for incompetence and impiety and had to pay a fine.
He died soon after, possibly by suicide.

Polybius compared people who took the advice of *manteis*
with those who were afflicted by chronic illness. Yet he also says
that the *strategos* (military general) should always have one of
them at his side – if not to find out what the future might have
in store, then at any rate in order to allay any outbreak of super-
stitious terror among their troops. Onasander, a first-century
CE military theoretician, insisted that the commander should be
able to read omens intelligently and also that he should summon
his officers to inspect the victims for themselves. 'Soldiers', he
says, 'are far more courageous when they believe they are facing
dangers with the good will of the gods; for they themselves are
on the alert, every man, and they watch closely for omens of

sight and of sound, and an auspicious sacrifice for the whole army encourages even those who have private misgivings.'[7] The early second-century CE general Frontinus went much further. Listing various stratagems to be used in war, he suggested that commanders trick their troops by staging the kinds of omen that would help lift their morale.[8] At a guess, his advice was followed many, many times.

On the whole, the evidence is mixed. Yet one indication that most people took omens seriously is that careful records were kept and that very few diviners were ever repudiated, let alone punished, for coming up with a wrong forecast. The most interesting view is the one put forward by the Roman historian Livy. His magnum opus, *Ab urbe condita libri* or *History of Rome* (27–9 BCE), covers a period measured in centuries. In it, he reports more omens than any other ancient historian does, including, to list but a handful, the birth of hermaphrodites among the Sabines, a two-headed boy in Veii, a one-handed boy in Sinuessa, and the birth of a baby girl with teeth already grown at Auximum. 'I am not unaware', he says,

> that, as a result of the same disregard that leads men generally to suppose nowadays that the gods foretell nothing, no portents at all are reported officially, or recorded in our histories. However, not only does my mind, as I write of ancient matters, become in some way or other old-fashioned, but also a certain conscientious scruple presents me from regarding what those very wise men of former times thought worthy of public concern as something unworthy to be reported in my history.[9]

Few present-day 'experts', when judging their predecessors' work, are as modest and as unassuming.

Another ancient historian who could never have his fill of omens was Suetonius, a contemporary of the emperors Trajan and Hadrian. A fine writer who excelled in gossip – his books included the *Physical Defects of Men*, now lost, and *On Famous Courtesans* – he says that Julius Caesar's death in 44 BCE was followed by the appearance of a comet. As so often, Suetonius explains, people interpreted it as a sign of some disaster to come. Others, however, saw it as Caesar's spirit ascending to heaven. Not surprisingly, this was the interpretation favoured by his successor, Augustus.[10]

The lives of subsequent Roman emperors were also studded with portents of every kind. Perhaps the most interesting case is that of Vespasian.[11] Coming from a family of no particular distinction, Vespasian chose a military career. Starting early on, his life was marked by more portents than that of any other emperor, bar Augustus. At the time of the birth of each of his children, an oak tree put forth a shoot that showed him the child's future. On one occasion a dog brought him a human hand. On another, an ox that had bolted burst into his dining room and then lay down submissively at his feet. A cypress tree on his father's estate, struck down by no visible cause, was restored intact the next day. Not long after the murder of Nero, when Vespasian was in his early fifties and commanding an army against the Jewish revolt, a statue of Divus Julius [Caesar] turned around of its own accord until it faced the east. In 69 CE, while staying in Alexandria, he successfully cured two men, one blind and the other lame (or, depending on the source, impotent). Some of these stories were reported not by some scribbler but by Tacitus, as sober, as cynical and as great a historian as they come. Briefly, Vespasian's ascent was well documented long before it actually took place. Never mind that at least some of the omens may have been manufactured retroactively in order to prove that, in reaching for and attaining the throne, he was a man of destiny who had the favour of the gods.

The life of the emperor Honorius (395–423 CE) was also accompanied by omens. However, by that time the empire had long been Christianized. Not surprisingly, Christian writers saw things in a different light. 'Omens', wrote St Augustine,

> are of force just so far as has been arranged with the devils ... [and] they are all full of hurtful curiosity, torturing anxiety, and deadly slavery. For it was not because they had meaning that they were attended to, but it was by attending to and marking them that they came to have meaning.

'They are', he concludes, 'of no significance apart from the previous arrangement in the mind of the observer.'[12]

Yet omens continued to play a major role throughout the Middle Ages. Gregory of Tours' *History of the Franks*, to mention but one of many, is full of them. In addition to the usual comets and eclipses, he speaks of stars that suddenly started moving in the wrong direction. There were also lights in the sky, mysterious bellowing sounds that could be heard for weeks on end, rains of blood, signs that appeared on vessels in peoples' homes and could be neither deciphered nor erased, and the like. Such signs, which 'usually announce a king's death or the destruction of a whole region', 'filled [his] heart with foreboding'.

Some two and a half centuries later, Einhard, Charlemagne's servant and biographer, provided a long list of the omens that bedevilled his hero towards the end of his life.[13] Among them were frequent eclipses of the Sun and the Moon as well as a black spot that appeared on the former and remained visible for seven days. Others were earthquakes – one of which caused part of the newly built palace at Aix-la-Chapelle to collapse – and a ball of fire that rushed across the sky, causing the emperor's horse to rear and throw its rider. Charlemagne himself, Einhard says, remained unfazed by all this. Nevertheless, a few months before his death, people began to notice that the words 'Carolus Princeps' on the legend inscribed around the cornice of the basilica he had built had faded and disappeared.

Giovanni Villani, a fourteenth-century Florentine chronicler who wrote a history of his native city, saw the 1348 earthquake in Carinthia/Friuli as a sign that the end of the world was near (for him, it was: not long thereafter he fell victim to the Black Death). Neither Nostradamus (1503–1566) nor the Renaissance princes and merchants who were his clients could have enough of comets, eclipses, deformed animals and similar apparitions.[14] Nor can one simply call Nostradamus a charlatan or an ignoramus. Having travelled extensively, besides his native French (he was born Michel de Nostredame), this astrologer and alleged seer had mastered Latin, Greek, Italian, Hebrew and Spanish, and perhaps Arabic as well. His letters abound with references to ancient authors, whom he regarded as the source of all wisdom. Throughout his life he never ceased adding to his knowledge by reading in such fields as poetry, astrology and history.

In a letter to his son César, Nostradamus reflected on what he was doing, which was obstinately, and perhaps vainly, trying to find a way to combine the will of God (without which nothing could be achieved), sorcery (which he roundly condemned), altered states of consciousness and the true insight he was seeking. Such insight, he concluded, could only be had on the basis of careful study.[15] Not surprisingly, his predictions were often wrong. Meeting with the widowed Queen Catherine de' Medici of France in 1564, he promised her peace, thus failing to foresee the outbreak of civil war just two years later. Next he claimed that her son, the future Charles ix, would live to ninety (he died at 24). Many of Nostradamus' quatrains – in which form he wrote his 942 *Prophéties* – were distinguished by both their high poetic quality and their vagueness, which made them applicable to almost any situation. Perhaps that explains why his various blunders did no lasting damage to his reputation.[16]

Nostradamus' slightly older contemporary Pietro Pomponazzi, who has been mentioned earlier, put it as follows:

I cannot ever remember having read in history books that any notable political change, or the life of any man worth mentioning, be it because of his virtue or his wickedness, did not take place without having those great celestial portents present at birth or at death, at the beginning or the end. And since such portents are given always or frequently, they must have a natural cause [and were not produced by either angels or demons, as many other scholars claimed]. Furthermore, it can also be argued that they draw from the power of celestial bodies from the fact that, as the histories tell, the astrologers forecast them or interpret them on the basis of the observations of the stars.[17]

Though we may not be able to say why certain omens relate to the events they portend in the way they do, Pomponazzi says, the fact that they do so is indisputable. Moreover, the greater the historical event, the more 'extraordinary and bewildering' the portents by which it is preceded, as made evident, first and foremost, by the appearance of the Star of Bethlehem at the time of Christ's birth.

Comets and new stars (nowadays we call them supernovas) also appeared in the heavens in 1585, 1593, 1596, 1604 and 1607. Each time one did, the outcome was interpreted as a warning. God, who most of the time was content to allow the world to run its own affairs without interference, was angry, and repentance was called for. 'Comets', wrote the German preacher Elias Ehinger when a new one appeared in December 1618,

generally mean war and the spilling of blood/dearth and death, and one fears that some years hence there will be great political upheavals with wretched wars and rebellions among the common man. And there will be great persecution. Great lamentation and misery will course through the whole world. With war, spilling of blood, robbery, murder and arson, great dearth and pestilence.[18]

Never was a warning better placed!

Similar statements could be multiplied a hundredfold. Both in Europe and in North America, Ehinger's contemporaries were unanimous that such phenomena called not just for interpretation but for prognostication.[19] As late as the second half of the seventeenth century it was taken for granted that any striking event, not only in the cosmos but earthquakes and freak storms, for example, had to have some kind of hidden meaning. In the end it was only the unfolding scientific revolution that caused belief in omens and portents to wane, turning acts of God into insurable risks, as one historian put it.[20] A major step in this direction was Edmond Halley's volume *Synopsis of the Astronomy of Comets* (1705). It showed that the one that had been observed in 1688 was the same as those that had appeared in 1601 and 1531. He also predicted it would return in 1758. In fact it did, though by that time he himself was dead.

An even more important step in the same direction was Benjamin Franklin's discovery, in 1749–52, that lightning was simply an electrical discharge. Far from acting as a messenger from another world, it was a naturally occurring phenomenon. And what was more, it was one that could be brought down to the earth and tamed. Two or three centuries earlier, saying so would have led Franklin to the scaffold. Now it both reflected what the philosopher and sociologist Max Weber, a century and a half later, called the 'disenchantment of the world', and pushed it along. Even so, the change was gradual, and catalogues of such events, along with their interpretations, kept being published (as they continue to be in the present day, especially online).

8

ON BIRDS, LIVERS AND SACRIFICES

To Plato, divination was proof 'not to the wisdom, but to the foolishness of man'.[1] Yet neither the Greeks nor the Romans ever took an important decision without trying to divine its consequences first. Private individuals of moderate means would turn to cheap fortune-tellers, who could be found on virtually every street corner, whereas rich and public persons consulted colleges of more or less specialized priests who were in charge of the process.

Among the numerous kinds of divination two stand out: ornithoscopy, or observing the flight of birds, and haruspicy, meaning the examination of the internal organs of sacrificial animals. Both had this in common: those who practised them, instead of passively waiting for an omen to present itself out of the blue (sometimes literally so), were trying to divine the consequences of specific actions they were about to take.

The idea that birds, either rising into the heavens or coming down from them, can act as messengers of the gods is an ancient one indeed. They do so both in the *Epic of Gilgamesh* and in the Book of Genesis, where Noah sends out first a raven and then a dove to find out what is going on in the world and whether the waters of the Flood have been receding. Ornithoscopy plays a key role in the opening lines of the earliest Greek literary work that has come down to us, the *Iliad*. Here the seer Calchas, 'the best of the bird-watchers who has knowledge of everything that has been, is, and will be',[2] resorts to it in order to discover which god has sent a plague to the Achaeans, and why.

At one point in the *Odyssey*, Odysseus' son Telemachus expresses the hope that his father will soon return home.[3] 'At once' a hawk is seen on the right, swooping down and carrying off a large white fowl. The seer Theoclymenus, who was present on the occasion, interprets this as meaning that Odysseus will return home and claim his own (the name of Odysseus' wife, Penelope, may have been derived from *penelops*, duck). As many passages in Aeschylus, Aristophanes and the poet Callimachus (310–240 BCE) confirm, ornithoscopy continued in use in post-Homeric times. Hesiod, in the concluding lines of *Works and Days* (826–8), says that happy is the man who can divine the future by birds. Sparta, Athens and perhaps other cities even had specially built observatories where experts in ornithoscopy carried out their work. An inscription found at Ephesus and dating to the period of the Greco-Persian Wars of 499–449 BCE gives us some idea of the way it was done. First, a question had to be formulated and submitted to the priests in charge. As the inscription explains,

> If the bird is flying from right to left, if it settles out of sight, it is lucky; but if it lifts up the left wing, then whether it rises or settles out of sight, it is unlucky. But if the bird is flying from left to right, should it settle out of sight in a straight line, it is unlucky; but if raising the right wing, lucky.[4]

Additional details are provided by Xenophon. An eagle screaming on one's right was considered a favourable sign, but mainly for great men, not for ordinary people. Furthermore, the one Xenophon saw was sitting, not flying. That fact was interpreted as foretelling trouble, for it was while the bird was rising that it was most likely to be attacked. Affected by the spectacle, and having made sacrifices to Zeus and received additional unfavourable omens from him, Xenophon refused the command over the Ten Thousand that had been offered him.[5] Both Julius Caesar and his successor Augustus held the office of augur as part of their official duties. Countless other examples could be adduced. Nor did the end of the ancient world and the rise of monotheism put an end to such ideas. Even today, some people believe that doves symbolize peace, eagles power and swans transformation, whatever that may mean.

Recent scholarship has shown that, contrary to earlier interpretations, the Homeric poems do not mention haruspicy. In Greek art it is first represented around 530 BCE; the earliest literary reference is found in Aeschylus' *Prometheus Bound*. Euripides in his play *Electra* attributed the origins of haruspicy to Prometheus, who handed it to man, a sacrilegious act for which Zeus later punished him. In fact it seems to have originated in ancient Mesopotamia early in the second millennium BCE. Inherited by the Assyrians, the art spread to Anatolia (the Hittites), Etruria, Greece, Rome and, moving in the opposite direction, China. But it missed Egypt, where it only came into fashion following that country's conquest by Alexander. Its spread enabled both ancient and modern historians to speculate about the links among all these peoples.[6]

Depending on the country in question, the principal animals used were tame ones such as sheep, goats and, in Rome, calves. Conversely, cocks, pigs and bulls were avoided out of fear their high spirits might contaminate their livers and cause false conclusions to be drawn.[7] Here and there we also hear of dogs and frogs being used; however, the context makes it hard to judge whether these references were meant seriously or in jest.[8] Once the sacrifice was completed and the animal killed, its spleen, stomach, kidneys, heart, lungs and the flow of blood under the knife were all subjected to minute examination. However, pride of place was awarded to the liver, which was regarded as the source from which the blood flowed. That is why, in Greek as well as the languages of the above-mentioned countries, the liver often had terms such as 'head', 'path' and 'river' attached to it.[9]

Strangely enough, in matters of divination this idea persisted even after Aristotle had shown it was not correct.

A healthy liver was supposed to show that the divinity to which the sacrifice had been made was present and was pleased with what he or she was offered. An anonymous second-century CE papyrus from Faiyum, in Egypt, explains the logic on which all this was based:

It [the region of the body governed by Jupiter] includes the breast as far as the stomach and the liver, in which reside fire, the mental faculty, and the appetitive faculty because the conversion into blood of the food which is introduced into the body is performed by the liver. It is for just this reason that the faculty of command is assigned to this portion; for truly the leader takes forethought for the state as the liver does for the body. If indeed the region of the liver becomes diseased, the whole body immediately becomes jaundiced or dropsical and like a corpse, because the blood is not properly managed. Therefore such things come to mankind from Jupiter, and therefore also the omens are observed in the livers of the victims by those who perform sacrifices, and appetites for food and sexual intercourse come from the liver.[10]

Particular significance was attached to the size and colour of the lobe (*lobos*, in Greek), as well as any stripes. Other significant features were density and smoothness. All this explains why archaeological digs in the Middle East have turned up hundreds of clay models of livers. In Italy, a bronze one was discovered. The earliest models date all the way back to the eighteenth century BCE. Some but not all carry lists of instructions, often divided by the part of the liver on which they are inscribed. Once the expert in charge had found particular signs on an actual liver, he could compare them to those on the models. Whether this was done only for purposes of study and teaching or also during the sacrifice itself is not clear.

As with the bird-watchers, most of the questions brought to the haruspices' attention appear to have been of the yes/no kind. To proceed or not to proceed? Will the outcome be good or bad? So important was the technique that, when the *lobos* was found to be missing, a campaign might be suspended and the army sent marching back home. This actually happened to the Spartan commander Agesipolis in 388 BCE. Nor was he the only commander who was compelled to cancel a campaign or delay it until the entrails finally brought a favourable message. It was a haruspex named Spurinna who, on the basis of a sacrificial animal that was found not to have a heart, warned Julius Caesar to beware of the coming Ides of March.[11] In vain, as it turned out.

Here it is important to note that the various forms of divination, like astrology and the interpretation of omens, but unlike shamanism, prophecy, dreams, oracles and necromancy, did not depend on people entering an altered state of consciousness of any kind, mysteriously travelling from one world to another and the like. Instead divination was a 'rational' art (*technē*, in Greek), coolly and methodically practised by experts who had studied it, often by going through an apprenticeship, and later spent years perfecting it. The Stoics in particular were in favour of the practice. To them divination provided proof that the gods existed, that they loved the human race, and that fate ruled over everything and could not be resisted.[12] Cicero in the book he wrote about the topic tried to convince his readers that it was either nonsense or fraud. Yet this did not prevent him from practising it as part of his duties as consul, an office he held in 63 BCE.

Divination by reading the entrails of sacrificial animals was still practised by Emperor Julian ('the Apostate') around the middle of the fourth century CE. Refusing to heed a warning that the signs were bad, he went to war against the Parthians, only to be defeated and killed.[13] When Christianity took over the empire its leaders, taking the opposite approach from that of the Stoics, worried lest divination cast doubt on God's omnipotence. Accordingly, they did their best to prohibit haruspicy as well as similar practices. They did not, however, succeed in making them disappear. Some remained in use during the early Middle Ages. Even today, in spite of all kinds of attempts to expose them as frauds, many forms of divination persist and flourish. In some East African societies this includes reading the future from the entrails of sacrificial animals.[14]

Other forms of modern divination are palmistry, scrying (gazing into crystal balls or other translucent or reflective objects), reading tea leaves, *o-mikuji* (randomly selecting pieces of paper with one's fate printed on them, practised in Shinto shrines in Japan) and so on. All are supposed to foretell the future of, and to, those who rely on them. Though all have been denounced countless times as having no scientific value or for being fraudulent, or both, all continue to be believed in by countless people.[15]

Nor is it always a question of the diviners convincing or bamboozling their clients. I myself used to know a lady who sometimes read Tarot cards at conventions as well as at parties and the like. At the time she was in her late thirties, very attractive, and possessed of what physicians would call a good bedside manner. Intrigued and attracted, people flocked to her to hear what she had to say, particularly in respect to their economic situation, health problems and, of course, any problems of the heart that affected them or their close relatives. However, she was never able to make up her own mind whether to take the cards seriously. On one hand she often referred to them as 'my nonsense'. On the other, she spent a lot of time and effort learning about them, studying them and improving her technique. Perhaps more important, she felt quite certain that her clients depended on her and were looking to her for solutions to their difficulties. Many of them did not have much formal education and had often led very hard lives. Worried that any bad things she might see in their future could have a negative effect on their psychological health, she ended up abandoning the practice.

9
THE MAGIC OF NUMBERS

The person who it was who first realized that numbers were not just arbitrary signs but could be used to capture important aspects of physical reality has long been forgotten. Certainly ancient Egyptian mathematicians, driven by the annual rise and fall of the Nile, which erased all surrounding landmarks, were anxious to find out ways of measuring and recording the area of rectangles, triangles and other forms. They likewise took an interest in calculating the volume of containers, useful for assessing taxes, which were paid in grain. And in angles, of course, without which the pyramids and other structures could not be built.[1] Their achievements in this last field have, in certain respects, never been equalled.[2] As we saw when we discussed astrology, numbers also governed the movements of the heavenly bodies, causing the Babylonians to take an interest in them. Even the Old Testament, which is anything but a textbook in mathematics, says that the Lord 'arranged all things by measure and number and weight' (Wisdom of Solomon 11:20).

But that was only the beginning. The discovery that musical scales are governed by numbers was attributed to the sixth-century BCE philosopher Pythagoras.[3] Pythagoras was born in Samos, an island in the Aegean Sea. He and his followers lived in Croton before being forced to flee to Metapontum (both of these are cities in southern Italy, which at that time was known as Greater Greece). The sect they formed was both mysterious and inclined to mysticism, with the result that there are many stories told about it, not all of them credible.

For the Pythagoreans, their master's discovery of musical scales led to the belief that 'all [or, depending on the translation, God] is number'. In their hands, numbers became the starting point from which to contemplate and grasp the meaning of everything in the universe. They even prayed to the tetractys (mystical tetrad), triangular figures made up of ten dots in four rows formed by the numbers 1 + 2 + 3 + 4 = 10:

> Bless us, divine number, thou who generated gods and men! O holy, holy Tetractys, thou that containest the root and source of the eternally flowing creation! For the divine number begins with the profound, pure unity until it comes to the holy four; then it begets the mother of all, the all-comprising, all-bounding, the first-born, the never-swerving, the never-tiring holy ten, the keyholder of all.[4]

Seeking admission, novices to the sect had to undergo an apprenticeship that lasted five years. At its end came an oath they swore to the tetractys:

> By that pure, holy, four lettered name on high,
> nature's eternal fountain and supply,
> the parent of all souls that living be,
> by him, with faith find oath, I swear to thee.

Under Pythagoras' system, integers were considered the work of the gods. By contrast, irrational numbers (meaning those with π, pi, at their head, which could not be expressed by dividing integers by each other) were regarded as abominations. By one story he even went so far as to have those of his followers who mentioned them executed. Odd numbers, being indivisible by two, were thought of as strong and male, and even, divisible ones as weak and female (this view still persists).[5] As an extension of this, every number was believed to have its own character and meaning. The number one was the generator of all numbers, as indeed it still remains. Two represented opinion; three, harmony, as well as the unity of past, present and future which helped men look into it. Four (others say, eight) meant justice; five marriage; six creation; and seven the seven planets or 'wandering stars'. Seven was also considered a sacred number worthy of being venerated. In all three monotheistic religions, sacred it remains.

A somewhat similar scheme is provided by Philo of Alexandria. Philo was a Jew who tried to defend his native religion by showing that it contained all the essential elements of Greek culture, Pythagoreanism included. Not surprisingly, he took one (God's number) as the basis of all other numbers. Two was the number of schism, three of the body. Four, which corresponds to the four elements as well as the four seasons, was the perfect number. Five was the number of sense and sensibility, and so on. Seven in particular he considered special, the freest, holiest and most important of all. But 50, 70, 100, 12 and 120 also carried a 'special' significance.[6]

Much better known than Philo was Plato. Plato's great objective, to which he dedicated his entire life, was to go beyond the often illusory world that is revealed to us by the senses so as to gain an understanding of the absolute one of ideas, by which it is governed. Mathematics, with its inexorable and immutable laws, he regarded as a critical stepping stone in that direction.[7] Which is why, by one tradition, he had an inscription placed over the entrance to his academy which read, 'let no one ignorant of geometry enter here'. In the *Republic* he suggested that the Guardians spend ten years of their lives, from age twenty to thirty, studying mathematics.[8] In the *Laws*, one of the last books he wrote, he calculated that his ideal city should have exactly 5,040 ($1 \times 2 \times 3 \times 4 \times 5 \times 6 \times 7$) citizens.[9] The reason he gives is that 5,040 can be divided into all natural numbers from 1 to 12 except 11. But it is also the sum of 42 consecutive primes (23 +

29 + 31 + 37 + 41 + 43 + 47 + 53 + 59 + 61 + 67 + 71 + 73 + 79 + 83 + 89 + 97 + 101 + 103 + 107 + 109 + 113 + 127 + 131 + 137 + 139 + 149 + 151 + 157 + 163 + 167 + 173 + 179 + 181 + 191 + 193 + 197 + 199 + 211 + 223 + 227 + 229). The number 42 itself has any number of quaint and interesting qualities.[10] One of Plato's modern translators says that, coming under Pythagorean influence during his old age, he seems to have felt that the city's well-being depended almost as much on the blessing conferred by that number as on justice and moderation.[11]

Plato's rough contemporary Polykleitus, whom many consider the second-greatest Greek sculptor after Phidias, came up with the Canon, meaning measure or rule.[12] According to its principles, numbers also govern what we perceive as beauty, specifically including that of the human body and face. The Canon itself has not survived. However, subsequent comments on it suggest that Polykleitus took as his basic unit what he considered the smallest part of the body, the terminal section of the little finger, and calculated all other body parts as multiples of it. Fingers had to be proportionate to the wrist, the wrist to the forearm, the forearm to the arm, and so forth.

Other artists, the most important of whom was the Roman architect Vitruvius (d. c. 15 CE), added their own relationships. As, for example, in declaring that, ideally, the body should be six times as tall as the foot is long.[13] Much later, the principle was taken up by several Renaissance artists who tried to fit the body into a circle or a square, and it has been confirmed by some modern studies regarding what is considered attractive, albeit that the specific figures they mention are not only different but seem to change from time to time and from one country to the next.[14] Architects applied a similar idea to buildings. The best-known example is the Parthenon, which is exactly 1.618 times as long as it is wide; 1 divided by 1.618 is the same as 0.618 divided by 1. This is known as the golden ratio, or phi. Famous artists and architects including Michelangelo and Le Corbusier have used it, and the UN

Headquarters in New York, designed by Oscar Niemeyer and built from 1948 to 1952, sports several examples of the golden ratio.

Starting with Galileo during the first half of the seventeenth century, one aspect of nature after another surrendered to the power of mathematics. That includes honeycombs, the form of drops of water and of snowflakes and of sand dunes, the spirals of sea shells, the shape of flower petals, the composition and qualities of every kind of material, the rate at which radioactive matter decays, and a literally infinite number of other things.[15] Not only did numbers relate to the external world, but they also seemed to play strange and unexplained games among themselves. Some numbers are positive, others negative. Some are primary, others not. Some are real, others imaginary. Some are considered rational in the sense that they may be expressed as fractions, others are not. Among these last are some of the most important of all, including, besides phi, pi, which as all of us learnt at school is the ratio of the circumference of a circle to its diameter, to say nothing of Fibonacci numbers and Gödel numbering, which fascinated Einstein during his last years.

I myself remember how, as a child of seven or eight, I was fascinated by the multiplication table that was printed on the backs of the standard notebooks we were made to use. Some numbers, such as 25, 35, 49, 63 and 81, only made a single appearance. Others, such as 12 (3×4, 2×6), 20 (5×4, 2×10) and 36 (4×9, 6×6), kept reappearing at different places. Some were primary – not that I knew the meaning of the term – and others were not. I felt there was something magical about it and spent many boring classroom hours trying to figure out how it all worked and what, if anything, it meant. Much later I discovered that mathematicians have engaged in the same pastime – that is, playing games with numbers so as to find out the special properties of a great many of them. Just check on Wikipedia: the number 0, which incidentally has many of the strangest qualities of all; and then on the numbers 1, 2, 3, and so on.

As one modern mathematician, echoing Plato, puts it, numbers and mathematics 'offer a pathway for consilience, or the unification of all fields of knowledge into a single tree; an ontology of information founded on the idea that computation is a universal solvent that can untangle any complex system, from human consciousness to the to the universe itself'.[16] By definition, anything that can be reduced to an algorithm (set of rules for calculation or problem-solving) can be predicted – even if it deals with things that have never been seen and cannot be seen, as in the case of elementary particles. And even if we do not have the slightest idea why a specific relationship between A and B exists, for example why gravity causes a falling object to accelerate at rate G and no other; even if the prediction is statistical, based on probability; in such cases we can predict not what will happen but the likelihood, numerically expressed ('the chance that x will happen is such and such'), that it will.

The special character of numerology is not the mathematics on which it is based, which as we shall see tends to be rather elementary (regardless of whether it is employed by an Archimedes or by a modern numerologist, one plus one always makes two), but in that its adherents invest numbers with meaning, which is to say treat them as symbols for things other than themselves. Doing so, they endow them with a mysterious, even numinous, character. Some numbers are considered to have certain powers and are influential, others are much less so. Some are lucky, others not. Some promise this, others that (as one would expect, the things they promise or do not promise vary very much from one culture to another). Some are associated with the planets or the signs of the zodiac, thus providing a link to astrology.

Numbers both reflect and affect the universe and everything in it in myriad different ways. Whether we know it or not, they also impact on the life of each of us. That is why, provided they are properly understood, they can help us predict what the future has in store. And also why, in the eyes of two modern numerologists who happen to be married to each other, numerology might 'prove to be more breathtakingly exciting than scientific mathematics'.[17]

A rather curious early example of the way numbers were used for prediction is a second-century CE text known as the *Oracles of Astrampsychus*. Named after a much older legendary Egyptian magician (with whom, of course, it has nothing to do), it is an off-the-shelf kit such as may have been used in any market square. It consists of a list of 92 questions, numbered from 5 to 103, which people might want to ask a fortune-teller, plus over a thousand possible answers. The client would ask the question that fitted him best and look up its number. Next the fortune-teller, using a complicated system of additions and subtractions, would arrive at the correct answer out of the thousand. Typical questions resembled those submitted to fortune-tellers at all times the world over: Will I become a senator? Will I marry a handsome prince? Will I survive the illness (no. 42)? Will I rear the baby? Will I be freed? Will I be sold? Will I sail safely? Answers were divided into good, bad and ambiguous. Many of the possible responses imply resignation to fate, such as 'wait', 'not yet', 'be patient' and 'don't expect it'.[18]

Here it is important to point out that neither the Old Testament nor any other ancient Middle Eastern document uses digits. Instead they spell out numbers. For example, Methuselah's lifespan covered 'nine hundred sixty-nine' years, not 969 (Genesis 5:27). The number of adult male Israelites who left Egypt was 'six hundred thousand', not 600,000 (Exodus 12:37). The same is true of contemporaneous texts like those of Homer and Hesiod. The first to hit on the idea of assigning numerical values to the letters of the alphabet were the Greeks, around 500 CE. Under this system alpha was 1, beta was 2, gamma 3 and delta 4. Iota stood for 10, kappa for 20, pi for 100, and so on all the way to omega, which stood for 800. The Greeks even went so far as to invent an additional letter, ϡ, pronounced *ss* or *sh*, which was assigned the value of 900.[19] For making all sorts of calculations much easier to carry out, the alphanumeric method can only be called brilliant. Presumably that is why it spread from the Greeks to the Jews. They called it *gematria*, a clear reference to the people from whom they had borrowed it.[20] The Romans and, much later, the Arabs also adopted it.

Asked to interpret a dream, an Arab numerologist (for example) would proceed as follows. First he would assign each letter in his client's name its numerical value. Next, nine was subtracted from each. If nine remained, then the dream had been of cities, which was a bad omen. If eight, it had been of travel; if seven, then of oxen, harvests and corn. Six related to angels and holy men, which denoted the completion of undertakings; five, horses and arms; four, the heavens and stars; three, that the person had divulged a secret to another; and two, that he looks to someone who will assist or benefit him in worldly affairs. Finally, one, a unit, recalled the idea of some king or great man, as being unique of its kind, and stood for success in one's desires and deliverance from trouble.[21] These elucidations were all derived, very ingeniously, from passages of the Quran in which such numbers occur; which in turn confirmed the need of the interpreter to be intimately and minutely acquainted with the contents of that volume.

Both during the Middle Ages and the Renaissance, numbers continued to be everywhere. Every number was assigned a multitude of things it stood for, whether in individual men and women or in the world as a whole. Perhaps because, for most people under ordinary circumstances, it marks the maximum number of things they can keep in mind at the same time, much the most popular number of all was seven.[22] It stood for completeness, perfection, the Universe (four, the Earth, plus three, the heavens), the day of rest after Creation, the days of the week, the seven churches, the Seven Sorrows of Mary, the planets, the Sacraments, the Deadly Sins, the Seven Virtues (three theological virtues plus four pagan virtues), the final days and end of the world, the seven trumpets and seven seals of the Apocalypse, the seventh age, the seven petitions of the Lord's Prayer, the seven journeys of Christ, the seven parts of the Mass, the seven ages of man, the seven last words of Christ, the seven tones of a scale and the seven types of good works. And so many other things as to baffle the mind. There were also eight beatitudes, each linked to one of eight dames. Even some poetry, notably the anonymous late fourteenth-century romance *Sir Gawain and the Green Knight*, was made to obey strict mathematical rules. They governed the relationship between its overall length, the number of verses and of lines, and so on.[23]

The forever changing and forever expanding outcome was an extraordinarily dense and complicated network in which everything was related to everything else.[24] Attempts to prohibit numerology, like those made by the jurist Gratian in his mid-twelfth-century legal book the *Decretum*, and also by his rough contemporary, the great Jewish scholar Maimonides, were to no avail. Numbers, one modern scholar has written, existed apart from mutability and human error. That was why they were closest to the language of the Creator, providing what some saw as the most important highway to approaching Him and understanding His work.[25]

On a more humdrum level, advice on how to use numbers for looking into the future was provided by one John Mirfield. Little is known of him; apparently he was a chaplain (or clerk) who, towards the end of the fourteenth century, worked at the hospital of St Bartholomew in London. A constant witness to death and the dying, he left behind a summary of his experience. To decide which patient would live and which one would die, he recommended the following procedure:

Take the name of the patient, the name of the messenger sent to summon the physician, and the name of the day upon which the messenger came to you; join all their letters together, and if an even number result the patient will not escape, if the number is odd then he will recover.[26]

The assignment of numbers to the current Latin alphabet is attributed to Heinrich Cornelius Agrippa von Nettesheim (1468–1535), a German polymath who wrote about theology, ballistics, mining and medicine, as well as a wide range of occult matters. As the scientific revolution took hold and spread, so did the use of mathematics in attempts to understand the world. Later scientists as eminent as the aforementioned Lord Kelvin went so far as to claim that anything *not* expressed, or capable of being expressed, in terms of numbers was 'meagre and unsatisfactory'.[27] No wonder numerology and numerologists flourished.

'Number vibrations', meaning the number to which each letter in your name vibrates, one early twentieth-century American numerologist claimed, 'are the mental language of nature.' That is why one should study everything indicated by '[one's] Birth Force as carefully as [one] studies music or astronomy. Study hotels, stores, wearing apparel which vibrate to the same number, not from a narrow point of view but from a broad outlook, and try all the things related to you.' For example, a horse vibrates to 11, while a lily vibrates to 22, 'showing that it is a master in the flower realm . . . We use these illustrations to show that it is not the number which is important, but the thing which speaks through number.' Your name, she goes on, is not just a gathering of letters arbitrarily assigned to you by your parents. It is, rather, 'the only mental assurance you have as to who you are and what you stand for in the community . . . The whole system of being, called the person, is represented by the name.'[28] That is why getting its numbers right is so very important. One present-day work on numerology proceeds in a somewhat similar manner.[29] The author starts by assuring his readers that their lives are governed by numbers – specifically, the dates of their birth. Character, relationships, life direction, finance and many other things are all affected. True, ultimately what decides is fate, but learning about numerology can help one prepare for what is coming and to move with or towards it, rather than vainly trying to oppose it.

The simplest way to use numerology, the author goes on, is by 'birth path numbers', meaning the day without the month or the year. Suppose you were born on the 18th of the month. Since 1 + 8 = 9, your birth path number is 9, known as the 'Primal Force'. People whose birth number starts with the number one are 'often' born leaders. 'If that is your life path number, it is recommended that you start projects from scratch and if you make mistakes, just learn from them . . . Make sure to take risks, be brave, and take full responsibility of our actions; only then will you receive true success in life,' the author writes. Number twos are romantic and gentle. Number three means creativity, number four trustworthiness and practicality. There is a chapter about compatibility and about attitudes to money. For example:

> Six is a symbol of provision and abundance. Material things aren't hard for them to achieve, and these include money. These people also often inherit family wealth, or are given money without them asking for it. These people also often receive gifts and recognition, and more often than not, succeed in whatever they put their minds to. They mostly never have to worry about cash flow, and their finances just stay stable for all time – no drastic highs or lows!

More advanced systems, the author suggests, also take the month and the year into account. Others correspond to the numbers used in astrology and Tarot cards, whereas others still have their own methods of assigning numbers to letters. The key number that governs everything is nine, a discovery said to go back to Pythagoras. Though our author does not say so, other sources claim that it derived its importance from the fact that it falls one short of ten, which, as we saw, is 1 + 2 + 3 + 4, the 'perfect' number.

Armed with this clue, one proceeds to list the letters of the alphabet as follows:

1	2	3	4	5	6	7	8	9
A	B	C	D	E	F	G	H	I
J	K	L	M	N	O	P	Q	R
S	T	U	V	W	X	Y	Z	

Some numerologists suggest that vowels should be dropped from the table and only consonants considered. By adding up the numbers of the letters that form one's name, repeatedly if doing so is necessary to obtain a single digit, one arrives at one's master number. The exceptions are 11, 22 and 33. Being master numbers that 'tickle our sensationalist nature', their digits should not be added up.[30]

By noting which single digit occurs most often in one's name, one can find out that person's character and talents. Character being fate, the road one can and should take in life, as well as the one which, on pain of failure, one should try to avoid, is unveiled. For example, those who have a 1 master number could be great politicians, actors or athletes because they are natural leaders and born warriors; 3 could be great painters, actors or artists of any kind. Suppose a person is called Sam Smith. S = 1, a = 1, m = 4, S = 1, m = 4, i = 9, t – 2, h = 8. The total is 30, and 3 + 0 = 3. The final outcome is a 'motivation number' that provides guidance concerning what we want to do and can do. In this particular case, three is 'the joyful spirit'. Such people 'like being around humorous, fun-loving people, and their joyful spirit also makes them easily noticed wherever they go'.

But those are only preliminary steps. By using similar methods, but focusing on one's initials rather than on one's day of birth or name, one can get one's 'balance numbers', those that give life 'balance and coordination'. If, for example, one's balance number is one, 'it means that you have to learn to draw strength from yourself – within yourself. However, you might also find it helpful to share your story and your feelings with family and friends – just learn to strike the balance between the two.' All this, one author says, will enable you to do 'the math of life – for love, for success, for fulfilment'.[31] Another teaches us that, in assuming that the day and time we were born determines our fate, people commit a bad error: the

> truth is the opposite – we determined when we would be born, before we were born, knowing deep in our soul the right mathematical day and time to come to this world. We determined our fate first and then the corresponding day and time. This determined our personal numerology including our life path number and destiny number.[32]

'By using a series of totals and subtotals of numbers, as well as grids, graphs and tables,' a third expert says, 'a numerologist can dissect a person to reveal their inner soul and outer ego; their internal and external personas; how they see themselves versus how other people perceive them; their past life and present destiny; how they operate physically, mentally, emotionally and spiritually; and much more.'[33] Not only in the West but in the Islamic world and East Asia, many people continue to take numerology seriously. In Korea it is practised in a ceremony known as *gut* (*kut*). In one of its forms it involves a *mudang* (female shaman) who answers questions by shaking a container with pine tree seeds. Those that fall out are ignored, those that stay in counted. Uneven numbers are fortuitous, even ones bad.[34]

Even as I was starting to research this book, I learnt that, in the United States, some Jewish people had been using numerology to prove that Hillary Clinton is an Amalekite and that Donald Trump would usher in the Messiah.[35] Here is how it works. Transcribed into Hebrew and using the numbers ascribed to them in *gematria*, the letters in the words Hillary, Rodham and Clinton each equal 255. The letters forming the word Amalekiah, for a woman from the nation of Amalek, also add up to 255. And the Amalek people are the hereditary foe of Israel, to whom no mercy must be shown.

But that is just half of it. The total of all three of Clinton's names is 765 (255 × 3) and – not by accident, of course! – that is the same value as *et tsara*, 'a time of terrible trouble'. The term comes from verse 12:1 in the Book of Daniel. It deals with the occasion when Michael, the guardian angel of Israel, will stand in defence of his people at a time of catastrophe. Clearly she means trouble: who knows what terrible things she might yet do? Never mind that when it comes to spelling non-Hebrew words, and names in particular, there are usually several different ways in which the letters may be transcribed. Doing so, one obtains wildly different results. For example, a woman from Amalek might equally well be called an Amalekit. In that case, the sum of the letters forming the word would be not 255 but 640.

By contrast, the sum of the Hebrew letters making up the name Donald Trump is 424, which is equal to 212 × 2. One expert in the field has noted that the sum of the letters in Bernie Sanders's name is 636, or 212 × 3. Enter the Ben Ish Chai (Yosef Hayyim), a rabbi who lived in Baghdad from 1832 to 1901. This 'authority on Jewish law and master kabbalist', as Wikipedia calls him,[36] interpreted the number 212 as meaning a difficult time for Israel. But there is more to it: 212 also matches any number of other words or combinations of words, including, most important of all, 'Messiah Son of David'. Halleluiah! Numerology, also known as arithmancy, is also mentioned in the Harry Potter series of books. There it is said to be a difficult subject that some students at Hogwarts, notably Harry's friend Hermione, take specifically in order to improve their ability to look into the future.

To sum up, numbers and the relationships among them have always fascinated people and do so still. Some of the greatest philosophers who ever lived saw them as a necessary part of the order of things, admirably placed there by nature, or God, or whatever else, for us to explore and, very often, enjoy. That is why, it is claimed, if only the correct way to juggle them can be found, they will tell us a lot about the most diverse things, starting with the movements of the heavens, musical scales and what does and does not please our aesthetic sense; and ending, if numerologists may be believed, with our own personality, future and any historical significance we may have.

Supporters of numerology have called it a 'very precise, measurable and almost scientific method of predicting the future', no less.[37] But not everyone sees these things in such a serious light. Here is a passage from what was once a worldwide best-seller, *The Story of San Michele* (1929), the memoirs of the Swedish doctor Axel Munthe:

> On Friday night the Farmacia [on Capri] was full of people gesticulating wildly in an animated discussion about their chances for the Banco di Lotto of to-morrow. Tetraquattro, sessantanove, quarantatre, diciasette!
>
> Don Antonio had dreamt his aunt had died suddenly and left him five thousand lire, sudden death – 49, money – 70! Don Onorato had consulted the hunchback in Via Forcella, he was sure of his terno – 9, 39, 20! Don Bartolo's cat had had seven kittens in the night – numbers 7, 16, 64! Don Dionisio had just read in the 'Pungolo'

that a camorrista had stabbed a barber at Immacolatella. Barber – 21, a knife – 41! Don Pasquale had got his numbers from the custodian of the cemetery who had heard them distinctly from a grave – il morto che parla – 48![38]

10

DECODING THE BIBLE

One important method people have long used for looking into the future is trying to gain access to the 'true' meaning of certain hallowed texts, including, above all, the Bible itself. Here the basic assumption, already found in the Talmud, was that God had deliberately placed hidden messages in the text for His people – whoever those might be – to decipher.

The process could be carried out in a variety of different ways. One was to comment on passages from books like Daniel or Revelation that seemed clearly prophetic in content and try to relate them to current events. Another was to look for prophetic meaning even where it did not seem to lie on the surface. The New Testament bristles with attempts to correlate every kind of detail from the life of Jesus with phrases and stories from the Old – as, to use the most important example of all, when Matthew (1:22–3) claims that Isaiah foretold the miraculous conception ('The virgin will conceive and give birth to a son, and they will call him Immanuel', 7:14).

One medieval French exegete argued that each verse of the Psalms corresponded to a year since the Incarnation, enabling him to calculate both the age of the world and the year in which it would come to an end. Subtler and more ambitious was the system of concordances between the chronology of the Bible and that of the Church worked out by Joachim of Fiore in his *Liber de concordia* (Book of Correspondences).[1] The Bible, he explained, is made up of two trees. The first grew from Adam and ended with the birth of Christ; the second started from Christ and would end with his Second Coming. Each tree contained 63 generations, divided into three groups of 21. Two of the New Testament trees – or 42 generations – had to pass before the onslaught of the Antichrist would get under way. The length of a New Testament generation was thirty years, because that was Christ's age when he got his first disciples. From this it was clear that the coming of the Antichrist would be in 1260 (42 generations of thirty years' duration each).

Further confirmation was received from the fact that, in Revelation 12, a miraculous woman is mentioned who fled to the wilderness, where God looked after her for 1,260 days (interpreted by Joachim as years). In the event, the year 1260 came and passed. But this slight miscalculation did not prevent Joachim's works from being consulted even as late as the first decades of the sixteenth century.[2] Had he not predicted (or so it was claimed) the coming of 'Karolus ein sun Philippi', 'a scion of the illustrious Caesarean line', who would chastise the papacy for all of its numerous abominable sins? And were not his prophecies supported by a host of other luminaries ancient and modern? And was not this prophecy horribly fulfilled when the troops of Charles v, son of Philip the Handsome of Burgundy, sacked Rome in 1527, forcing Pope Clement vii to shut himself up in the Castello Sant'Angelo? Yet Joachim himself, perhaps because he was aware of the perils facing anyone who claimed to have a direct line to God, insisted that he was not a prophet at all. All he had, he said, was the 'spirit of intelligence' to understand the mysteries of holy scripture.

Similarly, the widely held fear that the end of the world would come in 1666 goes back to the fact that 666 is mentioned as 'the number of the Beast' in Revelation 13:17–18. But this is just one of several interpretations that have been put forward. One is that 666 equals the sum of the letters used in *gematria* to spell out the words 'Emperor Nero' (r. 54–68 CE) in both Hebrew and Aramaic. When it was pointed out, on the basis of textual evidence, that the book was written after the destruction of the Second Temple in 70 CE and thus could not be understood as predicting Nero's rise, those in favour of the method were unfazed. They pointed out that the same letters, minus the word 'emperor', also matched the name of Domitian, who reigned from 81 to 96 CE. Never mind that transcribing the words could be done in different ways, with or without the titles added. Never mind, too, that some of the oldest surviving manuscripts say '616' rather than '666'. Nor have such notions become extinct since. Each time Christians feel Islam seems to pose a danger to their religion and them, ideas surface regarding the number 666 being associated with either the name Muhammad (spelt Maometis for the occasion) or the Quran.[3]

The idea that 666 really meant 1666 and that 1666 would bring about the end of the world is found for the first time in the work of Thomas Lupton, an Elizabethan purveyor of miscellaneous knowledge, in his 1597 book *Babylon is Fallen*.[4] From that point on it was referred to more and more often. There were also several attempts to combine 666 with 1260. One such was made by an English scholar and preacher, Thomas Goodwin (1600–1680). A dyed-in-the-wool Puritan, shortly before the outbreak of the Civil War Goodwin was forced to flee to Holland. However, during the years of the Commonwealth he was allowed to return. For about two years he served as chaplain to none other than Oliver Cromwell. For Goodwin, it was simple: all one had to do was add 406 (the approximate date of the Hun invasion and also of the instalment of the first pope, identified with the Devil, in Rome) to 1260, and everything was clear.

By 1666, Cromwell was dead and the Commonwealth no longer existed. Nevertheless, the number 1,666 had been bandied about so often that, when a fire destroyed large parts of London in that year, people were quick to turn to Goodwin's prophecy. The more so because, starting the previous year, a plague had killed an estimated 100,000 people, one-quarter of the city's entire population. The fact that 666 is the sum of the squares of the first seven primes ($2^2 + 3^2 + 5^2 + 7^2 + 11^2 + 13^2 + 17^2$) and has quite a few other 'magic' qualities probably helped.[5] Things did not end there. When Nancy and Ronald Reagan moved from the White House to the Bel-Air area of Los Angeles, they had the address of their new home changed from 666 to 668 St Cloud Road. In 2003, U.S. Route 666 in New Mexico was changed to U.S. Route 491. As the New Mexico secretary of transportation, Rhonda Faught, explained, 'The devil's out of here, and we say goodbye and good riddance.'[6]

Without a doubt, the most eminent among the multitudes who tried to use the Bible to calculate the date of the Second Coming and the establishment of paradise was Isaac Newton.[7] In 1704 he even wrote an entire volume, *Observations upon the Prophecies of Daniel, and the Apocalypse of St John*, devoted to the topic. Like many others, he started by postulating that each of the 2,300 'prophetick days' mentioned in the Book of Daniel really meant a year. Next, he tried to make up his mind as to the year with which to start. Was it 'the rise of the little horn of the He Goat' (Daniel 8:1–27), sometimes understood as 331 BCE, the year in which Alexander and his Macedonians overthrew the Persian Empire? Or 70 CE, when Jerusalem and the Temple fell to the Romans? Or 800 CE, when 'the Pope's supremacy commenced'? Or 1084, which marked the ascent to the papal throne of Gregory VII? Next, he more or less repeated the procedure on the basis of another number, 1,290, which is mentioned in Revelation.[8] Next, he used various abstruse calculations to reconcile the different results he got. Finally, he suggested 2060 as the most likely date of the Second Coming, but did not rule out later ones such as 2090, 2132, 2344 and 2374. Apparently flummoxed, he added that the Bible prophecy would not be understood 'until the time of the end', and that even then, 'None of the wicked shall understand.' To this day, commentators differ as to whether a biblical 'day' really means a year, or a thousand years (on the basis of

2 Peter 3:8–10), as well as to whether a week simply means seven days, a year, or seven years.[9]

Other methods of deciphering what the Bible 'really' said about the future abound. Gregory of Tours, with whom we are already familiar, provides one description of how it was done. The story is about Gregory's uncle St Tetricus, Bishop of Langres. He was trying to forecast the fate of Chram, the wicked son of the sixth-century Merovingian king Chlothar, whose father was King Clovis.

> The Book of the Prophets was opened first. There [his priests] found: 'I will take away the hedge thereof, and it shall be eaten up. When I looked that it should bring forth grapes, it brought forth wild grapes' [Isaiah 4:4–5]. Then the book of the Apostle was opened and they found this: 'For yourselves know perfectly that the day of the Lord so cometh as a thief in the night. For when they shall say, Peace and safety; then sudden destruction cometh upon them, as travail upon a woman with child; and they shall not escape' [1 Thessalonians 5:2–3]. Finally, the Lord spoke through the Gospel: 'And every one that heareth these sayings of mine, and doeth them not, shall be likened unto a foolish man, who built his house upon the sand. And the rain descended, and the floods came, and the winds blew, and beat upon that house; and it fell and great was the fall of it' [Matthew 7:26–7].[10]

And indeed so it came to pass; following a battle, Chram was captured by his father and burnt alive along with his wife and daughters. This example of cleromancy (lot casting; from the Greek *kleros*, a lot, and *manteia*, divination) is but one of several that appear in the text.

Something called a 'random Bible verse generator' can be found today on the Internet.[11] Click a button and a verse will appear on the screen in front of you. For example, 'God is our refuge and strength, an ever-present help in trouble' (Psalms 46:1) or 'For where your treasure is, there your heart will be also' (Matthew 6:21). The same method was used by some Jewish rabbis too. A person who was worried about the consequences of some course of action he or she was contemplating would ask a question, and in response the rabbi, opening the Bible at random, would find the answer in the first line of the text that revealed itself, starting, as is usual in Hebrew, from the right. Orthodox Jews still follow the practice from time to time, though apparently not all of them are prepared to do so. Nonbelievers will argue that all this is simply a question of chance and that nothing concerning the future can be learnt by such methods. Believers, though, claim that it is God's hand that guides them to the page or sentence in question – and gives them the insight needed to interpret it, of course.

Various other ways of using the Bible for predicting the future have also been proposed, and not just in the pre-modern world either. 'With correct instruction for reading the Torah,' we are told, 'Kabbalists can see their past, present, and future states.' They do so 'by gazing at these symbols [meaning not just the letters but the little dots and lines that appear above and under them, indicating the vowel sounds] in each of their combinations. But to see that, it is not enough to simply read the text. You must know how to see the codes.'[12]

Yet another method is to write down every second (or third, or fourth or fiftieth) letter of the text in the hope that they will add up to an intelligible message. This is known as the ELS (equidistant letter sequence) method and can be used either in the normal Hebrew way, from right to left, or else from left to right.[13] Advocates claim to have found predictions for virtually every major event of history, though whether it is just the Pentateuch or the Old Testament as a whole that should be used remains moot. Assuming, for the purpose of illustration, that the former is the case, here is how it is done.[14] First, the entire text is rearranged in a single queue sequence comprising 304,805 letters. Second, one chooses one or more events that one hopes are encoded in the text: the destruction of Hiroshima, say, or the Gulf War, or anything else. Third, one chooses letters that are one, two and three letters apart, and on up to ten, and then chooses further letters, at twenty to fifty letters apart, and so on; in this way, by utilizing a consistent number of skips, code words are found. Thus a text running, say, 'Brown Lunch Units Exist; SearcH our HOme to Enter', would yield 'blue shoe'. Supposedly it was by such methods that DivineCoders, described as 'an online community that is dedicated to searching for equidistant letter combinations in the Bible', discovered that God had embedded the words 'Prince Harry London' and 'Nixon Resigns' in the text.[15]

As anyone at all familiar with codes and coding knows, writing out a text that will correspond to another one in this way is exceedingly difficult. To believers, that was another proof that the messages discovered by using this method were, in fact, of divine origin. But that was only the beginning. An agnostic Jewish physicist, Nathan Jacobi, and an Orthodox Jewish engineer, Moshe Aharon Shak, say that they have discovered hundreds of ELSS. Among them are 'a plane will be lost' (said to predict the disappearance in March 2014 of Malaysia Airlines Flight 370), the outbreak of the Ebola epidemic later in the same year, and Hurricane Katrina in 2004.[16]

There also exists a considerable number of variations of Bible decoding. Each is advocated by a different school of thought and employs a somewhat different technique. One, known as *notarikon* (derived from the Greek meaning 'short writing'), goes back as far as the Talmud, during the early centuries CE. It consists in taking the first, last or middle letter in each word and joining them like beads on a string to form new words or even entire sentences. Another, called *themurah* (change), works by transposing letters.[17] The process can be, and in the past has been, carried out by hand. Like so many other things, though, the advent of computers has made it much easier.

Most of these methods have remained in the possession of a small number of enthusiasts who discussed them among themselves. However, back in 1997 an American journalist named Michael Drosnin made a splash by publishing *The Bible Code*.[18] This time, too, it was claimed that the code had been deliberately inserted into the text by God. From that time it lay dormant for three millennia, until an Israeli mathematician, Eliyahu (Ilya) Rips, hit on the idea of using a computer to break it. Rips, whom Drosnin described as a mathematical prodigy, first came to the world's attention in early 1969 when he tried to set himself alight in protest against the Soviet occupation of Czechoslovakia. However, he received only some superficial burns before the fire was put out. Diagnosed as suffering from schizophrenia, he spent some time in a closed mental hospital where he worked on complex mathematical problems. Released, he was permitted to go to Israel, where he made his discovery. Allegedly he passed the secret to decoding the Bible to the Israeli military, which used it in order to gain intelligence during the 1991 Gulf War (in which, however, Israel took no part). The Israelis in turn disclosed it to the u.s. National Security Agency, from one of whose analysts I myself first heard about it at some time during the early 1990s.

The following will explain how Rips's code is applied. First, the text of the Pentaeuch is written out one letter at a time without either punctuation marks or spaces between words, and without capitals, which Hebrew does not have. For example, the words, 'In the beginning God created the heaven and the earth. And the earth was without form, and void; and darkness was upon the face of the deep. And the Spirit of God moved upon the face o[f]' will look as follows:

i	n	t	h	e	b	e	g	i	n	n	i
n	g	g	o	d	c	r	e	a	t	e	d
t	h	e	h	e	a	v	e	n	a	n	d
t	h	e	e	a	r	t	h	a	n	d	t
h	e	e	a	r	t	h	w	a	s	w	i
t	h	o	u	t	f	o	r	m	a	n	d
v	o	i	d	a	n	d	d	a	r	k	n
e	s	s	w	a	s	u	p	o	n	t	h
e	f	a	c	e	o	f	t	h	e	d	e
e	p	a	n	d	t	h	e	s	p	i	r
i	t	o	f	g	o	d	m	o	v	e	d
u	p	o	n	t	h	e	f	a	c	e	o

At this point one can start checking whether some groups of letters, joined either horizontally or vertically (some say diagonally as well), form words that correspond to known historical events as well as any future ones one can think of. As with ELS, special software has even been developed to facilitate the search. It was by using this method that it was discovered, albeit only *post factum*, that the words 'Yitzhak [Rabin] was murdered' appear in the Bible.

Perhaps predictably, given the public interest in the issue, the method is said to have been used to predict an 'atomic Iran' (whatever that may mean) in the year 2017, as well as an Israeli attack on that country, and that the North Korean nuclear threat would set off an apocalyptic war of angels.[19] What follows is a more detailed explanation of the process that led to this conclusion:

> Using a special computer program to help him find these codes, the rabbi [Matityahu Glazerson] found the words 'Tsafon Korea' (North Korea). The message became even clearer as the rabbi found the letters *aleph, heh, resh,* and *bet* arranged sequentially. These letters form the acronym for '*Artzot Habrit*' (the United States in Hebrew).

Both of these codes were adjacent to the words '*Shoah Atomit*' (atomic holocaust). On the same grid of Bible codes, the rabbi discovered the word 'Gog', which he said hints at the possibility that North Korea is the nation that will bring the pre-Messianic war, prophesied to come 'from the North'.[20]

At various times, all these methods have been surrounded by the kind of statistics that 'prove' that, following the laws of probability, the chance that you or I would have come into the world is near zero. It is also worth noting that using them is not nearly as difficult as readers who are unfamiliar with Hebrew might think. There are three reasons for this. First, the Hebrew alphabet has only consonants but no vowels. As a result, the chance that any random combination of two or more letters will carry some kind of meaning is much greater than in English or any other European language; for the same reason, playing Scrabble in Hebrew is also much easier. Second, both methods can be applied not just to the Bible but to any book, regardless of its author and contents. Third, there are several *Free* Bible Code (emphasis in the original) search programs that claim to be superior to the one used by Rips. One of those even promises to work with Windows 95, Windows 98, Windows 2000, Windows NT, Windows XP, Windows 7, Windows 8 and Windows 10.[21] What else could one wish for?

Starting centuries ago, the result of this has been an astonishing amount of controversy involving scientists as well as rabbis.[22] Some rabbis claimed to know that God's mind (on which, of course, they were the experts) just did not work in this way. Plenty of others volunteered, or were enlisted, to explain why it did work. Early on, Rips himself was able to attract the support of a famous Israeli academic, Professor Robert Aumann, whose work on games theory won him the 2005 Nobel Prize in Economics. Himself a practising Jew, Aumann arranged for a lecture on the topic to be delivered at the Israel Academy of Sciences and even tried to have it published in a respectable statistical journal. Later he retracted his support, saying that he now considered the method very improbable. Rips himself was awarded the 1997 Ig Nobel Prize for improbable research. That, however did not and still does not prevent others from coming out with entire arrays of similar ideas.

PART III:
ENTER MODERNITY

11

FROM PATTERNS
TO CYCLES

The idea that, to look into the future, it is first of all necessary to study the past has been repeated so often as to become one of the clichés of our age. Among those who voiced it were the Spanish philosopher George Santayana ('whoever cannot remember the past is condemned to repeat it'[1]) and, it is said, President Theodore Roosevelt ('the more you know about the past, the better you are prepared for the future'). Even assuming that the past can be accurately and exhaustively known, though, rarely have those who have tried to use it for forecasting gone very far in explaining just *how* this can and should be done. The following pages are meant to describe four of the principal methods in question. Like much else in the present volume, the material is divided into two parts: before the eighteenth century and after.

Most of us today tend to take it more or less for granted that history is an arrow-like, ever-changing, non-repeating process. Having originated in the far past, perhaps even as far as the Big Bang, it runs in a straight line far into the future. In fact, however, that idea is a surprisingly recent one. As we shall presently see, in this form it only made its appearance around the middle of the eighteenth century. Before that date most people regarded history as the domain of again and again, or else of regularly recurring cycles, as Plato, Ibn Khaldun and many others thought.

Suppose history repeats itself and that the same circumstances always, or at least normally, lead to the same effects. In that case, the role of the unique and the exceptional is greatly

reduced. What remains are patterns that can be defined, identified and projected into the future. Colloquially known as
'experience', such patterns can, in principle at any rate, be used
to anticipate coming events. This view is very evident in the man
whom many consider the greatest historian who ever lived: the
fifth-century BCE Athenian Thucydides. A former general who
turned to writing history after his countrymen had cashiered
him, Thucydides was not primarily interested in forecasting
what might take place. Yet he explicitly based his work, and his
claim to eternal fame, on the assumption that human nature was
immutable and would always cause what had happened in the
past to recur.[2] Serving as president of the U.S. Naval War College
in the early 1970s, Admiral Stansfield Turner seemed to agree. He
threw out the existing strategic studies curriculum and replaced
it with one based on Thucydides; some of America's other war
colleges followed suit.[3]

Two millennia after Thucydides, a similar idea underlay
Niccolò Machiavelli's attempt to write 'effective' (or useful) history, as he called it – meaning the kind princes and their advisers
could read and profit from. For Machiavelli as for Thucydides,
all history was primarily a struggle for power. The reason why it
had lessons to offer was precisely because neither the nature of
power nor those who hungered for it, nor the methods they used
to obtain and maintain it, were subject to change. One outcome
was that, for Machiavelli, it did not matter whether an event took
place in the Roman Republic – on which he wrote at length and
from which he took most of his examples – or in his own day;
both were, at bottom, identical.

An even better example of unchanging patterns is provided
by the conflict between the few and the many, the rich and poor.
In the *Republic* and elsewhere, Plato voiced the idea that such
conflict would inevitably lead to civil war (*stasis*). Two and a
half millennia later, a great many of us still believe that such
is the case. The Book of Ecclesiastes, though forming part of a

completely different tradition, puts it as succinctly as it can be: 'What has been will be again; what has been done will be done again; there is nothing new under the sun' (1:9).

Patterns are one thing; cycles, another. Who first came up with the idea that time follows a cyclical pattern we do not know. Going back at least 5,000 years, it was current not only around the Mediterranean, in Egypt and Mesopotamia, but in China, where it held sway until the end of the nineteenth century, and among the Norse of Scandinavia. Proceeding independently, the Maya too developed the idea.[4] Very probably it arose in either of two ways. One possibility is that our remote ancestors started by observing the birth and death, growth and decay, rise and fall, of biological and social organisms. Another is that, watching the revolutions of the heavens and everything in them, they drew an analogy with things here on Earth. 'Archaic man', says Mircea Eliade in *The Myth of the Eternal Return*, 'modelled his sanctuaries, his settlements, in fact his entire life both religious and secular, on the celestial bodies and the divinities they represented. His commitment to repetition, and to the kind of foreknowledge it implies, was total.'[5] The fact that the earliest known time-keepers, the sundials made in Egypt during the thirteenth century BCE, were round may have helped. Seasonal variations apart, people could see with their own eyes how the shadow cast by the gnomon (from the Greek, meaning 'the part that knows') went round and round, returning to the same place each morning.[6] Most probably all these factors, the biological, the astronomical and the technological, worked hand in hand. And thus they made a joint contribution to the rise of astrology.

Among the ancient thinkers who took the view that time went in cycles, always returning to its starting point, was the Greek statesman Lycurgus. Others were the philosophers and historians Solon, Heraclitus, Herodotus, Empedocles and Polybius. Both the historian Livy, who thought that Rome was 'struggling with its own greatness',[7] and the poets Horace and

Juvenal subscribed to it. So, in the middle of the second century CE, did the emperor Marcus Aurelius.[8] Indeed it would hardly be too much to say that Roman culture and history were permeated by the fear, at times amounting to near-certainty, that the day was not very far away when the city would share the fate of its imperial predecessors. Growth and decadence, rise and fall, inexorable and inevitable, repeated over and over again.[9]

Many medieval sages, such as Honoré Bonet and, in the Islamic world, the towering figure of Ibn Khaldun, agreed. Others, remaining anonymous, came up with the *Rota Fortunae*, or Wheel of Fortune. Meant as a warning against hubris, the motif appears both in several so-called 'mirrors for princes', that is, the kind of literature that taught them how to rule, and in the well-known book of poems *Carmina Burana* ('The Wheel of Fortune turns / I go down, demeaned / another is carried to the heights'). Day Two of Boccaccio's *Decameron* refers to it, as do several of Shakespeare's plays.[10] Illustrations often show Fortune, in the shape of a blindfolded woman, busily turning the wheel round and round.

Pomponazzi, with whose views on omens and portents we are already familiar, put it as follows:

> That order will exist always in infinite ages, to infinity; it is not in our power, but in the power of fate . . . And we see that the earth which is now fertile will be barren, and the great and the rich will become humble and wretched, so the course of history is determined. We have seen the Greeks dominate the Barbarians, now the Barbarians dominate the Greeks, and so everything goes on and changes. So it is probable that he who is now a king will one day be a slave and vice versa . . . If then someone asks you, what kind of game is this? You would be well advised to reply that it is the game of God.[11]

He went so far as to raise the possibility that the development of religions, Christianity included, followed a similar pattern, thereby causing his books to be burnt by the Church and his life to be put in some danger.

Some cycles, comprising the rise and fall of dynasties, empires and peoples, were relatively short and only took centuries before they returned to their starting points. So, for example, the Egyptian Sothic or Sirius cycle, which, being based on the heliacal rising of the star Sirius, 'only' lasted 1,461 years. Even shorter, amounting to just 539 (77 × 7) years, was a cycle allegedly discovered by the French academic Gaston Georgel in his 1937 book *Les rythmes dans l'histoire*. Many others had more to do with cosmology than with human history or the future of politics and war, or the rise and fall of cities. Instead, they predicted that the cosmos itself would be destroyed, be reborn, develop and so on, in an endless number of cycles. Such, for example, was the teaching of the Greek philosopher Anaximander (*c.* 611–547 BCE). Or as one text attributed to the Buddha puts it: 'O monks, after hundreds of thousands of years, rains will cease. All seedlings, all vegetation, all plants, grasses and trees will dry up and cease to be . . . There comes another season after a great lapse of time when a second sun will appear.'[12] And a third, and a fourth, and a fifth, and a sixth.

Comparing time to a race in which horses and chariots are made to go round and round, Plato in the *Phaedrus* speaks of a cycle lasting 10,000 years. As each one came to an end, every soul was doomed to re-enter the race, going through exactly the same evolution down to the smallest details. Much later, this idea was taken over by early Islamic scholars. Zoroastrian, Buddhist and Hindu traditions all know of many different cycles of varying length. Among the longest, a single day (*kalpa*) of Brahma was supposed to last 1.28 billion solar years.[13] But even this was by no means the longest cycle of all. The larger the number of years inside each cycle, the stronger the impression one gets that at least some of them were not seriously meant. Instead they formed part of an elaborate game scholars played among themselves in order to see who could invent the largest ones of all.

Sticking to the fortunes of people and political entities, what almost all the above-mentioned authors, as well as a good many others, did have in common was a rough idea as to the way the cycles developed. First there emerged a people, rude but brave, cohesive, capable of quick and decisive action when necessary, and jealous of its traditions. United under an exceptionally able chief, such as Cyrus the Great, or Philip and his son Alexander, or Muhammad – perhaps the best example of all – or Genghis Khan, they rose, fought, defeated and subjugated their neighbours. In the fullness of time they established great empires. Having done so, though, sooner or later they surrendered themselves to city life – specifically, to luxury, indolence, song, wine and women. In Rome, for example, the number of days annually given up to games and spectacles grew from 66 under Augustus to 135 under Marcus Aurelius and 175 or more in the fourth century CE. The rulers' very wealth, originating in the taxes paid by the conquered population (a 'sort of perpetual penalty for defeat', as Cicero put it), turned them into an object of envy.

Neglecting their ancestors' traditions, they lost what was approvingly known as their 'manly vigour'. 'Men', says Polybius, 'turned to arrogance, avarice and indolence [and] did not wish to marry. And when they did marry, they did not wish to rear the children born to them except for one or two at the most.'[14] Tacitus, in contrasting his own people with the Jews, who did not kill off their children either before they were born or soon afterwards, agreed.[15] The fewer children people had, said Petronius, the easier they found it to move in society, and the higher their status.[16] And the smaller, naturally, their stake in society as a whole.

Nor were contemporaries unaware of the way fighting power was affected. Starting under Julius Caesar, one emperor after another set up bodyguards – *corporis custodes*, as they were known – made up entirely of Germanic soldiers.[17] Meanwhile the Romans, who for several centuries had provided the world's best soldiers, gradually ceased to enlist. To avoid serving, some even went so far as to mutilate themselves.[18] Abandoning the military virtues, increasingly they looked down on them and hired others, often foreigners, to do their fighting for them. By the last centuries of the empire, the army was made up almost entirely of such personnel. To make things worse still, they served under their own commanders. The outcome was a situation where fighters did not know how to rule and rulers did not know how to fight. Inevitably, the end was degeneration, defeat and downfall.

As late as the middle of the eighteenth century the idea that history worked in cycles continued to preoccupy the best European minds. Take one of the most famous of all, that of Charles de Montesquieu. His 1748 volume *The Spirit of the Laws* did as much as any other work to determine the coming political order both of his native France and of the American republic.[19] Standing at the cusp between the new and the old, Montesquieu had spent two years living in England, where he learnt to admire the prevailing balanced system of government. It had, he thought, allowed the country to 'progress the farthest of all peoples' on the road to piety, commerce and freedom. Still he did not completely discard the idea of cycles. Towards the end of his chapter on the topic, he wrote: 'Since all human beings have an end, the state of which we are speaking will lose its liberty; it will perish. Rome, Lacedaemonia and Carthage have surely perished. This state will perish when legislative power is more corrupt than executive power.'[20] This was the same Montesquieu who, in 1735, had published *Considerations on the Causes of the Greatness of the Romans and their Decline*, a book that, in its emphasis on the role of civic virtue and its inevitable decline, echoed the above-mentioned ancients almost word for word.[21]

When Frederick II of Prussia, who was Montesquieu's rough contemporary, commissioned 'Roman' ruins for his palace at Sanssouci he did so specifically in order to remind people of the cycles in question. Nor was he the only eighteenth-century ruler to do so. Much later, Albert Speer, Hitler's architect, embarked on a somewhat similar project.[22] What had gone up, they reasoned, would have to go down.

A few writers tried to use cyclical history to show that their own people were on the ascent and would soon occupy a much more important place in global society. Not surprisingly, eighteenth-century American writers were particularly likely to take this line.[23] Almost all of them agreed that the United States of their day belonged in the youthful stage of growth but was fast moving towards maturity. Who could know how far it might still go? Take the Reverend Thomas Barnard of Salem (1748–1814). Speaking on National Thanksgiving Day, 19 February 1795, he compared the prospects of the new United States with those of older European countries. The latter, he noted, had nothing to look forward to except 'decline and mortification, according to the course of human affairs' which were always going through cycles.[24]

Subsequent American writers joined the chorus, arguing that the centre of civilization was moving away from the Middle East, where it had first risen and where it had long lost its original glory. From there it had reached Europe, where it was very near its peak, and was on its way to North America, the land of the future and of Manifest Destiny. Ohio, which at the time was a frontier state, still has a community called The Center of the World. The name was dreamt up by a nineteenth-century entrepreneur, Randall Wilmot, who hoped it would become something of the kind and promoted it as hard as it could.[25] He was by no means the only one who tried to make his fortune in this way. When Henry Luce, publisher of *Time* magazine, famously proclaimed the 'American Century' in 1941, he was thinking along similar lines.

As was only to be expected, Russian writers working on the other side of 'old' Europe tended to resort to the same logic. Particularly interesting in this respect was Nikolai Danilevsky (1822–1885). A man of many talents, at various points in his life Danilevsky was active as a naturalist, economist, philosopher and historian. In 1869, locked in debate against 'Westernizing' Russian intellectuals, he published *Russia and Europe*, a monograph that quickly attained international fame. In it he listed ten different civilizations that each in turn had been born, achieved greatness, and finally fallen apart. Focusing on his own time, he contrasted what he saw as Roman-Germanic superficiality, impatience and brutality with Russian religiosity, honesty, spontaneity and, above all, willingness to suffer and to endure. Dating back only as far as the fourteenth century, Russian civilization was still relatively young. Provided it could resist the lure of the West and stick to its own pristine virtues, it was destined to outlast the latter. Turning itself into mankind's leading civilization, it would establish an empire that would put anything before it in the shade.

Nor is this view of cyclical history by any means dead even today.[26] As the current version goes, first came the so-called Rus empire, or Kievan Rus'. Founded about 980 CE by Vladimir the Great, it lasted until the middle of the thirteenth century, when it was dismantled under the Golden Horde. The subsequent period of subjugation lasted until 1480. That was when Ivan III of Muscovy formally emancipated himself from Tartar rule, founding what was to become the second Russian Empire. This empire lasted until 1917, when, brought to the brink of disintegration by the First World War, it gave way to the communist one. In 1989–91 that empire, having lost immense territories as well as half of its population, also fell apart.

Each time, the collapse was brought about not so much by external armies as by foreign, meaning Western, cultural values. Infiltrating Russia on the sly, so to speak, they undermined its pristine native virtues as described by Danilevsky and his most important successor, Ivan Ilyin (1883–1954). Each time, so bad was the situation that the empire had to be rebuilt almost from the ground up. Thus one cycle followed upon another. What gives this particular doctrine its importance is the fact that, in today's Russia, it has come to enjoy semi-official status. No less a person than Vladimir Putin himself has praised it several times. In 2005 he also saw to it that Ilyin's remains should be brought back from the place of his exile in Switzerland and reburied in Moscow's Donskoy Monastery. A more 'essentially Russian' burial ground could scarcely be found.

Optimists, however, were exceptional. For reasons that probably have more to do with psychology than with objective research, both in antiquity and in modern times most of those who took a cyclical view of history believed that the countries, cultures or civilizations to which they and their contemporaries belonged were in decline or would inevitably begin to decline at some not-too-remote point in time. Here is what one poet had to say about the matter:

In outline dim and vast
Their fearful shadows cast
The giant forms of empires on their way
To ruin: one by one
They tower and they are gone.[27]

The author was John Keble (1792–1866). His book *The Christian Year* was the most popular collection of English poetry in the entire nineteenth century, selling 375,000 copies in 158 separate editions. Today he even has an Oxford college named after him. Twentieth-century historians such as Oswald Spengler in *The Decline of the West* (1918) and Arnold Toynbee in *A Study of History* (1934–61) echoed his words. The former sought to show that Western culture, which had come into being around

1000 CE and which he called 'Faustian', had exhausted itself and, by about 2200, would follow its predecessors into the dustbin of history. The latter identified a total of thirteen, or nineteen, or 33 (depending on the stage he had reached in his work) important 'world civilizations'.

Each in his own way, both men sought to explore the laws that governed, and hence could be used to predict, the development of cultures and/or civilizations. Like Keble, both were enormously learned. Gathering the innumerable facts of history, they drove them in front of themselves like a herd of unruly sheep. Commercially speaking, the more successful of the two was Spengler. But it was Toynbee who, during the last decades of his long life, turned himself into an oracle on everything that had been, was, and would be. Including, not least, the fate of the empire into which he had been born and which, from at least 1918 on, was already showing unmistakable signs of approaching decline. Indeed he has been compared to Herodotus, Dante and John Milton.[28] Yet in the end neither he nor Spengler was able to convince his fellow scholars that he had found the true key to the past – let alone the future.

Both the idea that historical patterns repeat themselves – one that, in its simple everyday form, is known as experience – and that history itself moves in cycles are alive and well. One major late twentieth-century historian who based his work on a mixture of both approaches was Paul Kennedy in his best-seller *The Rise and Fall of the Great Powers* (1987). There he introduced his readers to something called 'imperial overstretch'. Imperial overstretch results when the size of an empire outgrows the resources available to defend it. Whenever such a mismatch has occurred, Kennedy argued, the outcome has been the decline and ultimate collapse of the empire in question. By way of examples he adduced the Spanish, British and American empires. Writing just two years before the end of the Cold War, he would no doubt have done well to include the Soviet Union too; not to mention ancient Rome, which by some interpretations was brought down by just such a process taking place from the last decades of the second century CE onward.[29]

Today, in the view of many, it is the U.S that, due to imperial overstretch, is in a state of decline. Spending more on defence than the next thirteen countries combined (as of 2019) and running huge budget and balance of payment deficits as a result, its power seems to grow increasingly hollow.[30] Whether President Trump's promises to reverse the process and make it 'great' again will be realized remains to be seen. As the cycle continues its westward movement, leaving America's shores for the Pacific and reaching for its other side, Washington may end up handing over the torch to Beijing as the rising force whose turn has come.

Societies, states and empires are not the only entities to which the idea of cyclic history, as well as attempts to use it in order to look into the future, has been applied. The best known is the business cycle. The idea that economic life has a momentum of its own that not only causes it to undergo periodic booms and busts but makes it predictable – in principle, at any rate – goes back to the first half of the nineteenth century. At that time it was advocated by a number of economists, the most prominent of whom was the industrialist and social reformer Robert Owen. Later it was taken up by Karl Marx, who argued that the cycle was a necessary part of the capitalist system of production. The swings, Marx predicted, would become more and more violent, causing society to grow increasingly polarized. As the rich grew richer (but fewer in number) and the poor, poorer (but more numerous), the outcome would be revolution and capitalism's final collapse. Whereupon all contradictions would be resolved and communism would take over.

Marx, a towering intellect, had what it takes to survey history as a whole. Not so lesser men, who accordingly set themselves more modest objectives. Starting in the last years of the nineteenth century, it became the shining goal of every economist to identify cycles (and have them named after themselves, of course). This gave rise to the Juglar cycle (duration 7–11 years), the Kitchin cycle (3–5), the Kuznets cycle (15–25 years) and the Kondratiev wave (45–60 years), to mention the most important ones only. Some economists followed Marx in trying to foresee where all this might lead in 'the end' (supposing, of course, there would be an end). But most were content to explain, as best they could, the way each cycle originated, developed and started afresh. Others still tried to extend the idea from economics to other social processes. Perhaps the best-known was the Italian sociologist Vilfredo Pareto (1848–1923). In his essay on the 'circulation of elites' he argued that the gap between the ruling and the ruled, wealth and poverty, had always existed and would always exist. Only the people who formed the elites, governed by a regular and hence predictable pattern, would change.[31]

Explanations as to what caused these cycles varied. Some cycles encompassed entire economies, others merely certain parts of them. Now it was the production of iron and construction, which were regarded as the key to everything else, to which the logic was applied; now it was employment; now commodity prices and freight rates; and now sales of corn, cotton and/or pork.[32] In societies that had been industrializing at a furious pace from about 1780 on, the output of steel in particular was considered critical to the economy. Until 1973, that is, when it suddenly ceased to be so in the most developed countries. As more people bought shares – between 1900 and the late 1920s, the number of Americans who did so increased twentyfold[33] – interest came to focus on the stock exchange. Both for its own sake and as a harbinger of things to come, it was studied countless times by countless people using countless different methods.

Though there was no agreement as to whether there was one 'wheel of retailing' or three, that sector too was supposed to follow a cyclical pattern.[34] Alas, gathering all the data and ensuring their accuracy proved to be next to impossible. In less developed countries this was because such data simply did not exist; in developed ones, because there was so much of it as to leave a great many analysts uncertain as to what was relevant, what was not, and in what ways.[35] In both cases, at least some of the data might be doctored or at least deliberately presented in such a way as to support this position or that. Often, the more data were gathered, the clearer it became that not all these cycles always moved either at the same speed or even in the same direction. While everything might be going down, usually it was possible to find at least some things that were going up. For example, even during the inflationary 1970s the real cost of computers and computing, like that of electronics in general, kept falling. During the great recession of 2008–9, spending on recreational goods remained stable. It may even have increased, probably because unemployment resulted in additional leisure time.[36]

A single, persistent and reliable 'master key' that could be used to predict the movements of all the rest was never discovered. Perhaps taking a leaf from Ptolemy, some economists did their best to devise cycles within cycles. Others took the developing sciences of meteorology, astronomy and even astrology as their models. Starting as long ago as 1878, this has led to numerous attempts to correlate business activity with sunspots.[37] Indeed it is the interaction between all those fields that explains why, starting around 1900, they came to share the term 'forecasting'. There have even been some periods – 1906–8, the late 1920s, from 1950 to 1969 and from 1993 until 2008 – when many leading economists and businessmen believed that 'modern' management methods, applied both by government and by private enterprises, had succeeded in breaking the cycle(s) and that, as a result, unlimited prosperity had begun or was about to begin and persist[38] – only to discover that recessions and even depressions still occurred and that the cyclical model, with its periodic ups and downs, remained the best way of looking into the economic future we have.

12

WITH HEGEL ON
THE BRAIN

tarting during the late Enlightenment, patterns and cycles
have been joined, and to some extent replaced, by the
view of time as a linear process, one that was moving in
a certain direction: from Creation towards an objective or goal
that had been predetermined by God. To be sure, the basic idea
was anything but new. The first to come up with it, somewhere
around the middle of the sixth century BCE, were the Jews.
Having witnessed the destruction of the First Temple and lost
their independent kingdom, they were forcibly exiled to Babylon.
The dramatic change in their situation resulted in a long period
of profound religious reform.[1] To them, however, the goal in
question would be reached not here on Earth but in another
world during the End of Days, also known as the Last Judgement.

One exposition of the idea is found in the Book of Daniel
(12:1–3): first there will be a war between the king of the South
and the king of the North, in the course of which the king of the
North will meet his end 'between the sea and the Holy Mountain'.
The text continues:

At that time Michael shall stand up,
The great prince who stands watch over the sons
    of your people;
And there shall be a time of trouble,
Such as never was since there was a nation,
Even to that time.
And at that time your people shall be delivered,

Every one who is found written in the book.
And many of those who sleep in the dust of the earth
    shall awake,
Some to everlasting life,
Some to shame and everlasting contempt.
Those who are wise shall shine
like the brightness of the firmament,
And those who turn many to righteousness
Like the stars forever and ever.

Just how the idea of linear time was transmitted to the surrounding peoples we do not know. Probably its spread had something to do with the fact that Palestine was occupied by Alexander in 332 BCE. Almost three centuries later, in 63 BCE, Pompey the Great occupied the country and made it part of the Roman Empire. A quarter of a century after that, the Jewish idea of time as having a beginning, a God-mandated direction and an end had become sufficiently familiar for the Greek historian Diodorus Siculus to refer to it as one of the two dominant views held by his contemporaries (the other one being that the world had always existed and would always exist). Albeit that he did not mention its Jewish origins.[2]

Many passages in the New Testament – Thessalonians 1 and 2, Corinthians and the Revelations of St John, to mention but a few – refer to the Messiah's Second Coming. Once it has taken place, the physical world in which we live will come to an end in much the same way as a candle burns out. Around 400 CE the idea was picked up by St Augustine. In his hands it became one of the two cardinal pillars of Christianity (the other being that Jesus is God). This in turn led to numerous, and still continuing, attempts to use biblical and ecclesiastical history to find out just how old the Earth was as well as speculation concerning the date when it would end, the way it would do so, and what, if anything would be left after that event.

When time ceased being propelled by God, a secular development that started during the first half of the eighteenth century, it still retained its linear character. A vital point most commentators have missed, however, is that direction and change are not the same. After all, it is possible for a rock, for example, to travel in this direction or that without changing one iota on the way. What really distinguished the last decades of the eighteenth century was not just a sense of direction but the introduction into history of change. The parent of change as an element, probably even the most important element, in our modern understanding of history was the Industrial Revolution. Before that time, so slowly had change proceeded that most people, immersed in their day-to-day lives, barely noticed it. Generation upon generation people lived on the land, often in the same house as their animals. They scratched a living and seldom left the villages in which they had been born. Periodic seasons of affluence and distress apart, life expectancy and living standards hardly increased. Now, however, it accelerated; by some calculations, over a little more than two centuries the 'black satanic mills' caused real global per capita income to increase by about thirtyfold.[3] And with industrialization came equally vast changes in other fields, including work, technology, population, social systems, living patterns, comfort, travel, education and health.

The first places that felt the impact of change were Europe's great urban centres. It was there that many of the factories and the workers who operated them were concentrated; it was there, too, that clocks and watches, which starting in the seventeenth century were provided with minute hands, became increasingly common, until every self-respecting bourgeois carried one. By the last quarter of the century England alone was producing 150,000 to 200,000 of them each year, many for export.[4] As if to illustrate the way the flow of history was now understood, some clocks began to bear the slogan *tempus fugit*. In Napoleon's words, time was more valuable than space. The latter might be recovered; the former, never.

So great and sudden was the transformation that not even the most remote populations, living in their villages according to their age-old traditions, were able to ignore it. Nor were the changes limited to Europe alone. Crossing the Atlantic, they were taken up by men such as Benjamin Franklin, Thomas Paine, Thomas Jefferson and John Adams. All four, and a great many others, came to discard the cyclical vision of history, gradually replacing it with a linear one leading from the past towards the future. No less important, especially in the long run, is the fact that the nineteenth century was the period of imperialism par excellence. As steamships, railways, rifles and quinine enabled the European presence and influence in other continents to take off and grow, hundreds of millions of people throughout the world started to have change forced upon them whether they wanted to or not.

As the young Karl Marx and Friedrich Engels wrote in *The Communist Manifesto* (1848), the bourgeoisie had taken over from the aristocracy as the dominant class. Now it was fast establishing a world market in which all countries and regions were linked to all the rest. Pressing forward relentlessly, its factories generated mountains of wealth wholly beyond the imagination of previous generations. On the way it accomplished wonders far surpassing Egyptian pyramids, Roman aqueducts or Gothic cathedrals. It also conducted expeditions that put all former exoduses of nations and Crusades into the shade. In the process it swept away all fixed, fast-frozen relations, along with their train of ancient and venerable prejudices and opinions – so much so, in fact, that many of them became antiquated even before they were able to ossify.

Seen from our special point of view, the injection of change into history was nothing less than revolutionary. Starting in ancient Babylon and Egypt, the questions that shamans, prophets, soothsayers, diviners and other seers and experts had tried to answer were almost always of the 'what if' type. A king might spend a fortune to have the Pythia tell him what would happen 'if' he went to war with a certain opponent. A merchant might ask Nostradamus what would happen 'if' he sent his ship on a trading mission to such and such a port. And a humble person living in some provincial town might buttonhole a cheap astrologer to find out whether he would marry his heart's desire and whether, in case he did, she would stay faithful to him. The events that were predicted in this way might be either good or bad, avoidable or not. Besides the End of Days, though, rarely did the question arise as to what *the* future might look like and in what ways it would differ from the present.

The way in which history was recast as the province of change was reflected in literature, specifically utopian ones. Following Augustine, medieval utopias had invariably been located in a time beyond history. Starting with Thomas More's early sixteenth-century *Utopia*, more and more often they were placed in some yet to be explored part of the world. As additional voyages were made and unexplored regions diminished in size and importance, increasingly this meant the South Pacific and the so-called, semi-imaginary Terra Australis. By the last decades of the eighteenth century, however, the existence, contours and general characteristics of Australia had become firmly established. Far from representing a better world, it was little more than a desert thinly inhabited by strange animals and what contemporaries could only regard as unredeemed, perhaps even subhuman, savages. The more geographical knowledge spread, the greater became the role of the future as the one place that, being unknown, could still contain a vision of an alternative society, good or, after the First World War, bad.

Among the first to place his utopia firmly in the future was the French writer Louis-Sébastien Mercier (1740–1814). His book *L'Ann 2440* was published in 1770 and quickly became a

European best-seller. It claims to tell the story of an unnamed man who, incensed by a conversation with a philosopher who points out the squalor and injustices of late eighteenth-century Paris, falls asleep. Waking up, he finds himself in the city of the future, where those problems have been successfully tackled and eliminated. In this way Mercier was able to skip over the question as to how his view of the future might be substantiated. A century later, the American journalist Edward Bellamy in *Looking Backward* (1888) used the same sleight of hand. So, a year later, did the English writer and designer William Morris in *News from Nowhere.*

Not content with this, others tried to establish better methods by which this new kind of future could be predicted. The first, which has since become easily the most popular of all, was to identify 'trends'. Curiously enough, the term is derived from the Middle English verb *trendan*, meaning, to turn, trundle, revolve or turn about. It is in this sense that Chaucer ('rollen and trenden with Inne hym self') used it in his translation of Boethius. During the sixteenth century it came to stand for a movement in a specific direction; but it was only about 1880 that its modern use, in the sense of a secular change in time, became at all common. From that point on it started the astonishing growth, documented by Google Ngram, that has turned it into one of the buzzwords of our age. Today, not a day passes when the media does not use it, not once but many times over.

Trends gave rise to extrapolation – another modern term. First mentioned around 1870 but starting its rise in 1920 or so, today extrapolation is everywhere. Indeed so much so that we find it hard to see how most people during most historical periods tried to look into the future without it. The number of fields that have been analysed by identifying trends and extrapolating from them, sometimes with success and sometimes without, is vast. Among them are births, deaths, populations (both human and nonhuman), migration, incomes, demand, sales, traffic (including accidents), energy consumption, greenhouse gases in the atmosphere, the number of working scientists, technological development, equality and inequality, and millions upon millions of other things. When gurus such as Steven Pinker, Yuval Harari, Larry Page and Ray Kurzweil claim that we are on the way to eliminating such things as poverty, illness and death they do not quote the word of God as the ancient Hebrew prophets used to do. Nor do they engage in all kinds of astrological calculations. Whether or not they are computer experts, it is always on extrapolation that they rely.

Even within a given field, though, not all trends necessarily point in the same direction. That is why putting them together while still giving each one the weight it deserves can be extraordinarily difficult. Some trends are big and global, others small, insignificant and only relevant to certain places or fields. Some are arithmetic, others, such as the one Thomas Malthus saw as governing the growth of populations, geometric or even logarithmic. Which means that, unless they are brought to an end, they will not take very long to reach the heavens and/or fill the Earth. A good historical example of such extravagant growth is provided by the introduction, at the end of the eighteenth century, of rabbits into Australia. Once the animals had spread into the wild they faced no natural enemies at all, allowing them to multiply until they became a serious pest. A more recent example is Bitcoin, which has, since its beginnings, led to an orgy of speculation with few parallels in history.

When people see, or think they see, a trend at work, typically their reaction is to join it in the hope of reaping the benefits it may bring. As they do so they push the trend forward, and vice versa. That is why extrapolation so often focuses on fields in which work is in progress, as the saying goes. The underlying assumption is that, if we can do this and that today, and provided we continue working in the same direction, we shall be able to do much more tomorrow. If only in order to obtain funding, at one time or another this reasoning has been applied to spaceships, fusion reactors, medicine, brain science, computer science, and other fields too numerous to mention.

Three signs make extrapolation easy to identify. First, as was already the case with Marx himself, whenever it is used one can be sure that 90 per cent of the text will deal with the past, not with the future. In this it differs from other methods, especially those that are based on altered states of consciousness. Second, there is bound to occur the oft-repeated phrase 'already now', or one of its variants, in the form 'starting so and so long ago, in such and such a place and such and such a field, *already now* we have moved along until we have reached point so and so.' Thus, for example, starting in 1800, or 1883 (a year of falling temperatures attributed to the eruption of the volcano Krakatoa in what is now Indonesia), or 1940 (an exceptionally cold year) or 1946 (another exceptionally cold year), 'already now' the world has warmed up by so many degrees. Starting in 1999, when a Japanese company released the first smartphone to achieve mass adoption within a country, 'already now' the number of devices in use worldwide is such and such. Already now computers can do this and that. The next stage is to draw a curve, iron out any irregularities and establish the direction in which the trend seems to be moving. This done, we expect it to point the way to the future.

Assisted by computers, which are very good at this kind of thing, so prevalent is this line of thought that it is hard to imagine a time in which it was not resorted to. A relatively early example was the 'law of acceleration' suggested by the historian Henry Adams, great-grandson and grandson respectively of two u.s. presidents who bore the same surname. Born in 1838, before he reached the age of six Adams had witnessed the emergence of four entirely new technologies: the ocean steamer, the railway, the electric telegraph and the daguerreotype. Scant wonder he believed in progress! In 1904, looking back over that progress, he tried to provide an objective measuring rod for gauging it. Not surprisingly he turned to the output of coal, which at that time was much the most important source of energy on which all production depended. During the nineteenth century, world output of coal had been doubling every ten years. Looking into the future, Adams expected 'the rate of progress' to become even faster during the twentieth century.[5] Fortunately he was wrong, or else everyone and everything would have been covered with soot long ago.

The key to looking into the future, it has been said, is to pick a single feature of the actual world, extrapolate it and spin out the consequences in as much detail as possible. H. G. Wells in *Anticipations* (1901) did just that. There he used extrapolation in order to predict, among other things, that developing means of transportation, especially motor trucks, would lead to the 'diffusion' of cities over the countryside. The outcome would be the creation of suburbs and exurbs, and the appearance of a new system of social classes similar to the one that, Wells thought, was 'already' becoming visible in the United States at the time. Referring to another work of his, 'A Story of the Days to Come', he said that it was 'essentially an exaggeration of contemporary tendencies: higher buildings, bigger towns, wickeder capitalists and labour more downtrodden than ever and more desperate'.[6]

A famous contemporary real-world example of extrapolation is Moore's law. Named after Gordon Moore, one of the founders of Intel, it predicted that the number of transistors in a dense integrated circuit, and with it computing power, would double every eighteen months or so. The 'law', formulated for the first time in 1965, correctly predicted the future of computers for about half a century. At that point the logistic curve, or S-curve, flattened and Moore's law went the way of all silicon.

For those interested in looking into the future, following all the trends is often impossible. Not only are there too many of them, but they often conflict with each other. That is why the third hallmark of extrapolation is the frequent identification of bellwethers (close synonyms are 'herald', 'harbinger', 'indicator' and 'predictor'). Originally the term referred to a castrated ram with a bell tied to its neck. Thus equipped, it led a flock of sheep that followed it wherever it went. Applied to u.s. politics, bellwether states are those whose voting patterns closely match those of the nation as a whole. In both fields, it is this correspondence that allows them to be used for the purpose of prediction, with the hope of saving an enormous amount of detailed research.

In the 1930s the bellwether state was supposed to be Maine. Currently the favourite is Ohio, which, starting in 1896, has voted as the nation did in all but two presidential elections (1944 and 1960) and which has had a perfect record from 1964 on. As they say, 'As Ohio goes so goes the nation' – as happened, once again, in 2016. Not everyone agrees. Some, using different starting points and different ways of calculating the results, have pointed to Florida, Nevada, Missouri, New Mexico or Tennessee as bellwether states. At one time or another almost one-half of all u.s. states have been pointed to as presidential bellwethers. Presumably that is why some analysts have done away altogether with using states to predict election results, beginning to look at counties instead.[7] Similar lists have been drawn up in the hope of predicting voting patterns in other countries.

The futurologist John Naisbitt in *Megatrends* (1982) listed five bellwether states: California, Colorado, Connecticut, Florida and Washington. Florida in particular was important to Naisbitt because, having the largest proportion of people over 65 years old, it pointed to future developments in all the rest. (The idea that it is not old beliefs but those who believe in them who die does not seem to have occurred to him.) Bellwethers have been used to anticipate future developments in other fields as well, including demography, education, healthcare and so on. In commercial life, bellwethers are firms whose stocks and/or performance seems to be closely related to that of the economy as a whole, thus supposedly indicating the existence of a trend for people to latch on to. For many years General Motors was the perfect example of a bellwether stock. What was good for GM was good for America, perhaps even the world; or so the common wisdom went. Today such firms are more likely to be FedEx – based on the belief that its balance sheet reflects the state of commerce, hence of productive activity – Amazon, Apple, Facebook, Berkshire Hathaway and others.

Closely linked to the discovery of trends was the other post-1750 historical method: dialectics. The basic idea underlying dialectics (from the Greek *dia* + *legein*, meaning 'to speak through', or against) goes back to a saying of Heraclitus, around 500 BCE, that all things originate in *polemos*, or 'strife' between opposites. A century or so later, Plato used it to characterize the most fundamental relationship of all, that between being and non-being, each of which both implied the other and could exist only by virtue of the other. Much later still it was picked up by medieval Christian scholars. They engaged in *disputatio*, a formal debating method designed to bring out the truth by successively piling up the pros and cons of any given proposition, for example whether the soldiers who crucified Christ and tortured the martyrs acted without understanding what they were doing, in which case they were innocent and their souls might still be saved; or knowingly and deliberately, in which case they would surely go to hell.[8] Especially in courts of law, the method is still in use even today. There was also a time, between about 1800 and 1900, when a number of authors tried to anchor dialectics in Newtonian mechanics – specifically the third law of motion, according to which every force generates an equal one acting in the opposite direction – but not with any great success.

The first to point to dialectics as the key to understanding historical change – and therefore, by implication, to any attempt to look into the future – was the early nineteenth-century German philosopher Georg Wilhelm Friedrich Hegel. In his hands dialectics was applied to history in general, and intellectual history in particular. An idealist through and through, Hegel's starting point was that it was Spirit (*Geist*), jump-started by the word of God during the Creation, that made history self-conscious, driving it forward and causing it to develop higher and higher forms. By definition, though, history did not obey the laws governing physical science. As a result, neither could history be reduced to the latter nor, much less, derived from them.

Rather, history followed a different path all its own. Any idea (thesis) that Spirit came up with and projected on the stage of history would quickly and necessarily give rise to its opposite (antithesis). As the two met and clashed, the outcome would be synthesis, made up of elements taken from both (for nothing was ever completely lost) and forming a new thesis. And so on, from one negation to the next, never staying in one place. The process could be observed at work in all living, as opposed to merely physical, processes, from the highest to the lowest, the largest to the smallest, incessantly and at all times and in all places.[9]

Where Hegel, reflecting the immense economic and social changes that were beginning to affect the Prussia of his day, really left his predecessors behind was in insisting that the historical process was not stationary like scales moving now one way and now in another, eventually finding equilibrium without undergoing any fundamental change. Instead, looking back over some 6,000 years of history – in his time, people still consulted the Bible for guidance in such matters – he saw history as dynamic. Unfolding in Newton's arrow-like time, always taking on new forms, it led away from the past through the present and from there into the future.

Pace Thucydides, Machiavelli and the rest, history never duplicated or repeated itself the way patterns and cycles do. Nor was it a question of the same event taking place time after time, as in the realm of physics. In the latter, H_2 and O always combine to form water. Water itself, as long as it is held under a constant pressure of one atmosphere and heated to 100 degrees Celsius, always turns into vapour. That is what it has done since the Big Bang, and that is what it will continue to do as long as the universe exists. Rather, as understood by Hegel history was a continuous process of changing and becoming in which every event was both unique and linked to everything else.

As has been said, Hegel's objective was to create a way of thinking about history that would relate to its predecessors the way a motion picture is related to a still photograph.[10] A critically important role in all this was played by what he called *Aufhebung*. Awkwardly translated as sublation, the ordinary meaning of the term is 'abolition' – as for example when we say that a particular custom, rule, law or institution was done away with. But it can also mean 'lifting to a new, and higher, level',[11] indicating the point at which change, ceasing to be merely quantitative, somehow becomes qualitative and transformative, leading to something new and in many ways unprecedented. As, for example, happens when an otherwise peaceful river turns into a raging waterfall. And as happened when the French Revolution broke through the existing order, seemingly so solid for centuries on end, as if it had been simply a giant cobweb. It was as if two and two, instead of always making four, suddenly made five, six, seven or three. Which of course is one reason why prediction is as difficult as it is.

By this view, the course of history, and therefore the future, is predetermined. Hegel himself was too committed to human freedom to make much use of dialectics in trying to forecast the course it might take. In a lecture series delivered between 1822 and 1830 and later published under the title *The Philosophy of History*, he went so far as to announce that America, 'the land of the future' where Spirit would first assume its next form, was of no interest to 'us here' in Berlin.[12] Not so for his most important follower, Karl Marx. The mature Marx saw in the American Civil War, about which he published several articles, a 'titanic struggle' between an old social order and a new one in the process of being born. Doing so, he readily romped where his master had hesitated to tread.[13] So much so, in fact, that his friend Engels, who incidentally wrote some of the articles in question for him, had to defend him against the charge of having 'Hegel on the brain'.

Marx's starting point was that, in unveiling the real nature of history and of dialectics as the way in which it proceeds from past through present to future, Hegel had been right.[14] Next, however, coming under the influence of another philosopher, Ludwig Feuerbach, he went on to turn Hegel on his head. Instead of thought driving action, Marx argued, it was 'life activity' that drove thought – and especially economic activity, or work, which, partly because it was reserved to man alone and partly no doubt because he personally always found it hard to make ends meet, he saw as the most basic and important activity of all.[15]

Born out of man's need to work and produce for a living, always jostling each other on their way into or out of history, the 'material relationships of production' developed in a dialectical way. Thus emergent slavery replaced 'primitive Communism' in which everyone was free and equal. Feudalism took the place of slavery; capitalism drove out feudalism; and Communism, returning in a much more highly developed form with every kind of modern technology at its disposal, would end up doing away with capitalism. Each of these four systems of production also developed a characteristic 'superstructure', meaning social classes as well as a body of religion, law, culture, art and thought intended to explain, justify and consolidate the rule of the upper classes over the lower ones. Each necessarily contained traces of the previous one. And, most important for our purpose, each also contained the germ of its own opposite within itself. When the time was ripe it would be negated by that opposite. As the old passed away, the new would emerge out of it like a butterfly from its chrysalis.

Here it is interesting to note that one major question that preoccupied Marx was whether the coming *Aufhebung* would be sudden, violent and cataclysmic or gradual and peaceful. Personally Marx, the scion of a middle-class family in the provincial town of Trier, Germany, was a born rebel. Having taken some part in the abortive revolution of 1848, initially he had no doubt that it would be the former type. During his last years, though, he was inclined to think that, in some countries at any rate, gradualism was the path history would take. About a decade and a half after his death, which took place in 1883, communists and socialists split over precisely this question. The basic building blocks having been put in place, ultimately it did not matter. Dialectics was supposed to make 'scientific' prediction possible, at least in principle. Writing for the communist newspaper *Pravda* in the summer of 1918, Lenin explicitly treated it as able to do so.[16]

Unlike so many of their predecessors and successors, neither Marx nor Hegel were interested in predicting what would happen to individuals. Instead, taking a grand point of view, they focused on vast, anonymous forces, whether spiritual or material, that affected the development of entire societies and even mankind as a whole. So impressive did Marx's followers find his system that they swore by it; at peak, they made one-third of humanity live under what they claimed was one of its forms.

To be sure, Hegel, Marx, Engels, Lenin, and even Lenin's self-proclaimed disciples Stalin and Mao Zedong, are all long dead. Yet arguably dialectics, applied to both spiritual and material factors and while taking due cognizance of the way they interact, still remains the best way to understand the way history unfolds over time. If so, then, understood as a method for making sense of the present and forecasting the future, it is by no means passé. That at any rate was the assumption underlying Francis Fukuyama's famous 1989 essay 'The End of History?'[17]

Examples of dialectics at work may be seen all around us. One such is the shift from craftsmanship, where individual workers produced non-identical items one by one; to conveyor-belt production, whereby many workers produce very large numbers of identical items; and from there to computerized factories, which need few if any people to manufacture an enormous number of things, each one as different from the rest as the products of craftsmen used to be. Each system is born and flogged forward on the road to perfection. Until, at some point, its negation appears out of nowhere (as it seems), taking over parts of its predecessor, discarding the rest, adding some new elements and recasting it so as to come up with something unprecedented and very often unexpected as well. As, for example, happened when the French Revolution broke through the existing order, seemingly so solid for centuries on end, and blew its remnants away as if they had been pieces of paper.

Another example is the growth in motor traffic. Starting around 1900, at first it gave those who had access to automobiles an unprecedented measure of mobility and freedom. What has not been said and written about young people who, escaping from their parents' supervision, could be found parked at the end of Love Lane? Later, though, the tables were turned, reaching the point where it now threatens to choke land transport and bring it to a halt. In London, for example, daytime traffic now proceeds at an average of 12.5 kilometres (7.8 mph) per hour, more slowly than a century ago and much slower than I myself, when I was still a young long distance runner in that very city, could and often did proceed.[18]

Still others are the rise of globalization, which, having emerged after the end of the Cold War with its sharp division between West and East, is now being confronted by its opposite, decentralization, regionalization and social fragmentation; and the Internet, which at first was supposed to make possible an entirely unprecedented measure of communication and expression but has now generated an equally unprecedented degree of censorship instead. The adverse reaction to political correctness, which itself was in many ways a reaction to the 'sexual revolution' of the 1960s and '70s, became manifest when Donald Trump was elected President of the United States.[19] Thanks to dialectics, all these events and many others were predictable, at any rate in outline. And some far-sighted people actually did predict every one of them.

. To retrace the steps we took in this chapter and the preceding one, when it comes to using history as the key for looking into the future four different methods are available. Of those, the first assumes that nothing ever changes and that everything always stays the same; the second, that change is cyclical and that history, always returning to its starting point, keeps repeating itself. As far as the written record allows us to see, both of these approaches go back at least as far as the fifth century BCE. Not accidentally, for that was when the very idea of history, meaning an 'enquiry' into things past with the intention of 'making sense' of them and ensuring they are not lost, was conceived for the first time. Between them they dominated the field until the effects of the Industrial Revolution started making themselves felt during the last decades of the eighteenth century. Both remain in frequent use even today.

The other two, which assume that history does not repeat itself and that change is the very stuff of which it is made, are of more recent vintage. Essentially they go back no further than the early years of the nineteenth century. One is to extrapolate from the past and the present, for which purpose it has to be assumed that history, like an arrow, proceeds in a certain direction. The other is to take into account both trends and the opposite ones to which they necessarily give rise; thus allowing not just for quantitative change but for qualitative development as well.

All four methods rest on the assumption that the best, indeed the only, way of looking forward is to use the rear-view mirror. Another thing they have in common is that they allow no room for altered states of consciousness of any kind: neither divine revelation nor dreams, nor raising the dead so as to learn what they may have to say, can tell us where history may be going (assuming it is going anywhere at all) and what it has in store for us. Instead they are based, or are supposed to be based, on the sober, objective and open-minded study of recorded facts and processes; processes such as, having receded from the present into the past, have been immutably fixed in it; and such as anyone, provided he or she empties his mind of *ira et studio* (anger and favouritism) and applies him- or herself, can access and interpret. The difficulty is to decide which method should be applied to what development at what time, as well as which one to use in dealing with a given problem, and how to combine all four. Marx himself came across this difficulty. So much did it exasperate him that, at one point, he claimed that events seemed to take place not once but twice. First as tragedy, then as farce.[20] To this question, no answer has been found or is likely to be found.

13

ASK, AND YOU'LL BE ANSWERED

Though there are always precedents, public opinion surveys are essentially a product of the post-First World War years. That was when George Gallup and others started developing them in the United States. The development of these polls rested on the idea that, if one were going to try and look into the future, one had better start by asking people what they were thinking and what they intended to do. That applied both to political questions and to economic ones, such as attempts to find out which commercial products people would prefer.

The first factor that led to the use of public opinion polls was the growth of modern mass society and democracy. History's first known poll was held in Pennsylvania in 1824. It showed, wrongly as it turned out, that Andrew Jackson would beat John Quincy Adams in the race for the presidency. From the United States, which acted as the pioneer, the method spread to other modern countries. Among the last to adopt it were Germany and Japan. In both the first polls were actually instituted by the American occupation forces in the years after 1945. In both, their use was partly a matter of questioning and undermining the power of the traditional elites. In the Soviet Union, the first tentative attempts to use surveys in order to find out where public opinion was going only got under way in the era of glasnost during the second half of the 1980s. Once they were introduced, the Soviet regime quickly entered upon its death throes.[1]

The second factor that contributed to the rise of polls was modern means of communication. First came postcards, the earliest of which began to be issued by various countries from 1870 or so. Early pollsters, such as the ones working for the magazine *Literary Digest* between 1916 and 1936, sometimes sent out millions of them. Names and addresses were taken from subscriptions, phone books and automobile registration records (later this method of unofficial voting became known as a straw poll). As the editors' correct predictions of the outcomes of the 1920, 1924, 1928 and 1932 presidential elections proved, it was not without success. In 1936, though, their prediction that Roosevelt's Republican opponent Alf Landon would win the election by a landslide proved spectacularly wrong. So wrong, in fact, that *Literary Digest* was discredited and had to close.

The flop, which became widely known, led to attempts to find better methods. Then as now, each firm had its own techniques. Some preferred face-to-face interviews, a procedure that, slow and horrendously expensive as it was, supposedly resulted in more honest answers. Others went to work in two stages, first on a small scale to iron out all kinds of problems, and then on a larger one. Enter technology, in the form first of telephones and then of the Internet. In recent years there has been a tendency to rely less on desktop computers, whose use is declining, and more on the ubiquitous personal computers, tablets, mobile phones and smartphones.[2] These devices allow many, often widely dispersed, people to be contacted quickly and effectively. They have also dramatically reduced the cost and, in the case of the last-named, enabled the responses to be processed automatically, rather than laboriously by hand as was the case during the early years.

In predicting the outcome of the 2012 elections to the u.s. presidency and Congress, research firms that relied at least partly on the Internet are said to have done better than more traditional ones that continued to work by telephone.[3] In the u.s. and other countries that use them, polls have rapidly been turning into an obsession; indeed they have become almost synonymous with public opinion, to the extent that, on occasion, it looks as though the purpose of holding an election is to find out whether the pollsters are right, rather than the other way around. Yet none of these improvements prevented polls from sometimes coming up with the wrong results, as happened, once again, during the 2016 presidential race.[4] So problematic is the technique that even a poll showing a ten-, twelve- or fourteen-point lead isn't necessarily enough to make a candidate's election safe.

Like other modern methods, the art of polling owes nothing to altered states of consciousness and everything to 'scientific' statistical calculation. Or so its proponents want the rest of us to believe. Essentially it consists, first, of formulating the questions to which one wants answers. Second, a sample of the population must be chosen in such a way as to eliminate, as far as possible, all kinds of biases, for example selecting too many people from one region and not enough from another; or too many young ones and not enough old ones; or too many affluent ones and not enough poor ones; or too many of those who use mobile phones as opposed to those who do not. The number of variables one can think of is practically infinite. As a result, commonly it is this part of the process that is regarded as the most difficult of all.

Third, some methods must be found to make people respond. Should they fail to do so, or should those who do choose to respond be unrepresentative in some way, even the best questionnaires will be of no use. One reason why the *Literary Digest*'s prediction of the 1936 election result failed as badly as it did was because only one-quarter of those who received the postcards bothered to provide their answers.[5] Doing so, they formed a self-selected group that was not representative of the population as a whole. Fourth, the results must be interpreted. That is all the more the case if, as often happens, respondents are presented not with simple yes/no questions but with a number of possibilities to choose from. Another problem is that people by no means always do what they say they will. That is why this method, like most others, is more accurate the nearer the future at which it looks.

For these and other reasons, there are some who argue that it is only a question of time before polling as we know it today will become obsolete.[6] After all, the world in which we live is awash with information being passed by every sort of computer to the next. Much of that information, indeed, is passed not to one computer but to many. That is why a growing number of pollsters, rather than reaching out directly to people, asking them questions and analysing the responses, have started using the considerably faster and cheaper method of cruising the Internet, or select parts of it, for information. Doing so, they gain direct access to what the members of targeted groups think – sometimes with permission, sometimes without, as for example in the case of Facebook and Cambridge Analytica (which was actually based in London) in 2018.[7] The procedure is an invasion of privacy, which is why, in many countries, it is illegal. But seen from the pollster's point of view it has the advantage that it eliminates any potential statistical difference between those who do respond to the questions they are confronted with and those who do not. The day may even come when artificial intelligence will allow the traditional yes/no questions to be replaced by more complex, open-ended ones. Or so those who participate in this game hope.

A minor – minor because the number of people asked as well as the surrounding publicity is much smaller – variant of polls is the so-called Delphi method. In one sense, the Delphi method is simply a continuation of the age-old process by which superiors asked inferiors for their views on this or that problem. In its modern form, it was invented by Project RAND (Research and Development, a California-based think tank initially supported by the U.S. Air Force) back in the mid-1950s. The method's original purpose was to assess the impact of developing technology on future warfare, a question that is still frequently being examined today. However, over the decades it came to be used to make any number of predictions in fields as different as business, economics, psychology and health science, among others.

Like all other forms of polling, Delphi is based on the assumption that the judgement of the many is better than that of the few.[8] Not because all the respondents rely on 'the best' method for looking into the future, or even the same one – but precisely because each has his or her own and uses it as he or she sees fit. So much so, in fact, that many of the methods are never explicitly put on the table; this is a method of prediction to make method irrelevant, one might say. Another assumption is that extreme views will tend to cancel each other out, resulting in a reasonable compromise. Both of these assumptions seem to have some evidence to support them. Unstated, but presumably present in the background, is the 'cover-your-ass' syndrome. If a prediction proves correct the person in charge will take the credit for the way he or she organized the enquiry. If it turns out wrong they may shift the blame by being able to point to the gathering of experts whose opinions they solicited and on which they had relied.

Some advocates believe that Delphi may be used when a problem is too complex to be subject to model-building (see below); and/or when too many people, of too many different backgrounds, are needed for face-to-face meetings to be held.[9] As will be evident, so much of what is involved is intuitive and/or arbitrary that the entire process is bound to be problematic. That is why this method is often used as a last resort. On the other hand, being cheap it may also be used as the first.

Having made up their mind to use the method, the directors of a given study will have to decide whether their approach is to be qualitative, quantitative or a mixture of both. Next they will either conduct a series of interviews, which may be more or less structured, and/or put together a questionnaire and send it to a body of experts who answer it as they see fit. In doing so, it is obviously important to ensure that those experts will be as knowledgeable, as 'objective', as representative (of what?) and as highly motivated as possible; under many circumstances this may be a tall order indeed. After the answers have been received, a second interview may be held, or else a second questionnaire, based on the first, sent out. And so on, as many times as is considered necessary (and as the participants will tolerate before they give up in frustration). A final possibility is to repeat the procedure by using another group of experts, then compare the results. All this is supposed to increase both consistency and reliability.[10]

There are also quite some variations. The director(s) may consult with the experts concerning the answers they submitted, or they may not. The experts may be asked to comment on their own degree of expertise, or they may not. They may be asked to explain how they arrived at their conclusions, or they may not. They may be allowed to see their peers' answers to the first questionnaire, or they may not. The process may be anonymous or it may be open. There may be a final conference where all the results are laid on the table in an effort to reach consensus, or there may not be. The number of possibilities is almost unlimited; but reaching a firm conclusion as to which one is preferable, almost impossible. As a result, some critics have argued that Delphi is not really a method for looking into the future at all. At best all it can do is prevent chaos by helping structure a group communication process.

Efforts to question relatively large numbers of people to find out whether the members of certain groups – for instance the young, the old, the educated, the innocent – can predict the future better than those of others go back to the 1930s.[11] While the outcome of the first such attempts was inconclusive, this did not prevent others from tackling the same problem. Among the most systematic efforts was one mounted by a Canadian-American professor of political science, Philip E. Tetlock, during the 1980s. His first step was to set up a unified framework that would allow correct forecasts to be clearly distinguished from those that were wrong. To this end he formulated his questions in such a way as to oblige respondents not only to provide yes/no answers but to say *when* the events that were being forecast would take place. For example, by asking not whether North Korea will have submarine-launched ballistic missiles in the future, but whether it will have them by a given date; or not whether NATO will come to include additional members, but whether it will have done so by a particular year. Next, by soliciting 28,000 predictions from 284 experts in various fields, Tetlock created a database that enabled him to separate 'hedgehogs', respondents who did not do well, from 'foxes', who did. A few of the latter could only be described as phenomenal.

But that was just the beginning. Tetlock's Expert Political Judgment project, as it was known, was brought to the attention of IARPA (Intelligence Advanced Research Projects Activity), a branch of the U.S. military charged with finding better ways of obtaining intelligence and analysing it. The latter helped organize and fund a follow-up project.[12] In his conclusions, Tetlock argued that, based on his results, good forecasting does not require powerful computers or arcane methods. Instead it involves gathering evidence from a variety of different sources; thinking probabilistically – that is, in terms of percentages; working in teams; keeping score; and being willing to admit error and change course if necessary. He also pointed to tournaments as a way to motivate participants and suggested that injecting accountability into the forecasting process could improve the accuracy of the responses he got.

Widely reported in the media, Tetlock's work even received the indirect support of then president Barack Obama. Obama was certainly the most intellectually inclined U.S. president since Bill Clinton and perhaps even since John F. Kennedy – one who, unlike his predecessor George W. Bush and his successor Donald

Trump, made decisions with his head and not simply with his gut. Considering a given project, he always asked his collaborators to use numbers to tell him what the chances were that it would work. As he said, he realized that 100 per cent certainty was never on the cards. He did, however, feel 'comfortable with uncertainty'. That was why, he added, it was so important to be willing to constantly re-evaluate decisions based on new information.[13] By one count, Obama applied the expert political judgement method to no fewer than 699 initiatives in six different fields (teenage pregnancy, home visiting, investment in innovation, social innovation funding, workforce innovation funding, and the Trade Adjustment Assistance Community College and Career Training programme). The total amount of money spent on these projects was almost $4.5 billion.[14]

Tetlock himself proceeded to what he called the Good Judgment Project, eliciting more than a million judgements about world affairs over a period of four years. On his way, he made a number of discoveries. First, some things were easier to predict than others. Second, people who were not dogmatic, did not automatically rely on what they thought they knew, did not answer off the cuff but spent some time and effort studying the questions they had been asked, and who were self-critical, did much better than the rest. Third, the best participants in the project did better than intelligence officers with classified information at their disposal. Moreover, the ways they arrived at their conclusions could be studied and taught. The closer the date of the event to be predicted, the more accurate the prediction as to whether or not it would take place; and the other way around. Answers to questions concerning events that might take place more than three to five years in the future had only an even (50 per cent) chance of being correct.

Not that I find that surprising.

14

THE MOST POWERFUL TOOLS

Today, the most powerful tools we have for looking into the future are models and the algorithms from which they are constructed. Modelling owes, or is supposed to owe, nothing to altered states of consciousness. To that extent, its use is similar to that of polls, history, the Bible, numerology divination, omens and, of course, astrology. As with these, the principle behind the modelling method is that the more 'objective' a model – in other words, the less room is allowed for the user's own perceptions and emotions to interfere with it – the better. A contemporary computer expert who, looking for work, claims to be filled by God and to be speaking in His name is hardly likely to get more respect from his peers than the impassioned habitués who used to populate London's Speakers' Corner on Sunday mornings. If, in addition, he behaves as shamans often do, drumming, singing, dancing, taking mind-altering substances and falling into a trance, he will garner even less.

Models can be very complex indeed. Essentially, though, they consist of two things. First there are lists of factors – nowadays often called variables – that, between them, are supposed to represent reality or some part of it. Second, and no less important, are the links between those variables. Those links, moreover, are almost always quantitative, meaning that, when component A changes or is tweaked by such and such an amount, not only must component B, C and D follow suit but they must do so by a particular amount.

The earliest, and for millennia almost the only, models were those that represented the movements of the heavenly bodies. Their purpose was to show not only the lunar phases, the positions of the planets, eclipses and the like, but lucky and unlucky days, feast days and so on. The oldest known example is the Antikythera mechanism, called after the island closest to the place where it was found in an ancient shipwreck on the bottom of the Aegean. It seems to date to the period between 205 and 87 BCE. Covered with salt and badly corroded, several decades had to pass until it could be reconstructed by modern scholars. Scholars have revealed that the device was able to show, in addition to the above, the relationship between the solar and lunar calendars as well as the dates of future Olympic Games. However, as the ancient world drew to an end the knowledge needed to construct such sophisticated machines was lost. It was only much later that more or less similar ones started to be built in China (the clock tower built by Su Song in about 1100 CE), the Arab world (Al-Jazari's castle clock, 1206) and Italy (the fourteenth-century Dondi clock). Another well-known example is the great astronomical clock of Strasbourg, which was originally constructed in the fourteenth century, though since then it has been rebuilt several times.

Almost by definition, models are based on mathematical calculations. The more relevant and inclusive the variables they consist of, and the more accurate the calculations that form the links among those variables, the better the model. Following the publication of Newton's *Principia mathematica* in 1687, which proclaimed a single set of simple laws to cover the movements of all bodies both here on Earth and in the heavens, the popularity of models of this kind soared. Some, based on the laws of physics, tell us for example exactly when a solar eclipse will take place hundreds of years in the future, how long it will last, and the geographical region in which our descendants will have to position themselves in order to witness it. Others go so far as to predict developments that will take place in the universe millions of years hence, for instance when a star will turn into a white dwarf, or a supernova into a black hole. Others, concerned only with vastly shorter periods of time, tell us what is about to happen in the submicroscopic world.

The earliest known attempt to extend mathematical modelling – as opposed to gathering statistics, a different if not unrelated task that goes back as least as far as the Bible (see 1 Samuel 24) – of the future from astronomy and physics to social life was made in the Roman Empire. The calculations of the early third-century jurist Ulpian seem to attempt to model the life expectancy of certain groups of people, though to which population his tables refer is not clear. His work, however, has survived only in the form of brief summaries in later sources, with the result that it is very difficult to make out. Ulpian's apparent objective was to predict how much the treasury, for which he seems to have been working, could expect to receive in taxes at future dates.[1]

Attempts to reduce risk by sharing it among several people, each of whom made a contribution to the common enterprise, go back as far as the first millennium BCE, if not further. However, it was only during the Renaissance that the Italian mathematician and 'degenerate gambler'[2] Girolamo Cardano (1501–1576) wrote the first works on probability, odds and risk management, and how to use them in betting. Work in this direction continued in the second half of the seventeenth century when probability theory and compound interest came to be better understood. The resulting models enabled men such as William Petty and Gregory King in England to try to estimate future national income as a basis for taxation and the sums the government could expect. What had long been a trickle of data, much of it fragmentary, disorganized and too disparate to be of use, grew far larger after the establishment around 1800 of the first national statistical bureaus in places such as France and Britain. Not accidentally, the term 'statistics', said to have been coined by the German scholar Gottfried Achenwall, itself also came into use about that time.[3]

During the 1880s some larger corporations joined governments in their attempts to obtain statistical information and put it to use. Increasingly conducting many kinds of operations in many places simultaneously, the corporations in question struggled to find a reasonable balance between decentralization and control. Consequently, they too started gathering and processing statistics concerning production, consumption, prices and many other things. Some even went ahead and set up special offices for the purpose. In the words of the English historian Henry Thomas Buckle, underlying the effort was the hope that, if only human affairs could be subjected to an examination as rigorous (meaning, based on 'social statistics') as that which had long been applied to the natural sciences, the laws on which they were based could be firmly established, and uncertainty as to the future eliminated or at least reduced.[4] The outcome was a vast increase in the use of models.

Both in the physical world and in social affairs, many models are probabilistic. The implication is that they have nothing to say about the future of individuals, but only about the groups of which those individuals form a part. Physicists cannot predict what a single molecule out of billions will do when the flask that contains them is heated, but they can predict – and with great accuracy – the average behaviour that results from the interaction of all of them combined. Similarly, insurers cannot tell just who is going to be involved in a traffic accident over the next year. But actuarial models can predict, given a group of people with certain known characteristics (age, sex, place of residence, type of vehicle, number of kilometres driven per year, previous insurance claims and so on), the chances of one of those individuals of being involved in a road accident. The same goes for having one's home burgled, developing a disease sufficiently serious as to require treatment, committing a crime and being arrested for it, and so on. It is on such models that insurance premiums are based. Judging by the enormous wealth of many insurance companies, and assuming it was attained by following the rules and not by circumventing or breaking them, probabilistic models are among the most successful of all. However, there are limits. First, since circumstances of all kinds change, the models tend to become less accurate as time goes by. Second, they cannot tell us anything about the fates of individual people. Which is why, officially at any rate, such models are not allowed as evidence in courts of law.[5]

Developing mathematical models has always been a tiresome business. First, the relevant factors have to be identified. A model of the world that includes *all* the relevant factors in that world would be identical with that world, and hence an early decision had to be made as to what to include and, which is quite as important, what to leave out. Next they have to be related to each other in specific ways; a difficult task, given that social reality is dynamic and that it is by no means certain that what is most important today will remain so tomorrow. That accomplished, data must be assembled, verified, arranged in usable form and collated. Finally, depending on the complexity of the issue, any number of calculations have to be made to see whether reality does in fact fit the models and vice versa. For hundreds of years, this had to be done laboriously by hand. During the last decades of the nineteenth century and the early ones of the twentieth this was often the task of women. Known as 'computors', they were considered particularly suitable for work that was painstaking, repetitive and boring.[6] Photographs shows entire rooms filled with these women, with perhaps only an older female supervisor and a couple of male visitors present.

It was during the 1920s that gathering statistics about virtually every aspect of social and economic life became commonplace. This was the case especially in the United States, where the secretary of commerce and subsequent president Herbert Hoover pointed the way. Hoover himself had used such methods to rise from a poverty-stricken youth to a man of immense riches. During the First World War, in his career as a philanthropist, he used them on a much larger scale, helping save occupied Belgium from starvation. Properly gathered, presented, applied and used, who knew what miracles they might still perform? Business analysts and consultants, claiming to provide their clients with every kind of forecast under the sun, flourished. Most only did so for a short time before history caught up with them. But some, including some of today's best-known firms, such as Booz Allen Hamilton and McKinsey & Co., survived.

The next crucial turning point in modelling and forecasting came with the introduction of computers during the years after the Second World War. Among the earliest, and most interesting, attempts was MONIAC (Monetary National Income Analogue Computer).[7] Also known, after its creator, as the Phillips Hydraulic Computer, it consisted of a series of transparent plastic tanks and pipes fastened to a wooden board. The entire apparatus was approximately 2 metres high, 1.2 metres wide and almost 1 metre deep. Each tank represented some aspect of Britain's national economy. Reflecting the enormous growth of the state during the previous few decades, at the top of the board was a large tank called the Treasury. Streams of coloured water, representing money, flowed from the Treasury to other tanks representing the various ways in which a country could spend its money.

For example, there were tanks for health and education. To increase spending on healthcare, a tap could be opened to drain water from the Treasury to the tank that represented health spending. Water then ran down the model to other tanks, representing other interactions in the economy. To represent the changing rates of taxation, varying volumes of water could be pumped from some of the tanks back to the Treasury. Other flows represented savings, income and other factors considered relevant. Additional ones, such as interest rates, could be readily added as desired. The actual flow of the water was automatically controlled through a series of floats, counterweights, electrodes and cords. From our point of view the decisive fact is that a series of controls enabled users to experiment with different settings and note their effects. This made MONIAC useful not just for teaching – its original purpose – but for attempts to predict the direction in which the economy was moving as well.

Needless to say, MONIAC did not design itself. Nor did any other computers, analogue or digital, act on their own in setting up models. That has remained the task of the humans who programme them, a job quite as tiresome as making the above-mentioned calculations. It could even be argued that, though computer languages have improved no end and many new ones have been devised, during the century and a half since Ada Lovelace worked with Charles Babbage on his 'analytical engine', the programming process itself has changed hardly at all.[8] What computers did do was to allow vast bodies of data to be processed at enormous speed, and if necessary repeatedly so in order to validate the results and see how tweaking one factor would affect all the rest. The effect was to refine – in the sense of taking more factors into consideration and making the links between them more accurate – the models and to vastly increase their number. This has now been taken to the point where anyone who does not use, or claims not to use, computers for setting up models and looking into the future is likely to be regarded as a fool.

As of the early years of the twenty-first century, extrapolation can lead to one, and only one, safe prediction to be made: that the use of numbers, computers and models for looking into the future will continue to increase. This is partly because they are in fact useful in enabling their users to figure out how numerous interrelated factors will play out, and partly in order to serve as symbols of progress, increase their users' prestige, and prevent laymen from realizing how uncertain much of the forecasters' knowledge really is. To repeat, many aspects of social life, both collective and individual, remain as impossible to model as they have ever been. To most people, moreover, the models, consisting as they do of equations, remain just as opaque and just as mysterious as the shaman's journey used to be. That is one reason why, even among the well educated and best informed, older methods still persist and will continue to persist as long as the idea of the future itself does.

15

WAR GAMES HERE, WAR GAMES THERE

War games here, war games there, war games, war games everywhere.[1] As this study draws to its end, the last method I want to discuss is games. Not all games, but the kind known as games of strategy or war games. The reason, as we shall presently see, is that the military were the first to use games for looking into the future. It was from them that it spread to economics and politics.

By a game of strategy, I mean one that involves a contest between two or more sides. Conversely, a contest may be called 'strategic' if it answers two conditions. First, each side must be free and able to pursue his own objectives while at the same time actively trying to interfere with the other's attempt to do the same. Second, and as a result, the moves each side makes depend on those of the other(s). Chess, basketball and of course war itself all fall under this definition. Other kinds of contests, such as races and those that are based on pure luck, generally do not.[2]

Some war games involve real-life players, as the Roman gladiatorial games and medieval tournaments did. Many others are played on paper, on some specially prepared board or, nowadays, on a computer. Those of the former kind sometimes involve violence, even deadly violence, as the two examples just given did. Some games are very large; others very small. Some make use of sophisticated technology, especially computers; others do not. From our point of view it doesn't matter; what does matter is the kind of interaction that takes place between the sides. It is one that many other human activities, including war and business, share.

War games are probably as old as war itself. Perhaps, in some ways, even older. A society that does not make use of them remains to be discovered. The purpose of designing and playing them has varied over time. Many tribal societies around the world used to have the kind of games that, played in the field, sometimes served as a sort of substitute war. The purpose was to have some fun, let off steam and, perhaps, resolve minor issues between neighbours.[3] The Roman gladiatorial *ludi* probably started as religious ceremonies. Later they turned into simple entertainment; *panem et circenses*, bread and circuses, as the poet Juvenal put it.[4] If certain modern scholars may be believed, during imperial times another purpose of holding them was to put the power of the emperors, under whose auspices they were held, on display for the population to witness.[5] The sources do present us with some references to soldiers being trained by and as gladiators, but this seems to have been exceptional.[6]

The rationale of medieval tournaments was similar. In addition, many of them also served as a sort of exchange where up-and-coming young aristocrats could display their martial prowess and senior ones choose which of them they wanted to take on as retainers.[7] If only because the idea that the future might be fundamentally different from the past did not exist, though, to anyone's knowledge none of these types were in any way meant to look into the future or predict it.

Military manoeuvres, intended to train troops as well as impress onlookers, are probably as old as the organized armies of kingdoms and city-states are. However, the idea of holding two-sided ones as part of an attempt to divine what future war might be like only seems to have arisen during the nineteenth century. Such manoeuvres involved real soldiers, who were normally armed with real weapons. In many ways, the one thing needed to make these manoeuvres 'real' would have been to replace dummy ammunition, such as bullets, shells and bombs, with the genuine articles. Some of the technology was experimental. Each in turn, this applied to machine guns, recoilless artillery, wireless, tanks, military aircraft and many other kinds of weapon. To this day, manoeuvres of this kind are one of the most important methods by which new technology can be tried out.

The scope within which manoeuvres were held grew and grew. At peak, on the eve of the Second World War, the number of participants sometimes reached into the hundreds of thousands.[8] The method was not without its limitations. Not only was there no real shooting, but the commanders on both sides tended to be handicapped by entire series of artificial rules meant to steer the proceedings in the direction those in charge considered the right one. To make sure the rules were obeyed, and also to determine the outcome of combat, umpires were used. Often this gave rise to disagreements as to whether the methods used by this side or that had been acceptable and a victory well earned.

Not all war games involved real troops or were played out of doors. Of those that did not and were not, much the most famous one is chess. First invented in sixth-century India, from where it spread to Persia, it was explicitly designed so as to model a clash between two opposing armies, each one consisting, as real ones did, of a king, a minister (*wazir* or vizier), elephants, cavalry, chariots and infantry. In the words of a Jewish poet in medieval Spain, Abraham ben Ezra (1089–1164):

> I will sing a song of battle
> Planned in days long passed and over.
> Men of skill and science set it
> On a plain of eight divisions,
> And designed in squares all chequered,
> Two camps face each one the other,
> And the kings stand by for battle,
> And 'twixt these two is the fighting.
> Bent on war the face of each is,
> Ever moving or encamping,

Yet no swords are drawn in warfare,
For war of thought their war is.

However, the analogy between chess and real-life warfare only goes so far. First, there was and is no attempt to model, and hence predict, such vitally important elements of war as physical effort and danger, friction, logistics or intelligence (chess is a game of perfect information where both parties have full and instant knowledge of every move each of them makes). Second, the movements of the various pieces are much too simple and much too stereotypical to represent what actually happens on campaign. Third, though the rules enable each piece to dominate a smaller or larger number of the surrounding squares, no piece is able to strike at distance (that is, without moving) as real troops often do. Fourth, the board is nothing like real terrain; except for the alternating black and white squares, all are exactly alike. Chess, needless to say, is a genial game that can be very attractive to those who play and watch it. But as training for war, let alone for looking into what form future campaigns may take, it is more or less useless.

The first known attempts to make chess more like real war got under way during the middle of the seventeenth century when Christopher Weickmann of Ulm, Germany, came up with what he called 'battle chess'. The idea was to make the board, the pieces and the moves correspond more closely to the terrain, troops and manoeuvres found in real war, thus rendering the game more useful for study and training.[9] During the eighteenth century a number of other men – there seem to have been no women among them – produced similar games. As time went on attempts were made to accurately model as many aspects of war as possible. This caused the games to become increasingly cumbersome and difficult to play. As with battle chess, they seem to have been used, to the extent that they were used at all, mainly for entertainment and training.

Some famous games of this type were produced early in the nineteenth century by a father-and-son team of Prussian officers by the name of Leopold and Georg-Heinrich von Reisswitz.[10] The games they invented were the first to be played not on any board but on a topographical map. Each piece represented not an individual, as in chess, but a unit of troops. The moves, capabilities and limitations of each unit were carefully calculated to correspond to real life as closely as possible. They were, moreover, matched to the kind of terrain on which they operated; for example, crossing a forest took longer than traversing open countryside did. The age-old method of making players take turns remained in force; however, in another rule designed to make the game more like real war, it was adjusted so that each turn now represented a certain number of minutes – the exact period varied – of real time. Finally, the younger Reisswitz in particular realized full well the role that chance plays in combat. That was why, to determine the outcome of clashes between units, he had the players resort to dice throws.

Some examples of the game can still be seen in some German museums. At the time they attracted the attention of King Friedrich Wilhelm III (r. 1797–1840). He played it with his sons, who later ascended the throne as Friedrich Wilhelm IV (r. 1840–61) and Wilhelm I (r. 1861–88). Prodded by the court, the game spread to the General Staff and the officer corps in general. The time came when every garrison had to own a set. The primary purpose of playing continued to be military training. Do, however, take note: by definition, training is a future-oriented activity. One cannot train without having at least a rough idea as to what one is training for. In other words, what the future may be like.

Thus encouraged from above, Reisswitz-type games were extensively played by professionals and amateurs alike, first in Prussia/Germany and then, following that country's great victories of 1864–71, elsewhere as well. Later, games could be and were designed to match any kind of environment in which war is or could be waged, be it land, sea, air or outer space. They could be made to reflect every level on which it is waged, from the tactical to the grand strategic. They also could be, and were, adapted to reflect every kind of new technology coming into use, starting with breechloaders and ending with tanks, dreadnoughts and ballistic missiles.

In the attempt to make them as realistic as possible, over time war games grew fantastically elaborate. To repeat, originally they were played on maps. Much later, during the 1970s, some of the maps were provided with hexes so as to make it easier to count the pieces' movements over them. To represent their capabilities and limitations the pieces themselves used a system of points. Depending on the arm they represented, for example armour or artillery or infantry, they would have a certain number of points for firepower (against particular targets, if so desired). To this would be added a number of points for defensive, for mobility under particular conditions, for joining up with other kinds of units, and so forth. Point systems could also be used to indicate the logistic situation, the state of morale (for instance by ranking it on a scale of one to five), the weather and so on. Additional dice, many of them with multiple sides, were also introduced.

The growing availability of computers from about 1980 on caused most games to move from the board to the screen. By permitting the players, on whom more in a moment, to act simultaneously rather than taking turns, it also did a great deal to make play more realistic. The necessary, often quite complex, calculations, instead of being performed by hand, were now carried out by the computer itself. Often this enabled games that used to take up hours of time (and endless little pieces of paper) to be played in mere minutes. Games, however, continued to be governed by, indeed consist of, interacting rules, now known as algorithms, in this case, of models of what real war, including future war if so desired, would be like.

So fundamental is this issue that it is worth repeating. Models, we have seen, are at bottom nothing but clusters of factors that interact with each other on the basis of rules. Taken together, the factors and rules are supposed to represent reality or some part of it. War games are also clusters of factors that interact with each other on the basis of rules. Taken together, the factors and rules too are supposed to represent reality or some part of it. So what is the difference? This is where strategy comes in. Take a contest between two or more sides. The factors that give the contest its 'strategic' character are that each side is free and able to pursue its own objectives while actively trying to prevent the other from doing the same, and that as a result of this, the moves each side makes depend on those of the other(s).

To return to MONIAC as a simple example, each time the flow of liquid, representing one factor, is changed, other changes will automatically follow. Provided the model is properly calibrated to reflect the way the economy works, it will be able to make a prediction. In a game, too, each move will be responded to by one or more others. Those changes, though, will not be brought about merely by the rules acting blindly on their own. Instead they will be governed by the players' purpose, which, in most cases, is victory, as, for example, by destroying the opponent(s) as in chess, or by gaining a certain number of points after a certain number of moves or within a particular period of time, as in many other games. War games, in other words, are models that differ from the rest in that their behaviour is determined, in large part, not by their intrinsic qualities but by the players' training, attitude and so forth. Whether the player is human or, as in many games, a computer, does not really matter.

By one estimate, globally war games are on track to become a $200-billion-a-year industry.[11] As has been the case from the Stone Age on, probably the vast majority were designed and organized for the purpose of entertainment. Others, however, are used to test every kind of military operation and predict its outcome, as far as possible. As mentioned, the pioneer in the field was the Prussian/German General Staff. Well before the end of the nineteenth century, while planning each campaign they used to hold one or more war games, of which there were several kinds. The objective was to see how things might develop; how they might change if particular factors, such as the number of troops or their equipment, were altered; what the opponent's moves might be like; how they might react to certain moves on the blue (friendly) side; what the final outcome might be; and so on.

Naturally, the vast majority of war games, those played by the Prussian military included, have disappeared into limbo. So much so, in fact, that a perennial complaint about them is the lack of sufficient time and attention to properly study any lessons for the future they may offer. However, the details of a few can still be found in archives and elsewhere. The most famous war game of all was probably one held in Berlin in 1894. The newly appointed chief of staff, General (later Field-Marshal) Alfred von Schlieffen, intended to throw the bulk of his forces against the French in the west. Desirous to know what, as he did so, would happen on Germany's eastern border, he had his officers war game the most likely campaign that would ensue. Twenty years later, in the autumn of 1914, the battles of Tannenberg and the Masurian Lakes, as they came to be known, followed the game's moves with uncanny accuracy.[12] Decades afterwards, German officers were still pointing to these episodes as outstanding proof of what war games, properly and competently handled, could reveal about the future.[13]

This method of looking into the future having vindicated itself, during the Weimar Republic, the Third Reich and Second World War the German military continued to enact war games on a regular basis. So, for example, on the eve of the 1940 campaign against France, when every echelon of the military, from the General Staff to at least as far down as division headquarters, held them, often repeatedly, so as to come up with the best solution. Such was also the case prior to Operation Sea Lion (the planned 1940 invasion of Britain, which was aborted as a result), the 1941 campaign in North Africa and the invasion of the Soviet Union in the same year. The officer in charge of the last-named games was the deputy chief of the Army General Staff, Friedrich Paulus – the same who, in 1942–3, was to become famous by presiding over the debacle at Stalingrad.[14]

The games in question were held in two series from November 1940 to February 1941. The first series showed a) that the Wehrmacht would be able to reach its most important objective, Moscow, but only barely; b) that, in case the armies did reach the objective, it would be impossible to supply them; and c) that losses would be very heavy indeed. All this proved to be spot-on. However, so determined was Hitler to mount the campaign that the General Staff probably did not even present him with the results. In February 1941 another round was held. This time the outcome, namely that the Red Army would be destroyed, though more satisfactory to the planners, proved totally wrong. Three years later, in September 1944, a case occurred when a game predicted the future so accurately that, when the enemy (the Americans) made a sudden move, the officer in charge, Field Marshal Walter Model, ordered it to continue – only this time with real troops, using real communication arteries for moving over real terrain.

In the U.S. and elsewhere, the armed forces also took up the method. The U.S. Navy during the interwar period was particularly keen on it, regularly holding games to simulate a war against Japan. Later no less an officer than Admiral Chester W. Nimitz, commander of the U.S. Pacific Fleet in the Second World War, claimed that, with the exception of the kamikaze attacks of 1944–5, their games had accurately predicted every kind of scenario that actually took place. Perhaps even more important were the games held by the Imperial Japanese Navy. One round, held in September–October 1941, confounded the pessimists by perfectly predicting the way the successful attack on Pearl Harbor would unfold. Another, held in the spring of 1942, predicted that the coming attack on Midway would be a disastrous failure. However, the admirals of the Imperial Japanese Navy decided to ignore that outcome, arbitrarily refloating some aircraft carriers which, the dice used to determine the outcome of the combat showed, would be sunk. Much to their chagrin, the campaign turned out just as the games had predicted.[15]

The Second World War over, there was a growing tendency to extend the use of war games from the military into the field of economics. So much so, in fact, that in the hands of Nobel Prize-winning war gamer and economist Thomas Schelling and others, on occasion the scales were turned: war itself came to be treated as if it were a mere extension of economics. Gaming was used to look at every kind of possible future, from the anticipated impact of more (or less) taxation and/or saving, changes in interest rates, regulation and/or investment, on this or that kind of business; to what the establishment of a casino might do to the economy of this or that town or region.

As with all war games, the great advantage of the method was that, instead of simply bringing out what a single person or team might imagine the future to be like, it addressed changing challenges – injected by the umpire – as well as the element of competition. Doing so, it forced participants to question 'known truths' and deal with all kinds of scenarios they had never thought about. Following in the Reisswitzs' footsteps, some games were designed to bring in the element of chance. Today this is known by the grandiloquent name of Monte Carlo simulation. It is performed not by rolling dice but with the aid of the now usual computers churning out random numbers.

Increasingly after 1960, gaming as a method for looking into the future became a standard part of the life of business organizations that valued it and could afford it. This in turn gave rise to an entire industry whose mission was to organize such games for use in other industries.[16] Typically games are set up to look three months to ten years into the future. The data on which they are based, and the plans they come up with, are real; that is why, in industry as in the military, the departments responsible for them tend to be among the most secretive of all and why relatively little information is available on them. From the little that is available it would seem that their success in accurately 'getting' the future right and forecasting what it would be like is spotty. At times they work, at others not.

Much more problematic was the application of war gaming to politics. Gathering quantitative information and writing equations so as to get a good hold on the way a military operation is going to develop, the opponent's reactions, the immediate outcome and the broader effects it may have is difficult enough. The same applies to both micro- and, even more so, macro-economics. Doing the same in respect to an ongoing political process – or even to a political process that has long since come to an end, such as the collapse of the Roman Empire – is much more difficult still. How does one quantify the impact of soft power, or persuasion, negotiations, blackmail or threats? Or honesty, or guile? It is hardly an accident that none of the great classic texts on politics has much use either for games or for the algorithms on which they are based. That applies as much to Kautilya's *Arthashastra* as to Plato's *Republic*, Aristotle's *Politics* and Machiavelli's *The Prince*.

Quantification being as difficult as it is, attempts to war game the future of politics differ from those made in both economics and war in that there are neither rules nor dice. Instead they take the form of what has been called, disrespectfully, BOGSATs (Bunch of Guys Sitting Around a Table).[17] Some BOGSATs have the participants literally gathered around a single table inside a single room. In others they are separated by a partition, enabling the members of each team to confer in private before communicating with the other. In these computerized days, each player will probably have a laptop to help them access relevant facts of various kinds, making the table look like a snake's nest. Communication proceeds in writing, and normally there is an umpire to control the proceedings. In some games the umpire acts as an honest broker, simply passing information from one team to another, while in others he may take a more active role, for example deciding which information to pass to whom, distorting it – to reflect Carl von Clausewitz's dictum that information in war is always uncertain – and even shaping the debate by throwing in questions of his own.

Once again, determining how successful and useful such games have been in predicting the future is very difficult. A famous case in point are the Sigma I-64 and II-64 exercises held at the Pentagon in spring and autumn 1964 respectively. In both cases, the objective was to predict, as far as possible, the Viet Cong and North Vietnamese reaction to u.s. intervention in the ongoing civil war in Vietnam. In the first round the 'blue' players included some of the most important movers and shakers of u.s. defence policy, or their representatives. Presumably they wanted to be on the winning side. Who played 'red' is not recorded. However, apparently the most senior official was the CIA Deputy Director for Intelligence, Ray Cline, who was no Southeast Asia expert. During the second round the members of the 'blue' team were even more powerful. Except perhaps for a few kings who took part in some medieval tournaments, probably in the whole of history no higher-ranking group of men has ever played a war game of any kind. As mentioned, it is not clear who played 'red', but they seem to have been a group of medium-level experts on defence and foreign policy.

In the event, the first series predicted that a u.s. bombing of North Vietnam could not be kept secret as some, rather preposterously, suggested it should be. It also predicted that such a campaign, launched without appropriate political justification, would lead to massive protests both outside and within the u.s. and that it might cause the Soviet Union 'to change the ground rules of the Cold War' by taking aggressive action in Latin America. Of the three predictions, the first two turned out to be spot on. The third did not.[18] The conclusion that emerged from the second series of exercises was that an incremental bombing campaign against North Vietnam, like the one that was actually launched, would not compel the North Vietnamese to throw in the towel. Instead the outcome would be a growing American involvement attended by serious foreign and domestic political problems. In the event, both of these games, having failed to fulfil the expectations of those who ordered them to be held, were simply put aside.

A somewhat similar round of games, called Desert Crossing, was held by the Clinton administration in 1999.[19] This time the target country was Iraq, which at that time was suffering under sanctions and being bombed on a regular basis. Yet the regime refused to collapse. Seventy military, diplomatic and intelligence officials took part in the exercise; some did so by representing their own government, some by representing those of other countries that would be affected in one way or another, and some by playing the role of Saddam Hussein and his senior subordinates. The games suggested that, to really get a hold on Iraq, no fewer than 400,000 troops would be needed (in fact, the u.s. never really had even half as many). They also suggested that driving Saddam Hussein from power would not necessarily result in political stability; that any replacement regime was likely to be considered more 'American' than 'Iraqi' and thus be unable to control the country; that the outcome would be fragmentation along religious and/or ethnic lines, leading to chaos created by rival forces bidding for power; and that a long-term u.s. presence was likely to cause problems with America's regional allies.

In the event, the games followed their predecessors into the dustbin – indeed so much so that, when the officer in charge,

General Anthony Zinni, tried to call attention to them just prior to Operation Iraqi Freedom (the 2003 invasion of Iraq), no one knew they had ever taken place. It was only at the end of 2006 that they re-emerged; and then only with the aid of a Freedom of Information Act request by the National Security Archive, an independent research institute and library located at George Washington University.

Had Cassandra been invited to participate, she would not have been surprised.

PART IV:

THE LORD OF THE

UNIVERSE

16

LOOKING BACKWARDS

Retracing our journey, it is clear that attempts to look into the future and see what it may bring go as far back as the human eye can see. They appear to form an indispensable part of human nature, one that separates us from other animals – many of which share it to a limited extent but none of which seems to have come close to us in this respect – and also from machines, which, being made of dead matter, are incapable of anticipating anything at all. Probably there never has been, nor ever will be, a society that did not have methods of doing so or did not try to devise them as best it could. A stronger argument against materialism, the hoary idea that we ourselves are 'nothing but' machines, could hardly be thought of.

As I said in the Introduction, the number of methods that have been devised for looking into the future is very large, from the age-old form of shamanism to today's mathematical models, many of them so complex that even those who created them and fed them into computers are unable to predict which way they will go. Some never went beyond the small, not seldom esoteric, tribes and sects in which they were invented and practised; others spread until they came to be studied and practised all over the global village. Often, several different methods were used by different people or even by the same people at the same time and place. They grew out of each other, influenced each other, and migrated to and fro between different civilizations, as shamanism, prophecy, the interpretation of dreams, necromancy, astrology, numerology and of course extrapolation, dialectics, polls, modelling and war games all did. Very often they over-lapped, so that drawing a sharp line between them is impossible. Yet the core problem, to find out what the future was going to bring and what it would be like, has always remained.

Starting in antiquity, there has never been a shortage of dis-putes as to which method of prediction is the right one, either in general or under specific circumstances and for specific pur-poses. As in practically every other form of human endeavour, what one man took as beneficial, another regarded as anath-ema. This was so much the case that the authorities sometimes imposed the death penalty on those who practised some of the methods in question. In most societies this was due to the fear that prophecies, especially such as promised evil things to come, might lead to political instability. To this, monotheistic societies added the clash between human foreknowledge and the omnipo-tence of God. Nor are such prohibitions necessarily passé even today. An interesting case in point came to light in August 2017 when Andreas Georgiou, Greece's former chief statistician, was convicted in court for arguing that the future of his country's economy was not quite as bright as the politicians, anxious to secure further loans from the European Union, were claiming.[1]

Reflecting the societies that devised and made use of them, the methods in question were not static but developed over time. Which is to say that they were affected, even governed, by the culture that gave birth to them. Culture is a set of interlocking attitudes and beliefs that is inculcated into people from their moment of birth on. Escaping from culture is very difficult, often impossible; so axiomatic do its tenets appear that most people, most of the time, do not even realize that they exist. This explains why, across time and place, the vast majority of people, specifically including some of the most intelligent and best edu-cated, believed in things that we modern, educated Westerners would regard as unadulterated nonsense. This includes the kind of nonsense that was used in order to try and understand what the future might bring. Conversely, there is every reason to think that, had the ancient Israelites, Greeks or Romans been confronted with today's mathematical models, they would have shaken their heads over so much foolishness.

Another thing all the methods for looking into the future had in common was the heavy use they made of symbolism and allegory. The same also applied to some of the methods that did not require a transition from one state of mind to another, including astrology, divination, the interpretation of omens and portents, and numerology. All were based on observing certain phenomena, either natural or mathematical, and trying to decipher the symbols they were believed to carry.

Some of those who used the methods in question spoke directly to anyone willing (and, on occasion, unwilling) to listen to them. Others, such as the Pythia and those who experienced prophetic dreams, had their visions or prophecies delivered at one remove, so to speak, at the hand of experts who specialized in interpreting them. No doubt there were also occasions when they doctored them to suit either themselves or their clients; those who failed to do so might well put their lives in danger. However, to repeat what I said about prophecy fraud, this topic lies beyond the scope of the present study.

The critical turning point in the history of humanity's attempts to 'dip' into the future and see what it might have in store appears to have taken place from about 1650 to 1780, a period that comprised first the scientific revolution and then the Enlightenment. The period opened with Thomas Hobbes's denunciation of 'apparitions' and 'visions' as either 'fancy' or 'knavery' not worth the attention of serious people; passed through Thomas Paine, who like many of his contemporaries identified reason with God, meaning that it was to be relied upon for all purposes, anticipating the future included; and ending, symbolically, with the more extreme French revolutionaries, such as Jacques Hébert and Maximilien de Robespierre, who enlisted the aid of the state in trying to abolish God and enthrone Reason in His stead.

In all this, the most important single development was the rather sudden decline in the status of 'enthusiasm' and related spiritual phenomena. As far back as we can look, one very important – in many societies the most important – method for looking into the future was to enter into some kind of altered state of consciousness (ASC). This was something shamanism, prophecy, oracles, the interpretation of dreams and necromancy all had in common. All considered it necessary to take leave of the ordinary world, travel into a different one and get in touch with supernatural beings, be they spirits, gods or God himself. Or the dead, who would then answer questions or speak through one's mouth.

As *Homo ecstaticus* went into decline, no more were those who would look into the future expected to take drugs, dance until they collapsed, foam at the mouth, lose consciousness, utter incomprehensible phrases or perform miracles by way of proving their powers. No longer were they supposed to go on a mysterious voyage, visit some unknown country, meet with various spirits, speak in the name of the Lord or arrange a conference with Him. This was taken to the point where, especially among the elites of the most advanced countries, anyone who did or claimed to do such things was more likely to be declared insane than to gain recognition as a prophet.

Three factors led to the change. The first was the expansion of science, especially but not exclusively physical science, into domains that previously could be understood, if at all, only in supernatural terms. The second was an ongoing process of secularization, which in many places put great emphasis on an orderly life, sobriety and reasonableness.[2] The third was the steady expansion, during those very years, of bureaucratic (the term itself goes back to the 1760s) methods of control with their emphasis, in addition to the previous three, of consistency, regularity and dependability.[3] Prediction, in other words, shed the sacred-magic-otherworldly quality that had characterized it for so long. From focusing on the *in*credible – as Tertullian, referring to Christ's Second Coming, put it,[4] it is certain because it is impossible – it shifted to an attempt to appear as credible as possible. On the way it became, or pretended to become, subject to the ordinary rules of reason in the same way as many other things also did. Nor did those who tried to exercise that reason any longer need to prove themselves by performing miracles.

None of this is to say that any of the earlier methods disappeared immediately or completely. To the contrary, one of the most impressive things about many of them is their extraordinary longevity and their ability to survive into the modern, supposedly rational and supposedly scientific, world. This has been the case especially at times of great turbulence, uncertainty and stress, and especially, but by no means exclusively, among the religious, the less educated and those living in straitened circumstances. That ability, in turn, is based precisely on the heavy use they make of symbolism, metaphors and allegory, all of which can enter the consciousness much more directly, attract many more people and leave stronger impressions much more easily than science, with its often arcane experiments and mathematical formulae, can. As the founder of analytical psychology, Carl Gustav Jung, might have said, it is symbols, along with the ASC in which they are rooted, that make our minds tick.

Even today, many people still consult psychics and mediums of every kind. As of 1995, horoscopes figured in 70 per cent of American daily newspapers, where two-thirds of all readers consult them at least once a week. Twenty years later, American fortune-tellers were said to be taking in about $2 billion a year. In Italy the number of fortune-tellers of every kind is said to have quintupled since the great recession struck in 2008: one-quarter of the entire adult population regularly consults them, at an annual cost of €8 billion.[5] As I was writing this book I learnt that Israel's founder and first prime minister, David Ben-Gurion, repeatedly went to the trouble of consulting with a 'psychic' woman. Her name was Sally Linker and she lived in dire poverty in Tel Aviv, where she surrounded herself with rags and cats. One time she told him that in four days he would feel better; on another occasion she said that two of his enemies, while they believed they had the power, would not succeed in bringing him down.[6] As we have seen, he was not the only head of state who sought this kind of advice, either regularly or just on occasion.

While old methods were discarded or at least relegated to the margins, new ones made their appearance. Among the first and, as countless references to it show, most important was the one based on history. As long as history meant 'again and again', which it mostly did before about the middle of the eighteenth century, using it for looking into the future could only involve either repetitive patterns or cycles. As the Industrial Revolution began making its impact felt, though, the idea that some of the most important things did not change and would never change became less and less tenable. Increasingly even human nature, which most previous authorities had considered to be static, started being understood as the product of history, and hence subject to change. So much so, in fact, that some scientists regard this very malleability, and the consequent ability to live and even prosper under a wide range of conditions, as the most important constituent of our nature. The outcome was the view of history as an arrow-like process that led from the past through the present into the future. This meant the future not as the Apocalypse (as first Hebrew and then Christian prophets, each in their own way, had understood it from the sixth century BCE onwards), but the future here on Earth.

In its turn, the idea that the essence of history was change gave birth to attempts to discern how that change came about and where it might lead. This meant doing one of two things. Either one identified trends and extrapolated from them – the method that, applied to a seemingly infinite number of fields both large and small, has since become the most common by far – or else, going one step further, one used dialectics in an attempt to figure out the way various trends, coming from different and often opposite directions, might interact. In theory at any rate, such methods owe nothing to ASC, symbolism or allegory. God, the spirits, dreams and the dead were also bid goodbye. That was precisely why Karl Marx insisted on calling trend identification and the dialectical method 'scientific', a claim many of his followers have continued to repeat up to the present day. Once again, though, the emergence of these two methods of using history did not mean that the older ones were forgotten or fell completely out of use.

A relatively recent forecasting method is polling in its various forms. Of all the methods in use, it is the most democratic. This explains why the first place in which it was tried was early nineteenth-century America. It also owes something to the development of modern methods of communication, beginning with postcards and passing through the telephone to computers and the Internet, and as such only started being used on any scale during the early decades of the twentieth century. Polling rests on the assumption that the judgement of the many, provided they form a proper sample, is more likely to be accurate than that of individuals. It also rests on the notion that extreme views tend to cancel each other out, especially over the course of time. The voice of the people is the voice of God; to which one can only say, Amen. It was the perceived shortcomings of surveys that led to the development of the Delphi method on one hand and Philip Tetlock's Good Judgment Project on the other. Each in its own way, they represent attempts to do away with simple nose-counting and bring expertise back into the process.

Today's most prestigious method used for looking into the future consists of constructing mathematical models, whether such as are actually built or such as only exist on paper (the case, presumably, for the great majority) and are never translated into cogwheels or computer chips. At the most basic level, models are simply lists of variables and the ways they interact. As far as possible, though, those relationships are expressed not with words but with the aid of sets of rules or algorithms. The earliest models, going back thousands of years, were meant to represent physical phenomena, specifically the movements of the Sun, Moon, planets and fixed stars. Their function in governing the calendar apart, their primary use was in astrology; not infrequently the two things were fused to the point of being inseparable.

As we saw, historically the first field to feel the impact of models on forecasting was insurance. Of all known forecasting methods, they have been among the most successful. However, there is a catch. This success has been achieved at the expense of giving up any attempt to forecast the future of individuals. We can be reasonably certain about what percentage of persons, falling into such and such a category, will be involved in a road accident or contract a given disease or fall victim to a robbery. It is, indeed, on just such models that many aspects of public policy, from healthcare to police work, are based.[7] What we cannot tell is who will be affected – precisely the question that, for most of us who are not insurance brokers, public health officials or police officers, is the most important of all.

Other attempts to construct mathematical models of the way society, and specifically demographics, works, started being made during the years around 1650. During the second half of the nineteenth century, owing to much-improved data-gathering methods devised and used by offices that had been specially established for the purpose, they started being applied to entire populations and economies. Still, what really enabled models to attain the status they enjoy today was computers. Their introduction meant that once the algorithms had been written – meaning, once the computers had been programmed – enormous amounts of data could be processed at enormous speed, repeatedly and at very low cost.

Some models do more than allow those who design and use them to tweak the various factors that constitute them in a variety of ways. They do that, of course; but they also involve a strategic interaction between opposing sides, human or artificial (in the form of computers). Such models are known as war games. The first to develop them and use them systematically in an attempt to understand what future campaigns might be like was the Prussian/German military around the middle of the nineteenth century. Later they spread to other armed forces too. After the Second World War, attempts were made to extend war games into other fields. One was business, where, owing to the great role numbers play in it, they had a great future in front of them, even though few attempts had been made to see how accurate they really were. Another was politics; to which, it turned out, war games were useful in terms of training but less so for predicting the future.

Every one of these methods has been surrounded by endless hype. Some of the claims made on their behalf were based, if not on what we today regard as sound principles, at any rate on good faith. Others involved outright trickery and fraud, both of which are as prevalent today as they were in the days when Frontinus recommended that commanders resort to carefully controlled forms of divination to encourage their troops and make them fight harder.

Such being the case, it is good to keep in mind the warning issued by Alfred Russel Wallace, Darwin's contemporary in developing the theory of evolution:

> It is . . . in the interest of truth that every doctrine and belief, however well-established or sacred they may appear, should at certain intervals be challenged to arm themselves with such facts and reasoning as they possess, to meet their opponents in the open field of controversy and do battle for the right to live. Nor can

any exemption be claimed for those beliefs which are the product of modern civilization and which have, for several generations, been held by the great mass of the educated community; for the prejudice in their favour will be proportionally great.[8]

17

WHY IS PREDICTION
SO DIFFICULT?

A number of people, among them Mark Twain and the nuclear scientist Niels Bohr, have been credited with saying that 'predicting is difficult, especially of the future'. As the sheer number and variety of the methods that have been devised for doing so show, that has always been true and will likely remain true. To repeat, I have no intention of examining the problems that attend each method separately. All, specifically including the most sophisticated modern ones, have their advantages and their disadvantages. As the repeated, and sometimes catastrophic, emergence of so-called 'black swans'[1] – things that, by most logical reasoning, should not have happened but did – proves, though, in a great many cases the latter outweigh the former. Perhaps that is because, unless errors happen to cancel each other out, for a prediction to come true both the assumptions on which it rests and the details it contains must be correct.

Difficult as looking into the future is, some parts of it are more difficult than others. Other things being equal, three factors govern the degree of difficulty. First, the greater the role of psychological and social factors, as opposed to physical ones, in shaping both the present and the future, the harder that future is to foresee. This is the case the other way around, too, though there are at least two major exceptions to the rule. One is the weather. True, weather forecasting methods have improved considerably since the spread of telegraphy enabled the first crude ones to be devised during the last decades of the nineteenth century. However, it is still only for the coming week or so that the information they provide is at all reliable. Nor, in a great many cases, is there anything to prevent conditions from changing completely within a period of a few hours or even less; which is why some weather stations have been switching to predicting it hour by hour.[2] The other is earthquakes, a field in which a century of investigation has led to virtually no progress at all. True, the fact that not all regions are equally susceptible to quakes has been known for centuries, even millennia. Yet in those that are more so, earthquakes may occur at any time and without warning to speak of. So far there have been no demonstrably successful predictions of large earthquakes, and the few claims of success are controversial, to say the least.[3]

Second, there is the question of detail. The more detailed a forecast, the more likely it is to go wrong. That is why futurologists, starting at least as far back as the Greek oracles, are so often content with providing no more than outlines or vague contours; and also why probabilistic forecasting has been invented and developed. Third, generally the more remote the future we are trying to foresee, the more complex the chain of events that leads to it, and the less accurate our forecasts. Starting around 1940, this fact gave birth to the expression 'the foreseeable future'. As a look at Google Ngram shows, since then its rise has been meteoric. Not that the foreseeable future is always what the term implies; very often it is a mere preliminary either to nonsense, a lack of imagination (change without change, as it has been called), or both.

Here I want to look at some difficulties all methods have in common: first, those that are rooted in our own nature; second, those that originate in the nature of the future; third, those that stem from the imprecise ways in which most predictions are expressed; fourth, those that have to do with time; and fifth, those that result from the difference between an unknown future and a known one. In what follows I shall try to explain each of the five in turn.

To begin with, such is our nature that, in our attempts to gain knowledge – any knowledge, regardless of the thing to be known – our principal method is observation, carried out by our senses, either with or without the benefit of instruments and experiments. Of this method the philosopher John Locke wrote that it was the *only* way in which we can gain knowledge.[4] Nor was he by any means the first to hold that view. Be that as it may, there is little doubt that observation, whether as practised by ourselves or by others who inform us of their conclusions, accounts for a very large part of whatever knowledge we possess or think we possess. Yet when it is a question of looking into the future it is of no avail. What has not yet happened or come into being cannot be observed, let alone experimented with.

In the field of physics, we can at least rely on the laws of nature. They give us assurance that, as long as conditions do not change, the same thing will happen again and again. Elsewhere, the best we can do is to call on trends and extrapolation. That, in many cases, is a dangerous thing to do indeed. The following limerick puts it very well:

A trend is a trend is a trend
The question is, will it bend
Or be driven off course
By an unforeseen force
And come to a premature end.

Worse still, extrapolation refuses to take *Aufhebung* into account. So much so, in fact, that the word has no proper equivalent either in English or in any number of other European languages (though in philosophy it is usually given as 'sublation'). As a result, extrapolation cannot encompass qualitative change. All it ever does is to assume more (or less) of what already is. (Which, incidentally, is a cardinal reason why so much science fiction is as boring as it is: instead of having characters use bullets to slay monsters and kill one another here on Earth, writers have them use all kinds of mysterious rays to do the same in interplanetary or intergalactic space. Big deal.)

Next, we must ask whether we humans are capable of making any 'objective' forecasts at all. It is of course true that we are reasoning creatures. Reasoning, in the sense that we can very often distinguish means from objectives and causes from consequences, and, within each pair, relate the former to the latter. What we cannot do is look into the future without, first, taking into account the most obvious aspects of what we already know, or think we know; and second, excluding all the things we do not know and/or are unable to grasp.

In fact, there is much more to each of us than pure reason. Not only are we prone to error, but every thought we have in our mind is a product of our memory, whether accurate or not. It is also intimately mixed up with, and to some extent a product of, our emotions, including greed, hope, joy, elation, love, hate, despair, fear, grief, anger and resentment, to name but a few. Forming a true witch's brew, these emotions in turn are shaped in part by the circumstances in which we find ourselves and which go a very long way to govern our points of view and form our opinions. It may even be true, as Nietzsche said, that thought itself is nothing but the shadow of our feelings – a feeble, often almost desperate attempt to rationalize them and to justify them to ourselves and others.[5]

Some of us are optimists, others pessimists. Some are sanguine, others uncertain. Some are highly strung, others have what is commonly known as strong nerves. Moreover, there may very well develop a feedback loop: those who are repeatedly right, for example, may become overconfident, causing them to close their minds and commit a growing number of errors. Those who are repeatedly wrong may, if they are intelligent, reconsider and start moving in the opposite direction. To use Tetlock's terminology, foxes may turn into hedgehogs and hedgehogs into foxes. And this is before we take into account our drives and hormones, including such as were passed to us by our genes and of whose very existence we may not be aware.

Behind all of this are our brains. All of the brain's components, from the most recent to the oldest and most primitive, are in constant touch with, and impact, one other. They do so, moreover, in different ways at different times. That is why there is no such thing as an impression formed, or a thought conceived, or a decision made, or an action taken, by the cerebral cortex alone.[6] Briefly, when everything is said and done, objectivity is, objectively speaking, impossible. No two people have ever seen the future (or anything else) in exactly the same light. Willy-nilly, the first thing we bring to bear on it is our own highly changeable, highly capricious, not seldom inexplicable and unfathomable state of mind.

Our tendency to resort to heuristics, meaning mental shortcuts, and to 'understand' whatever we find in front of us by either referring to existing patterns or inventing new ones (often even when none exist) does not help either.[7] Nor shall we solve the problem by devising models and algorithms and, assisted by computers, handing it over to them to crunch. That is because those models and algorithms necessarily reflect the human minds that created them. It is they, the humans, who, on the basis of their biases, decide what to put in and what to leave out; as well as in what order to arrange what is left, which may critically affect the outcome, and also, perhaps the most important question of all, what relative weight to attribute to each of the various factors and how to shape the links among them.

That even applies to the kind of artificial intelligence programs that sometimes surprise their creators by doing things in ways those creators never thought of. A good example of the problem is in the area of automated trading. By one estimate, as of 2017 nearly 45 per cent of all trading on the stock exchange was done electronically. Other sources put the figure much higher still. Untold billions have been spent on the systems in question. One advantage of making the switch to electronic trading is that the replacement of analysts by engineers can lead to savings, since one of the latter can take the place of four of the former.[8] Another is that trading can proceed with fewer technical errors, at a speed no human can remotely match, and at vastly reduced cost. It is also much easier to retrace the process so as to find out what led to certain decisions, good or bad, and tweak the rules if necessary.[9]

Yet there is no proof that machines are better at forecasting the future of stocks (let alone other, less quantifiable, things) than the people whose jobs they have taken. Some experts feel that automatic trading, far from generating greater profits for those who rely on it, tends to latch on to so-called 'flash events'. This refers to short-term fluctuations such as the one that, on 1 August 2012, caused one firm to lose four times its annual income within half an hour, bringing down its stock and ultimately forcing it to merge with another company so as to save itself.[10] Nor is it a question of simply increasing or reducing individual stocks in a way that is totally out of proportion to the 'real' value of individual firms. Taking a more general view, flash events increase the fragility of the market. Their occurrence can make any reasoned attempt to look at what may be coming all but impossible, and may very well help create a situation where some people prefer not to invest but keep their assets in liquid form instead.

Complex as these problems are, those raised by the nature of the future itself may be even more so. Here the key question is whether the future exists at all, in the same sense as the present does and the past once did. Bertrand Russell, one of the twentieth century's most important philosophers, thought so. His argument was that, supposing the present is real, and since there is no clear dividing line between it and the future, the future too must be real. That being the case, then – in principle at any rate – the future should be foreseeable.[11] To use the metaphor of the unrolling carpet, trying to foresee the future would be like looking for the part of the pattern that is still hidden: a difficult task, admittedly, but one that, given the right equipment (perhaps some kind of hitherto unknown X-rays), is not in principle impossible.

But not everyone agrees with this line of thought. Other philosophers have argued that the future is not any solid reality coming towards us like an express train, but simply a set of more or less tenuous premonitions, or guesses. Impossible to locate – where *is* that future we are talking of? – they are mere fancies, generated somehow by our brains, whose ill-understood activity they reflect. As such they are part of what is sometimes known as 'psychological time'.[12] Loosely floating about, they do not necessarily have any kind of link with the external world. This, if modern brain scientists may be believed, is also the case with dreams, and like dreams too, they assume as many different forms as there are brains. If such is indeed the case, then obviously the number of futures is as large as that of the people who come up with them. Or much larger, in fact, because, as Goethe's *Faust* puts it, 'two souls, alas, exist in my breast'.[13] And foreseeing which of the myriad possibilities will come true is impossible except with the aid of pure luck or, at best, that vague thing known as intuition.

It may be true, as the early nineteenth-century French polymath Pierre-Simon Laplace wrote – and as materialists had argued thousands of years before him – that all events are predetermined in the sense that they are caused by those that went before them. As a result, a 'demon' with a perfect understanding of all existing things, as well as the links among them, should be able to form an equally perfect knowledge of the future.[14] Yet however great the scientific advances that have been made over the last two centuries, there is no sign that such knowledge is any closer today than it was two hundred years ago. For every mystery that scientists solve, there is another one that reveals itself. Nor, while trying to anticipate the future, is there any way we can take account of things we do not know we do not know.

Much worse still, we now have Heisenberg's uncertainty principle, the so-called observer effect, and chaos theory to tell us why such knowledge is impossible to attain.[15] The uncertainty principle says that, at the subatomic level, either the position of an elementary particle or its momentum is measurable, but not both together. The observer effect, which is an extension of that principle, says that the very attempt to observe something causes it to change. The smaller the observed object, the more true this is.

Chaos theory maintains that very small differences in initial conditions can, by way of a chain of events too complex to master, lead to wildly divergent outcomes. This leads to that strange, but for all practical purposes real, hybrid: deterministic randomness.[16] For example, particles smaller than one-thousandth the width of a human hair may intensify storms, increase the size of clouds and cause more rain to fall.[17] A butterfly fluttering its wings in Beijing, it has been said, may give rise to a hurricane in Florida. Or else, depending on what happens somewhere in between those two places, either cause it to be diverted to Haiti or prevent it from forming altogether.

Even in the field of physics, therefore, there is some reason to doubt that all events are predetermined by those that went before them. Or, at any rate, that we shall ever know enough to make anything like perfect prediction possible. And this is before, switching from physics to psychology and sociology, we allow the question of a free will, whether individual or collective, to enter the equation. Does a free will, which at least the higher living creatures capable of looking some way into the future seem to possess to some extent and which enables them to choose for themselves where they want to go and decide what they intend to do, exist? Suppose it does and that it is capable of influencing what is going to happen next: doesn't that mean that any attempt to predict the future will be foredoomed?

Whether this is really so I am not going to discuss. Depending on the way his thought is interpreted, the first to claim that the free will was merely an illusion was the Greek philosopher Epicurus around 300 BCE. Since then any number of thinkers, some of them very famous indeed, have taken the same position. Nowadays, finding a formula that, somehow circumventing the free will, will at some future time render human thoughts and actions predictable has become the shining goal of every brain scientist; as well as of technology giants such as Amazon, Google and Facebook, and of the police forces and intelligence agencies that rely on similar technology, of course. Yet the question of how to explain human behaviour, both individual and collective, without taking into account 'the ghost in the machine', as it is sometimes called, has not changed one iota. For all the talk about brain cells and dendrites and axons and synapses and chemical facilitators and electrical discharges, in many ways it is no whit closer to a solution today than it was twenty-something centuries ago.[18] Indeed trying to solve the problem is a bit like trying to catch a mirage; the closer one gets, the further it recedes.

Strictly speaking, a prediction should be either 100 per cent right or 100 per cent wrong. Either we are involved in a road accident or we are not. Either it rains or it does not. Either a war breaks out or it does not. Any prediction that falls in between is, in a certain sense, not a prediction but an attempt at evasion. In practice, however, outside the realm of physics – and sometimes, as in that of meteorology, even there – the vast majority of predictions fall in between these two extremes. One situation 'may very well arise', another 'probably' will not. One event is 'likely' to take place, another is 'unlikely' to do so. The price of stock x 'could' go up or down (on Bloomberg, every second sentence seems to have 'could' in it). The problem is that different people, based on their different temperaments and perhaps on their different states of mental and physical health, will almost certainly understand such terms in very different ways. What appears a risk worth taking to some, others will see as a dangerous gamble. What some consider as easy as pie, others will regard as a mighty obstacle.

The standard way to deal with this problem is by using percentages.[19] Instead of 'tomorrow it will rain', the weatherman says 'there is a 60 per cent chance of rain'. Instead of saying 'war will break out', the intelligence officer will tell his boss, 'there is a 10 per cent chance that that there will be war.' Seen from the point of view of the person who makes them, such predictions have the advantage that no one can quarrel with them; whether or not it rains or a war breaks out, they are always right. But what does 60 per cent, or 40 or 20 per cent, or any other figure, really mean? That, once again, depends on the mental make-up of the person who watches the forecast or listens to it, their social position, and so on. A 60 per cent chance of rain may very well cause one person to take his or her umbrella along, and another to leave it behind. A 10 per cent chance of war will appear quite high to one commander but quite low to another.

The following anecdote, apocryphal or not, will illustrate the problem as well as it can be. Back in the late 1970s, Israel's General Rafael 'Raful' Eitan, who was known for his sneaky sense of humour, was serving as chief of staff. At one point he had to authorize an air force operation. Asking those responsible about what the weather was going to be like, he was told there was a 20 per cent chance of rain. 'Wrong,' he said, 'it's 50 per cent. Either it rains, or it doesn't.'

Another difficulty confronting successful prediction is posed by time. In more than one of his works, Friedrich Nietzsche refers to what he calls *der ewige Wiederkehr*, the eternal return.[20] Nor was he by any means the first or only philosopher to do so; at least one of them, the French socialist agitator Louis

Auguste Blanqui (1805–1881), tried to prove its existence by using mathematical methods. The underlying idea is simple. Suppose, with Newton, that space and time are infinite, whereas the number of things that have existed, do exist and can exist is not. In that case, those things must necessarily recur an infinite number of times – including, as Nietzsche says in one of his notes, 'every pain and every pleasure, every friend and every enemy, every hope and every error, every blade of grass and every ray of sunshine once more, and the whole fabric of things which make up your life'.[21]

Even a clock that has stopped running must show the correct time twice a day. If Nietzsche is right, then it follows that any prediction, however reasonable or outrageous, must come true sooner or later, including, perhaps, that the Moon will turn into cheese, or vice versa. But the opposite also applies: a prediction that is not accompanied by a definitive statement as to when the predicted situation or event is going to come about cannot be disproved. Questioned, all one needs to say is, 'Wait, and you will see.' That is just what hosts of 'end of the world' visionaries have been doing for the last three millennia or so,[22] and what, starting with Thomas Malthus in 1796, many of those who predict overpopulation and a shortage of resources that will lead to general impoverishment, famine and war have been doing and are doing right now. Each and every time, their prophecies did not come about. Each and every time, they simply postponed the date.

The same applies to Marx's more fanatical followers, from Rosa Luxemburg ('capitalism . . . will become impossible'[23]) to Nikita Khrushchev ('we shall bury you'), who spent much of the first half of the twentieth century in particular looking forward to the 'inevitable' triumph of communism. Even today, some people still persist in seeing Marxism as 'the philosophy of the future'.[24] Given that the date has been postponed several times already, Ray Kurzweil's prediction concerning the singularity, when machine intelligence overtakes our brains, may also be going that way. It was in order to deal with this problem that Tetlock initiated his Expert Political Judgment project – only to come up with the idea, which is hardly new, that the best way of gaining a good understanding of the future is to employ the best (meaning the most inquisitive), most open-minded and least dogmatic people.

An excellent example of the fallacy of prediction *sine die* is the so-called Doomsday Clock. First proposed in 1947, its creators, the editors of the *Bulletin of Atomic Scientists*, hoped to use it in order to warn the public against the danger of nuclear war and press for disarmament. In all the seventy years of its existence its hands have never stood further away from midnight than seventeen minutes. In late 2017, the fracas in which Donald Trump called Kim Jong-un 'Little Rocket Man' caused them to be set at two and half minutes to midnight. Two and a half out of 1,440; very close indeed! But not once in its history did the clock say when the war it predicted would break out. The next day? In a year? Five years?

The point is not trivial. Knowing that stock *x* will rise is one thing. Knowing that it will do so on day *y*, is something else entirely. If we know something is coming the very next day, we will have time to make only limited preparations. If we expect it to come five years hence, the precautions we can take are of a different kind and will proceed at a different pace. As time went on and a nuclear holocaust did not materialize, this lack of precision made it clear that the Doomsday Clock was a mere gimmick and that its ability to tell how close or far away a nuclear war is was exactly zero. Perhaps that was why the editors of the *Bulletin of the Atomic Scientists* decided to change the way they set the hands of their clock. To be sure, they keep proclaiming that nuclear war is not far away. However, some years ago they started taking into account all kinds of other dangers as well, including global warming, biosecurity and cyberwarfare.[25] No doubt it is only a question of time before terrorism and an asteroid hitting Earth will be added as well.

Finally, suppose that all the difficulties can be overcome and that the future can be known. In that case, we shall find that a known future is a very different beast from an unknown one. According to the logic of dialectics, the fact that everybody 'knows' something can often serve as an indication that it is not true or will soon cease to be true. Conversely, if the future is unknown, or at any rate unimagined, we cannot even try to move either towards it or away from it. That is just what the aforementioned 'black swans' are all about. The only choice we have is to go on with our lives, take some reasonable precautions, such as not putting all our eggs in the same basket (or, to the contrary, making the basket as strong as we can), hope for the best and allow events to run their course.

For those who believe in fate, knowledge of the future is of no use even when they succeed in obtaining it. Having been told what fate had in store for him, Oedipus did his best to escape it, but to no avail, as he ended up killing his father and marrying his mother precisely as the oracle had predicted. Quite some prophecies are self-fulfilling. Herodian, the early third-century Graeco-Roman historian, tells the following story about his contemporary, the emperor Caracalla. Like so many other important people, Caracalla at one point asked some soothsayers about the manner in which he would die, only to learn that he would be succeeded by one of his generals, Macrinus. When Macrinus by chance came across a letter carrying this prophecy to the emperor, he was forced to kill him so as to save his own life.[26]

If we know that something is inevitable – say, that the Sun is steadily emitting more radiation and on its way to incinerating us all – what is the point of trying to prevent it or even think about it? On the other hand, as far back as the lives of the biblical prophets, many predictions were conditional and explicitly designed to make people change their behaviour. By doing so they could avoid the very future that had been predicted for them: repent, or you will go to hell. At times, as in the days of King Josiah, the warning worked (2 Kings 22). The same is true today. If enough people know, or think they know, that a certain stock is going up or down they may very well help it do so by buying or selling it. If pollsters convince enough people of their prediction regarding the outcome of an election, then this knowledge has a good chance of influencing the outcome of the election in question. This may happen, for example, if voters, convinced that the outcome has already been decided, join the bandwagon, deliberately try to resist it or simply do not turn up.[27] It has even been argued that polls can do as much to shape public opinion as to find out what it says.[28]

Herding, as this is known, can apply not only to ideas concerning the future but to the methods involved in forming those ideas. Such methods, provided they are published, may start acting like infectious diseases, passing from one predictor to the next. Once everyone uses the same system, the most probable outcome is going to be ever more violent ups and downs. Herding is said to have played a critical role in bringing about the 2007–8 economic crisis.[29] A well-known app such as the navigation software Waze, by suggesting that a road is congested, can cause drivers to seek other routes, thus relieving that very congestion. And the other way around, of course.

In other words, there are a great many cases in which knowledge of the future, whether accurate or not, will cause it to change. The New Testament puts it as succinctly as it can be: 'If the owner of the house had known when during the night the thief was coming, he would not have left his house to be broken into' (Luke 12:39). If we can predict, then very often we can also prevent what we predicted from coming true. Again, the point is anything but trivial. Had the United States military known of, or at any rate imagined, the planned Japanese attack on Pearl Harbor, then that attack would not have come as a surprise. As the responsible commander, Husband E. Kimmel, later wrote, he would have taken a whole series of precautions.[30] At a minimum, the number of American casualties would have been greatly reduced, and Japanese ones substantially increased. It is even possible that, if Japanese intelligence were to have got wind of the fact that its plans had been leaked or guessed and that the Americans were ready, the attack might not have come about at all. One reason why Israel did not mobilize its forces on the morning of 6 October 1973, in the face of intelligence regarding an impending Arab attack, was the fear that, by doing so, it might spark off the very war it was hoping to avoid.

18

IS OUR GAME IMPROVING?

Given how numerous and complex the problems are, is there any reason to believe that we today are better at making predictions than our ancestors were? Earthquakes aside, in the case of phenomena that are governed by the laws of physics the answer is a resounding yes – otherwise, little if any of the tremendous technological progress that got under way from the seventeenth century onward would have been possible. Thanks to the widespread use of satellites and computers, even weather forecasts, far from perfect as they remain, are said to be considerably better than the ones we used to have a century or even a generation ago. The same applies to probability theory and, in medicine (a field this volume has barely touched upon so far), prognosis. To be sure, hardly a day passes without some patients 'unexpectedly' dying and/or 'miraculously' recovering from this or that disease. But at any rate, the days when poor John Mirfield had to resort to numerology in order to guess which of his charges would live and which ones would die are largely over.

However, in other fields, including many of those that directly affect the life of every single person on our planet, the answer is almost certainly no.[1] Reverting to the image of the future as a train, one reason for this is that it seems to come at us at a speed too high for a solid assessment to be possible. No sooner do we understand, or think we understand, the present than it disappears and is replaced by something else – at times something radically different. Had it not been for our failure to improve our game, such age-old methods as shamanism and astrology would scarcely have survived the drumfire of criticism to which, starting at least as early as the ancient Greeks, they have been subjected.

Be that as it may, black swans, meaning events that by the laws of statistics should not have taken place but nevertheless did, are no less sudden, no less common and no less critical today than they have ever been. Or so the Second World War Nazi extermination camps; the 9/11 attacks; the 2004 Indian Ocean earthquake and tsunami; the 2005 New Orleans hurricane and flood; the 2011 Fukushima disaster; and the 2016 election of Donald Trump seem to show. Indeed it would hardly be too much to say that changes of the kind political scientists like to call 'earthquakes' continue to take place almost daily. The same applies to the economic field. Or else, by using simple extrapolation, each and every one of us would have become filthy rich long ago. One could indeed argue that extrapolation, which, owing to the Newtonian way in which we perceive history, has now become the most common prediction method of all, by failing to take account of qualitative change is also the most misleading one.

In general, few of us ever take any kind of action unless we expect a favourable outcome. Except perhaps when it was a question of outwitting the taxman, no entrepreneur has ever started a new business expecting to lose money. Yet now as ever, depending on the source you believe, a large percentage of business enterprises are forced to close within three, five or ten years. For every stock-exchange dealer who gets it right there must be another who gets it wrong. That is why, as an analyst I know told me, one only has to be right 51 per cent of the time. Doing this over a long period, it turns out, is very hard; doing much better than this is so difficult and so exceptional as to border on the phenomenal.

The fact that Warren Buffett sits on top of nearly $85 billion is no argument to the contrary. He himself is literally one in a billion, just as John D. Rockefeller, Nathan Rothschild, Louis De Geer, Jakob Fugger and Marcus Licinius Crassus – he who said that you weren't rich until you drew sufficient interest on your money to maintain an army[2] – were. Almost half a millennium before Crassus there lived a certain Lydian by the name of Pythius, son of Atys and grandson of Croesus, whose name is still synonymous with wealth. Herodotus says that Pythius hosted Xerxes' five-million-strong host, marching from Persia to Greece, 'in a most magnificent fashion'. In response to the king, who was surprised by his generosity and questioned him, he said that he still had more than enough money left to live on.[3] Even this list does not include the long line of more or less absolute rulers, who, starting with the Egyptian pharaohs and passing through the Roman emperors all the way to Vladimir Putin, have always been the richest people by far. True, some of today's forecasting methods are infinitely more complicated and infinitely more expensive than their predecessors. On the whole, though, there is no reason to believe that they are more successful.

Even in physics, the most basic domain of all, Heisenberg's uncertainty principle and chaos theory remain in force today and will very likely continue to do so in the future. Perhaps the best proof of all comes from military history. In any war, only one belligerent can emerge victorious – meaning that fully half of all belligerents, having failed to foresee what the future will bring and to act accordingly, will end up being defeated, perhaps even annihilated. Probably the proverbial monkey could have done as well! Yet after more than 10,000 years – the period, archaeologists tell us, that has passed since war first made its appearance – armed conflict still shows no signs of abating. A science of the future, as it has been called, is as far away as it has ever been.

19

A WORLD WITHOUT
UNCERTAINTY?

S
o far in this volume we have treated the difficulty of looking into the future as the Great Enemy and presented
some of the methods people have devised in the hope of
abolishing or at least reducing it. Towards the end we sketched
some of the obstacles to understanding what is coming and why
doing so is as difficult as it is. So difficult, in fact, that it is doubt-
ful whether we today, for all the science and technology at our
disposal, are better able to predict the future than our ancestors,
in a shamanic trance or watching the heavens as 'Chaldeans',
were. Approaching the end, though, it is interesting to turn the
question on its head and embark on a thought experiment. We
can ask, first, what Laplace's demon, and of course today's 'Big
Data' experts, would need to know in order to do away with
uncertainty and correctly predict everything that will happen.
Second, what a world with no uncertainty, supposing it is possible, would do to us as human beings; and third, what such a
world would be like.

Assume, as determinists of all ages have always done, that
anything that ever happens, without exception, does so because
it has to – that is, for a cause. In such a case, the answer to the
first question becomes obvious: the information at the demon's
disposal would have to be perfectly comprehensive. It would also
have to be perfectly correct, accurate and up to date ('real-time',
as it is nowadays known); all the way from, as Queen Elizabeth I's
astrological adviser John Dee might have said, the nature, where-
abouts and movements of every single elementary particle

anywhere in the universe, past and present, right down to what is happening in each one of the hundred billion or so cells and trillions of connections (synapses) that make up the brain of each and every one of us. All the links between all these things, of whatever kind, would also have to be completely understood, both in themselves and in relation with all the rest.

In such a world, the kind of change that is not brought about by intent but governed solely by the laws of physics, such as is always taking place in the tectonic plates, would still be possible. Flow and ebb, eruptions and earthquakes would still take place. Temperatures would still go up and down, storms would still start blowing and cease doing so, and asteroids would still crash into planets. Stars would still be born and, having consumed their fuel, collapse and cease to be. However, the distinction between accidents on the one hand and necessary events on the other would disappear, leaving only strict causation to govern everything. All questions regarding the future – supposing there is anyone left to ask – would be answered before they are asked; and all divergent (divergent in the sense of leading in a different direction) thoughts and actions, assuming they are somehow possible at all, prevented not after they were contemplated or committed but before; most probably, if it is true that thought is simply the reflection of certain electrochemical processes in the brain, by doing away with both the brain and its owner (as H. G. Wells in one of his less-known novels, *Men Like Gods* of 1923, imagined would be the case).

To carry the idea a little bit further, the very fact that we know everything about the future would prevent 'everything' (including us) from taking any road other than the one on which, through no decision of our own, we are destined to travel. Frozen like insects in amber, we would be left without most, if not all, the things that distinguish us from mere dead matter, computers specifically included. The mystery of the unknown, the thrill of anticipation and the challenge of dealing with the unexpected would all disappear. So would imagination – when the future is certain, who needs imagination? – intentionality, purpose and the ability to choose the objectives we want to achieve. Likewise, thought about the best way of achieving those objectives would disappear. And hope, of course. There would be no conscious life capable of making decisions, nor what has been called 'the magnificent unpredictability'[1] of human behaviour, both individual and collective – the very unpredictability, based on our *not* knowing the future, that comprises the essence of life and which, perhaps more than anything else, gives the latter whatever flavour it has.

But even that is not half of it. Language, including not just words (either spoken or written) and sentences but mathematics and computer programs as well, works by selecting certain sounds or signs and making them represent – stand for – other things. However, by so doing it necessarily opens up a gap between itself and the things it refers to.[2] This is the very gap that so often causes different people, even such as use the same language, to misunderstand one another. Conversely, a perfect understanding of everything presupposes that this gap be closed. The signifier, meaning language, would have to be identical with the signified – that is, the world and all that is in it, not least including thought. For not only is language anchored in thought, but thought itself can be and often is thought about. In other words, the knower, his thought, the language in which he expresses that thought, and the known would have to be one and the same.

Outside that one thing, if a thing it is, there would be no-thing. Not even empty space, for Einstein and relativity have taught us that space too is a 'thing', one that exists independently of any objects it may contain; has such and such qualities; is capable of being warped and even twisted by gravity; and so on. Nor even time, for time is but one aspect of space and inextricably bound up with it. Which of course means that the past and future, even assuming that they really exist and are not simply constructs of the human mind, would also go by the board – leaving nothing but an eternal present.

Briefly, abolishing uncertainty concerning what will happen in the future would mean a return to whatever there was, if there was, before the Big Bang. An infinitely small, infinitely dense point, perhaps: one that contains the entire universe within itself and yet, being absolutely self-contained, comes with a horizon no greater than itself. One that, assuming it thinks at all, is at once the subject and the object of its own thought, eternally and incessantly contemplating itself. The following lines, written by an anonymous author at some point during the Middle Ages and later incorporated into the Jewish prayer book, express the idea as perfectly as it can be. Except that they are much more poetical, they read as if they were taken from some work by Stephen Hawking:

> The Lord of the Universe who reigned
> before anything was created.
> When all was made by His will
> He was acknowledged as King.
> And when all shall end
> He still all alone shall reign.
> He was, He is,
> and He shall be in glory.
> And He is one, and there's no other,
> to compare or join Him.
> Without beginning, without end
> And to Him belongs dominion and power.

If such a transformation were ever to take place, it would undoubtedly form the most important 'singularity' since the Big Bang. Infinitely more important than the development of artificial superintelligence that Ray Kurzweil, extrapolating from the advances in computing that have taken place over the last few decades, has been trumpeting. And infinitely more important than an encounter with an extraterrestrial civilization, however advanced.

Whatever he and other contemporary prophets may say, there seems to be no danger of this happening any time soon.

REFERENCES

INTRODUCTION

1 Sophocles, *Antigone*, 589–90.
2 See, above all, F. Brentano, *Psychology from an Empirical Standpoint* [1874] (London, 1995), pp. 88–9.
3 S. Herculano-Houzel, 'The Human Brain in Numbers: A Linearly Scaled-up Primate Brain', *Frontiers in Human Neuroscience*, 9 November 2009, www.frontiersin.org.
4 F. de Waal, *The Bonobo and the Atheist* (New York, 2014).
5 See, for a short discussion, A. Ault, 'Ask Smithsonian: Can Animals Predict Earthquakes?', www.smithsonian.com, 10 August 2016.
6 J. Balcombe, *What a Fish Knows* (Kindle edition, 2016), passim.
7 C.D.L. Wynne, *Do Animals Think?* (Princeton, NJ, 2004), pp. 59, 229.
8 T. Hobbes, *Leviathan* [1652] (London, 1952), p. 130.
9 J.-J. Rousseau, *Émile* [1762] (Portland, OR, 2009), p. 413. Thanks to Eldad, my son, who drew my attention to this passage.
10 See, for example, R. J. Szczerba, 'Fifteen Worst Tech Predictions of All Time', www.forbes.com, 5 January 2015.
11 D. B. Redford, ed., *The Oxford Encyclopedia of Ancient Egypt* (Oxford, 2001), vol. II, p. 301.
12 See on this A. M. Weaver, 'The "Sin of Sargon"', *Iraq*, LXVI (2004), p. 63.
13 U. Koch-Westenholz, *Mesopotamian Astrology* (Copenhagen, 1985), p. 12.
14 Ptolemy, *Tetrabiblos*, 1.2.
15 See, on this curious story, 'Berlin's Wonderful Horse', *New York Times*, 4 September 1904.

1 A VILLAIN OF A MAGICIAN

1 See, for these and other interpretations of the term, S. Krippner, 'The Epistemology and Technologies of Shamanic States of Consciousness', *Journal of Consciousness Studies*, VII/11–12 (2000), p. 93; also B. Laufer, 'Origin of the Word Shaman', *American Anthropologist*, XIX (1917), especially pp. 363–7.

2   J. Narby and F. Huxley, *Shamans Through Time* (New York, 2001), p. 18.

3   See on this L. D. O'Malley, 'The Monarch and the Mystic: Catherine the Great's Strategy of Audience Enlightenment in *The Siberian Shaman*', *Slavic and East European Journal*, xli/2 (Summer 1997), pp. 224–42.

4   See, on the attempts to conserve and revive shamanism, M. Harner, 'The History and Work of the Foundation for Shamanic Studies', *Shamanism*, xvii/1–2 (Summer 2005), pp. 1–4.

5   M. Eliade, *Shamanism: Archaic Techniques of Ecstasy* [1951] (Princeton, nj, 1972), p. 7.

6   M. van Creveld, *The Rise and Decline of the State* (Cambridge, 1999).

7   See J.-P. Chaumeil, 'Varieties of Amazonian Shamanism', *Diogenes*, xl/158 (June 1992), pp. 101–13.

8   F. McClenon, 'Shamanic Healing, Human Evolution, and the Origin of Religion', *Journal for the Scientific Study of Religion*, xxxvi/3 (September 1997), pp. 345–54.

9   See, on this aspect of the matter, A. R. Radcliffe-Brown, *The Andaman Islanders* [1922] (New York, 1964), p. 15; also W. Arens, 'Evans-Pritchard and the Prophets', *Antropos*, vii/1–2 (1983), pp. 1–16.

10 C. D. Worobec, *Possessed: Women, Witches and Demons in Imperial Russia* (DeKalb, il, 2002), p. 79.

11 W. H. Kracke, 'He Who Dreams: The Nocturnal Source of Transforming Power in Kagwahiv Shamanism', in *Portals of Power: Shamanism in South America*, ed. E. Jean Matteson Langdon and Gerhard Baer (Albuquerque, nm, 1992), pp. 1–16.

12 Arnold Ludwig, quoted in A. P. Garcia-Romeu and C. T. Tart, 'Altered States of Consciousness and Transpersonal Psychology', in *The Wiley-Blackwell Handbook of Transpersonal Psychology*, ed. Harris L. Friedman and Glenn Hartelius (London, 2013), p. 129.

13 Max Planck Institute, 'Trance State of Consciousness is associated with a Specific Brain Network Signature and Perceptual Decoupling', Press Release, www.cbs.mpg.de, 8 July 2015.

14 See, for a more detailed explanation, A.-L. Siikala, 'The Siberian Shaman's Technique of Ecstasy', *Scripta Instituti Donneriani Aboensis*, xi (1982), pp. 103–21.

15 J. M. Allegro, *The Sacred Mushroom and the Cross* (London, 1970).

16 See P. Hadot, 'Shamanism and Greek Philosophy', in *The Concept of Shamanism: Uses and Abuses*, ed. Henri-Paul Francfort and Roberte M. Hamayon (Budapest, 2001), pp. 389–401; also W. T. Stace, *A Critical History of Greek Philosophy* [1920] (Kindle edition, 2018), loc. 3835.

17 See J. M. Cruikshank, 'Legend and Landscape: Convergence of Oral and Scientific Traditions in the Yukon Territory', *Arctic Anthropology*, XVIII/2 (1981), pp. 67–93.

18 R. R. Desjarlais, 'Healing Through Images: The Magic Flight and Healing Geography of Nepali Shamans', *Ethnos*, XVII/3 (September 1989), p. 289.

19 See J. J. O'Hara, Sostratus *Suppl. Hell.* 733: 'A Lost, Possibly Catullan-Era Elegy on the Six Sex Changes of Teiresias', *Transactions of the American Philological Association*, CXXVI (1996), pp. 173–8.

20 Aristotle, *Eudemian Ethics*, 1248b.

21 Sophocles, *Oedipus Rex*, 284–5.

22 See, for what follows, R.G.A. Buxton, 'Blindness and Limits: Sophocles and the Logic of Myth', *Journal of Hellenic Studies*, C (1980), pp. 28–9.

23 Euripides, *Hecuba*, 1036 and 1260–95.

24 See A. L. Miller, 'Myth and Gender in Japanese Shamanism: The *Itako* of Tohoku', *History of Religions*, XXXII/4 (May 1993), pp. 343–67.

25 J. Y. Lee, 'The Seasonal Rituals of Korean Shamanism', *History of Religions*, XII/3 (February 1973), pp. 271–87.

26 Lee E-Wha, *Korea's Pastimes and Customs*, trans. Ju-Hee Park (Paramus, NJ, 2001), p. viii.

27 S. Osborne, 'Baba Vanga: Who is the Blind Mystic Who "Predicted the Rise of ISIS"?', *The Independent*, 8 December 2015.

28 See 'Category: Fictional Blind Characters', https://en.wikipedia.org, accessed 28 March 2019.

2 IN THE NAME OF THE LORD

1 See for example 2 Kings 9:6–11, Hosea 9:7 and Jeremiah 29:8–9.

2 For this entire question see also R. R. Wilson, 'Prophecy and Ecstasy: A Reexamination', *Journal of Biblical Literature*, XCVIII/3 (September 1979), pp. 321–5.

3 'Prophecy in the Old Testament', Lexicon of Jewish Culture [in Hebrew], http://lexicon.cet.ac.il, accessed 28 March 2019.

4 See 1 Chronicles 29:29.

5 2 Samuel 12 and 1 Kings 1:1–22.

6 1 Kings 11:19–39 and 17:1–4, 7, and 12–3.

7 See, for example, Isaiah 2:2–3 and Hosea 3:4–5.

8 See, for what follows, J. Blenkinsop, *A History of Prophecy in Israel* (London, 1996), locs 1070–127.

9 Ibid., loc. 1102; G. Dossin, 'Sur le prophétisme a Mari', in *La divination en*

Mésopotamie ancienne (Paris, 1966), pp. 85–6. The translations are by Blenkinsop.

10 See, for this entire story, K. Radner, 'The Trials of Esarhaddon: The Conspiracy of 670 BC', *Isimu*, VI (2003), pp. 165–84.

11 See, for the inscription, J. Hoftijzer and G. van der Kooij, eds, *Aramaic Texts from Deir 'Alla Documenta et Monumenta Orientis Antiqui*, XIX (1976).

12 Plutarch, *Alcibiades*, 17.4.

13 Plato, *Phaedrus*, 244b.

14 Cicero, *On Divination*, 1.114.

15 Cicero, *On Divination*, 1.31.66–7.

16 1 Maccabees 9:27, 4:44–6 and 14:41.

17 Bava Batra 10b.

18 See on this entire topic L. S. Cooke, *On the Question of the 'Cessation of Prophecy' in Ancient Judasim* (Tübingen, 2011), and B. D. Sommer, 'Did Prophecy Cease? Evaluating a Reevaluation', *Journal of Biblical Literature*, CXV/1 (Spring 1996), pp. 31–47.

19 Thessalonians 2; Acts 11:27, 13:1, 15:32; and 1 Corinthians 12–14. See, about the entire question of prophecy in the early church, J. L. Ash, 'The Decline of Ecstatic Prophecy in the Early Church', *Theological Studies*, XXXVII/2 (1976), pp. 226–52.

20 See for example I. A. Ahmad, 'Did Muhammad Observe the Canterbury 95 Meteoroid Swarm?' *Archaeoastronomy*, XI (1989), p. 95.

21 See Islam/Religion, 'The Prophecies of Muhammad', www.islamreligion. com, accessed 28 March 2019.

22 Gregory of Tours, *The History of the Franks* [573–94], trans. Lewis Thorpe (Harmondsworth, 1974), pp. 465–7.

23 According to the anonymous *Liber Mirabalis* (1524): see www. bibliotecapleyades.net, accessed 28 March 2019.

24 See R. E. Lerner, 'Medieval Prophecy and Religious Dissent', *Past and Present*, LXXII/1 (August 1976), pp. 8–9.

25 See B. Newman, 'Hildegard of Bingen: Visions and Validation', *Church History*, LIV/2 (June 1985), pp. 163–75.

26 *Analecta Sacra*, ed. J. B. Pitra (Monte Cassino, 1882), vol. VIII, p. 576, Letter No. 164.

27 J. Gerson, 'On Distinguishing True from False Revelations', in *Early Works*, trans. Brian Patrick McGuire (Slough, 1998), pp. 334–64.

28 See, for Gerson's strictures on female prophetesses, his two treatises, 'De probatione spirituum' and 'De distinctione verarum visionum a

falsis', both in Jean Gerson, *Oeuvres complètes*, ed. Palémon Glorieux, Paris, 1960–1973, vols IX, pp. 177–85 and III, 36–56 respectively.

29 See, for what follows, J. N. Bremmer, 'Prophets, Seers, and Politics in Greece, Israel, and Early Modern Europe', *Numen*, XL/2 (May 1993), pp. 168–71.

30 A. Prosperi, 'Dalle "divine madri" ai "padri spirituali"', in *Women and Men in Spiritual Culture*, ed. E. S. van Kessel (The Hague, 1986), pp. 71–90.

31 J. Bilinkoff, 'A Spanish Prophetess and Her Patrons: The Case of Maria de Santo Domingo', *Sixteenth Century Journal*, XXIII/1 (Spring 1992), pp. 21–34.

32 J. Calvin, *Commentary on Jeremiah 27:15*. See, on this entire topic, W. Berends, 'Prophecy in the Reformation Tradition', *Vox Reformata*, LX (1995), pp. 30–43.

33 M. Luther, *Werke*, Kritische Gesamtausgabe (Weimar, 1883–2009), 46, 60, 34–40.

34 R. W. Scribner, 'Incombustible Luther: The Image of the Reformer in Early Modern Germany', *Past and Present*, CX/1 (February 1986), p. 41.

35 See P. Mack, 'Women as Prophets during the English Civil War', *Feminist Studies*, VIII/1 (Spring 1982), pp. 18–45.

36 See C. Burrage, 'Anna Trapnel's Prophecies', *English Historical Review*, XXVI/103 (July 1911), pp. 526–35.

37 Quoted in D. Leverenz, *The Language of Puritan Feeling: An Exploration in Literature, Psychology, and Social History* (New Brunswick, NJ, 1980), p. 1.

38 W. Frijhoff, 'Prophetie et societe dans les Provinces-Unies aux XVIIe et XVIIIe siècles', in *Prophites et sorcièrs dans les Pays-Bas, XVIe–XVIIIe siècles*, ed. M.-S. Dupont-Bouchat et al. (Paris, 1978), pp. 263–362.

39 J. Green, *Printing and Prophecy* (Ann Arbor, MI, 2011), passim.

40 *The Doctrines and Covenants of the Church of Jesus Christ of Latter-day Saints*, 87 and 84:44.

41 Ibid., 97:10–12.

42 'Saint Athanasia of Egaleo: The Visions and Misspellings of the Virgin Mary' [in Greek], www.crashonline.gr, 2 January 2018.

3 ORACLES, PYTHIAS AND SIBYLS

1 Cicero, *On Divination*, 1.3.

2 Quoted in Origen, *Against Celsus*, 8.45.

3 Plutarch, *On the Pythian Oracles*, 405c.

4 J. Z. de Boer and J. R. Hale, 'New Evidence for the Geological Origins

of the Ancient Delphic Oracle (Greece)', *Geology*, xxix/8 (August 2001), pp. 707–10.

5 Plutarch, *On the Pythian Oracles*, 438b.

6 Herodotus, *The Histories*, 1.47.

7 See, for a list of pronouncements, 'List of Oracular Statements from Delphi', https://en.wikipedia.org, accessed 20 June 2019.

8 Plutarch, *On the Pythian Oracles*, 11.

9 Herodotus, *The Histories*, 1.50.

10 Plutarch, *Alexander*, 14.6–7.

11 Heraclitus, Fragment 92.

12 Plato, *Phaedrus*, 244b.

13 There is a list of such occasions at 'Sibylline Books', https://en.wikipedia.org/wiki, accessed 20 June 2019.

14 According to Tacitus, *Annals*, 6.12.

15 Plutarch, *Quaestiones Romanae*, 83.

16 See on this C. C. Coulter, 'The Transfiguration of the Sibyl', *Classical Journal*, xvi/2 (November 1950), pp. 65–6.

17 St Augustine, *City of God*, 18.23.

18 See on this episode R. Raybould, *The Sibyl Series of the Fifteenth Century* (Leiden, 2016), p. 37.

19 See J. L. Malay, 'Performing the Apocalypse: Sibylline Prophecy and Elizabeth i', in *Representations of Elizabeth i in Early Modern Culture*, ed. A. Petrina and L. Tosi (London, 2011), pp. 175–92.

4 A DREAM TO REMEMBER

1 Aristotle, *On Divination in Sleep*, 1.463a31-b1.

2 C. Lac, 'A Brief History and Scientific Look at Dream Analysis and Interpretation', www.skepticink.com, 17 October 2013.

3 See J. M. Siegel, 'Rem Sleep: A Biological and Psychological Paradox,' *Sleep Medicine Reviews*, xv/3 (June 2011), pp. 139–42.

4 L. Oppenheim, 'The Interpretation of Dreams in the Ancient Near East', *Transactions of the American Philosophical Society*, xxxvi/3 (1956), pp. 250, 274–5, 293.

5 See D. Ogden, *Greek and Roman Necromancy* (Princeton, NJ, 2001), passim.

6 Polybius, *The Histories*, 33.21.3.

7 Herodotus, *The Histories*, 1.108.

8 Plutarch, *Alexander*, 2; Cicero, *On Divination*, 1.22; Suetonius, *Caesar*, 81.

9 Aristophanes, *The Wasps*, 52–4.

10　Herodotus, *The Histories*, 7.15.

11　Pindar, Fragment 116b.

12　Xenophon, *Cyropaedia*, 8.7.21; Cicero, *On Divination*, 1.63–5; Aeschylus, *Eumenides*, 104; Iamblicus, *On the Mysteries of Egypt*, 3.3.

13　Plutarch, *Quaestiones convivales*, 8.10.2.

14　Athanasius, *Contra gentes*, 31.38–44.

15　Juvenal, *Satires*, 6.546–7.

16　Plato, *Laws*, 909e–910a.

17　Galen, *Corpus medicorum graecorum*, 16.222–3.

18　On Artemidorus see S.R.F. Price, 'The Future of Dreams: From Freud to Artemidorus', *Past and Present,* CXIII/3 (November 1986), pp. 3–37.

19　The most recent bilingual Greek–English edition is D. E. Harris-McCoy, *Artemidorus' Oneirocritica: Text, Translation and Commentary* (Oxford, 2012).

20　Ibid., 2.25.

21　Sahih Muhammad ibn Ismail al-Bukhari, *The Translation of the Meanings of Sahih al-Bukhari* (Lahore, 1979), 9.91.

22　See, for the following paragraphs, N. Bland, 'On the Muhammedan Science of Tâbír, or Interpretation of Dreams', *Journal of the Royal Asiatic Society of Great Britain and Ireland*, XVI (1856), pp. 119–40.

23　I. R. Edgar, 'The Inspirational Night Dream in the Motivation and Justification of Jihad', *Nova Religio*, XI/2 (November 2007), pp. 59–76.

24　This story is found in A. Lines, 'Sick Videotape Proves bin Laden was the Evil Mastermind Behind the Horrors of Sept 11', *The Mirror*, 14 December 2001.

25　On Tertullian see P. C. Miller, *Dreams in Late Antiquity* (Princeton, NJ, 1998), pp. 66–70.

26　See S. F. Kruger, *Dreaming in the Middle Ages* (Cambridge, 1992), pp. 40–41.

27　See, for a translation and a commentary, S. M. Oberhelman, *The Oneirocriticon of Achmet: A Medieval Greek and Arabic Treatise on the Interpretation of Dreams* (Lubbock, TX, 1991).

28　Kruger, *Dreaming in the Middle Ages*, pp. 45–52.

29　Ibid., p. 109.

30　See H. Goldberg, 'The Dream Report as a Literary Device in Medieval Hispanic Literature', *Hispania*, LXVI/1 (March 1989), pp. 21–31.

31　See on this episode R. Boone, 'Empire and Medieval Simulacrum: A Political Project of Mercurino di Gattinara, Grand Chancellor of Charles V', *Sixteenth Century Journal*, LXII/4 (Winter 2011), pp. 1027–49.

32 D. Barrett, *The Committee of Sleep: Dreams and Creative Problem Solving*, Department of Psychiatry, Harvard Medical School, Boston, MA, n.d, www.researchgate.net/publication/265122910, accessed 1 April 2019.

33 See R. Lewinsohn, *Science, Prophecy and Prediction* (New York, 1961), pp. 120–23.

34 For example, Alchera Dream Software, at http://mythwell.com; and many others.

35 See 'What Do Dreams Mean? Software Provides Dream Interpretation to Learn Their Meanings', www.healthynewage.com, 28 January 2016.

36 All these quotes may be found in G. Holloway, *The Complete Dream Book* (Kindle edition, 2006), locs 243, 327, 549, 740, 1110–15, 1153–8.

37 M. Lennox, *Llewellyn's Complete Dictionary of Dreams: Over 1,000 Dream Symbols and Their Universal Meanings* (Kindle edition, 2015).

5 CONSULTING THE DEAD

 1 See for example 'Dying Words: The Last Words Spoken by Famous People at Death, or Shortly Before', www.corsinet.com, accessed 28 March 2019.

 2 This and the following paragraph is based on I. L. Finkel, 'Necromancy in Ancient Mesopotamia', *Archiv für Orientforschung*, XXIX–XXX (1983–4), pp. 1–17.

 3 See, for what follows, B. J. Collins, 'Necromancy, Fertility and the Dark Earth: The Use of Ritual Pits in Hittite Cult', in *Magic and Ritual in the Ancient World*, ed. P. Mirecki and M. Meyer (Leyden, 2002), pp. 224–6.

 4 See, for all of these, B. B. Schmidt, *Israel's Beneficent Dead: Ancestor Cult and Necromancy in Ancient Israelite Religion and Tradition* (Tübingen, 1994).

 5 See, for these and other interpretations, H. E. Mendez, 'Condemnations of Necromancy in the Hebrew Bible: An Investigation of Rationale', MA dissertation, University of Georgia, Athens, GA (2009), pp. 57–62.

 6 See Exodus 22:1; Isaiah 8:19.

 7 Mishnah Sanhedrin 7, which deals with the punishments meted out to various kinds of criminals.

 8 M. Ben-Chaim, 'Consulting the Dead', www.mesora.org, accessed 28 March 2019.

 9 Strabo, *Geography*, 15.2.39.

10 Aeschylus, *Persians*, 739–41.

11 Quoted in D. Ogden, *Greek and Roman Necromancy* (Princeton, NJ, 2001), pp. 243–4.

12 Virgil, *Aeneid*, 6.756–902.

13 Ibid., 6.847–53.

14 Plutarch, *Cimon*, 6.4–6.

15 See S. I. Dakaris, 'The Acheron Necromancy Excavation', *Greek Archeological Society Records* [in Greek] (Athens, 1964), pp. 44–53.

16 See on this N. W. Slater, 'Posthumous Parleys: Chatting up the Dead in the Ancient Novels', in *The Greek and the Roman Novel: Parallel Readings*, ed. M. Paschalis et al. (Eelde, 2007), pp. 57–69.

17 Lucian, *Pharasalia*, 238–40.

18 Heliodorus, 'An Ethiopian Story', trans. J. R. Morgan, in *Collected Ancient Greek Novels*, ed. B. P. Reardon (Berkeley, CA, 1989), pp. 19–24.

19 Apuleius, *The Golden Ass*, 2.28–9.

20 Gerald of Wales, *Giraldi Cambrensis opera*, ed. John S. Brewer (London, 1861–91), vol. VI, pp. 57–60.

21 M. D. Bailey, 'From Sorcery to Witchcraft', *Speculum*, LXXVI/4 (October 2001), pp. 960–67.

22 C. Marlowe, *The Tragic History of Doctor Faustus*, introduction, line 24.

23 See D. B. Morris, 'Gothic Sublimity', *New Literary History*, XVI/2 (Winter 1985), pp. 299–319.

24 See, for Britain, L. Hunt, 'Necromancy in the UK: Witchcraft and the Occult in British Horror', in *British Horror Cinema*, ed. S. Chibnall and J. Petley (London, 2001), pp. 82–96.

25 See on this J. Oppenheim, *The Other World: Spiritualism and Psychical Research in England, 1850–1914* (Cambridge, 1985).

26 See Arthur Conan Doyle, *The New Revelation: The Coming of a New Spiritual Paradigm* (London, 1918).

27 See P. J. Bowler, *Reconciling Science and Religion: The Debate in Early-twentieth-century Britain* (Chicago, IL, 2014), p. 35.

28 A. Conan Doyle, *The History of Spiritualism* [1926] (Kindle edition, 2010), loc. 46.

29 On Caton see M.A.B. Brazier, 'The History of the Electrical Activity of the Brain as a Method for Localizing Sensory Function', *Medical History*, VII/3 (July 1963), pp. 204–6.

30 See, on C. F. Varley's links to spiritualism, B. J. Hunt, 'Varley, Cromwell Fleetwood (1828–1883)', *Oxford Dictionary of National Biography* (Oxford, 2004).

31 See, for what follows, A. Einstein, 'Aether and the Theory of Relativity', 1922, www-history.mcs.st-andrews.ac.uk, accessed 28 March 2019; also Adam Amorastreya, 'The End of the Aether', 16 February 2015, https://resonance.org, accessed 25 October 2019.

32 Anon., 'Spiritualism and Electromagnetism', www.mathpages.com, accessed 28 March 2019.

33 Conan Doyle, *The History of Spiritualism*, locs 154, 159.

34 C. P. Scheitle, 'Bringing Out the Dead: Gender and Historical Cycles of Spiritualism', *Omega*, L/3 (2004–5), pp. 329–34.

35 See E. Gomel, 'Spirits in the Material World: Spiritualism and Identity in the Fin De Siècle', *Victorian Literature and Culture*, xxxv/1 (2007), pp. 201–2.

36 See B. Bearak, 'Dead Join the Living in a Family Celebration', *New York Times*, 5 September 2010; and A. Bennett, 'When Death Doesn't Mean Goodbye', *National Geographic*, 31 March 2016.

37 See, for an overview of the topic, C. Zaleski, *Other World Journeys: Accounts of Near-death Experiences in Medieval and Modern Times* (Oxford, 1987).

38 'Near-Death Experiences of the Hollywood Rich and Famous', www.near-death.com, accessed 28 March 2019.

39 See S. Taylor, 'Near Death Experience and DMT', *Psychology Today*, 28 October 2018.

40 'Seven Surprising Truths Near-death Experiences Reveal about the Universe', 30 October 2017, https://bibledice.wordpress.com.

41 B. Greyson, 'Near-death Encounters With and Without Near-death Experiences: Comparative NDE Scale Profiles', *Journal of Near-death Studies*, vIII/3 (Spring 1990), pp. 151–61 (p. 157); see also 'The Future and the Near-death Experience', www.near-death.com, accessed 26 March 2019.

42 See www.near-death.com, accessed 28 March 2019.

43 'Most People Believe in Life after Death, Study Finds', *The Telegraph*, 13 April 2018; L. J. Francis and E. Williams, 'Paranormal Belief and the Teenage World View', *Journal of Research on Christian Education*, xvIII/1 (2009), pp. 20–35.

44 D. W. Moore, 'Three in Four Americans Believe in Paranormal', https://news.gallup.com, 16 June 2005.

45 C. Ikonen, 'Michael Jackson Speaks Beyond the Grave to Reveal "Truth about Death"', www.dailystar.co.uk, 24 February 2018.

46 See, for an overview, Francis and Williams, 'Paranormal Belief'.

47 'True Miracle: "Brain Dead" Boy Revives after Parents Sign Consent for Organ Donation', www.rt.com, 7 May 2018.

48 S. Shemer, 'Israeli Scientists Uncover Innovative Method to Read Memories – Even after Death', www.nocamels.com, 16 April 2018. For a more detailed account see D. Mukherjee et al., 'Salient Experiences are Represented by Unique Transcriptional Signatures in the Mouse Brain', *Elife*, 7 February 2018, DOI: 10.7554/eLife.31220.

6 SEARCHING THE HEAVENS

1 See A. Marshack, *The Roots of Civilization: The Cognitive Beginnings of Man's First Art, Symbol and Notation* (London, 1972), p. 81.

2 See J. M. Steele, 'Eclipse Prediction in Mesopotamia', *Archive for the History of Exact Sciences*, LIV/5 (February 2000), pp. 412–54.

3 Quoted in J. L. Cooley, 'Propaganda, Prognostication, and Planets', in *Divination, Politics and Ancient Near-Eastern Empires*, ed. A. Lenzi and J. Stökl (Atlanta, GA, 2014), pp. 7–32.

4 Quoted in F. Rochberg-Halton, 'Elements of the Babylonian Contribution to Hellenistic Astrology', *Journal of the American Oriental Society*, CVIII/1 (March 1988), p. 54.

5 See U. Koch-Westenholz, *Mesopotamian Astrology* (Copenhagen, 1985), p. 13.

6 Josephus, *Jewish Antiquities*, 1.166–8.

7 See, on the various connotations of 'Chaldean', A. Y. Reed, 'Abraham as Chaldean Scientist and Father of the Jews', *Journal for the Study of Judaism*, XXXV/2 (April 2004), pp. 119–58.

8 See J. C. Greenfield and M. Sokoloff, 'Astrological and Related Omen Texts in Jewish Palestinian Aramaic', *Journal of Near Eastern Studies*, XLVIII/3 (July 1989), pp. 201–14.

9 See J.E.S. Thompson, 'Maya Astronomy', *Philosophical Transactions of the Royal Society*, CCLXXVI/1257 (May 1974), pp. 87–8.

10 On Carneades see A. A. Long, 'Astrology: Arguments Pro and Contra', in *Science and Speculation*, ed. J. Banes (Cambridge, 2005), pp. 165–92.

11 On Bardaisan and his essay see Tim Hegedus, 'Necessity and Free Will in the Thought of Bardaisan of Edessa', *Laval théologique et philosophique*, LIX/2 (2003), pp. 333–44. The essay itself is available at www.newadvent.org, accessed 28 March 2019.

12 St Augustine, *Confessions*, 7.6.8.

13 See on this S. J. Tester, *A History of Western Astrology* (Woodbridge, 1987), pp. 151–3.

14 Abu Ma'shar, *The Abbreviation of the Introduction to Astrology*, trans. and ed. C. Burnett et al. (Leiden, 1994).

15 See J. Samso, 'The Early Development of Astrology in al-Andalus', *Journal of the History of Arabic Science*, III (1979), pp. 329–30, at www.medievalists.net, accessed 28 March 2019.

16 According to H. Lemay, 'The Stars and Human Sexuality: Some Medieval Scientific Views', *Isis*, LXXI/256 (March 1980), p. 127 n. 1.

17 Geoffrey Chaucer, 'The Wife of Bath's Prologue', ll. 609–20. See also B. F. Hamlin, 'Astrology and the Wife of Bath: A Repinterpretation', *Chaucer Review*, IX/2 (1974), pp. 153–65.

18 Joseph Crane, 'Chaucer's Wife of Bath Needs a New Astrological Chart', www.astrologyinstitute.com, 20 March 2017.

19 Lemay, 'The Stars and Human Sexuality', p. 133.

20 R. Lewinsohn, *Science, Prophecy and Prediction* (New York, 1961), p. 84.

21 J. S. Lucas, *Astrology and Numerology in Medieval and Early Modern Catalonia* (Leiden, 2003), p. xix.

22 Regiomontanus, 'Oratio Iohannis de Monteregio', *Opera Collectanea*, ed. F. Schmeidler (Osnabrück, 1972), p. 52.

23 Quoted in A. Warburg, *Heidnisch-antike Weissagungen in Wort und Bild zu Luthers Zeiten* (Hamburg, 1919), p. 85.

24 See J.G.H. Hoppman, 'The Lichtenberger Prophecy and Melanchthon's Horoscope for Luther', *Culture and Cosmos*, I/3 (Autumn–Winter 1997), pp. 49–59.

25 D. A. Phllips, *The Complete Book of Numerology* (Kindle edition, 2005), loc. 2545.

26 R. Dunn, 'The True Place of Astrology among the Mathematical Arts of Late Tudor England', *Annals of Science*, LI/2 (1994), pp. 151–63.

27 See for example A. B. Lang et al., 'Activity Levels of Bats and Katydids in Relation to the Lunar Cycle', *Oecologia*, CXLVI/4 (January 2006), pp. 659–66.

28 See D. Lehoux, 'Observation and Prediction in Ancient Astrology', *Studies in the History and Philosophy of Science*, XXXV/2 (June 2004), pp. 227–46.

29 See, out of a vast literature, J. Chotal et al., 'Variations in Personality Traits among Adolescents and Adults According to Their Season of Birth in the General Population', *Elsevier*, XXXV/4 (September 2003), pp. 897–908; and S. Knapton, 'People Born in Summer are Taller than Those with Winter Birthdays', *The Telegraph*, 12 October 2015.

30 Quoted in Tester, *A History of Western Astrology*, pp. 68–9.

31 On Pomponazzi see E. Garin, *Astrology in the Renaissance* (London, 1976), pp. 12–14.

32 W. Soakland, 'Supernova and Nova Explosion's Space Weather', *Journal of Earth Science and Engineering*, VII (2017), pp. 136–53.

33 S. W. Hawking and G. F. Rayner Ellis, *The Large Scale Structure of Space-Time* (Cambridge, 1973), p. 1.

34 W. Shumaker, ed., *John Dee on Astrology: Propaedeumata Aphoristica, 1558–68* (Los Angeles, CA, 1978), pp. 130–31.

35 Brian Baulsom, 'What is the Logic Behind Astrology?', *Quora*, 4.3.2017, www.quora.com, accessed 28 March 2019.

36 G. Dean and A. Mather, eds, *Recent Advances in Natal Astrology: A Critical Review, 1900–1976* (London, 1977), pp. 442–3.

37 N. Campion, 'How Many People Actually Believe in Astrology?', http://theconversation.com, 28 April 2017; B. Hays, 'Majority of Young Adults Think Astrology is a Science', www.upi.com, 12 February 2014; National Science Foundation, 'Chapter 7. Science and Technology: Public Attitudes and Understanding', www.nsf.gov/statistics/seind14, accessed 28 March 2019.

38 According to G. van Rheenen, *Communicating Christ in Animistic Contexts* (Pasadena, CA, 1991), p. 66.

39 See R. Harmanci, 'How Nancy Reagan Became Forever Linked with Astrology', www.atlasobscura.com, 6 March 2016.

40 'Star Wars – the Discount Model', *The Economist*, 8 January 1998, www.economist.com.

7 CLEAR AND MANIFEST

1 Francesca Rochberg, 'Natural Knowledge in Ancient Mesopotamia', in *Wrestling with Nature: From Omens to Science*, ed. Peter Harrison et al. (Chicago, IL, 2011), p. 13.

2 Semonides of Amorgos, 1.1–4.

3 Theognis, 133–6 and 141–2.

4 Thucydides, *The Peloponnesian War*, 5.54.1, 5.55.3, 5.56.1; Xenophon, *Hellenica*, 3.4.3, 3.5.7, 4.7.2, 5.1.3, 5.3.14, 5.4.37, 5.4.47, 6.5.12.

5 Arrian, *Anabasis*, 4.4.3.

6 Cicero, *On Divination*, 1.4.3.

7 Polybius, *The Histories*, 2.17.2 and 9.12–20; Onasander, 25.10.

8 Frontinus, *Stratagemata*, I.11.14–15.

9 Livy, *Roman History*, 43.13.1–2.

10 Suetonius, *Caesar*, 88; Cassius Dio, 45.7.1; Servius, *Commentary on the Aeneid*, 6.81.

11 See R. Lattimore, 'Portents and Prophecies in Connection with the Emperor Vespasian', *Classical Journal*, xxix/6 (March 1934), pp. 441–9.

12 St Augustine, *On Christian Doctrine*, 2.23–4.

13 Einhard, *Vita Caroli*, 32.

14 S. Gerson, *Nostradamus* (Kindle edition, 2012), locs 2096–101.

15 Mario Reading, *Nostradamus: The Complete Prophecies for the Future* (Kindle edition, 2015), locs 28–132.

16 Gerson, *Nostradamus*, loc. 378.

17 Quoted in E. Garin, *Astrology in the Renaissance* (London, 1976), p. 100.

18 Cited in B. Roeck, *Eine Stadt in Krieg und Frieden: Studien zur Geschichte der Reichstadt Augsburg* (Göttingen, 1993), p. 523.

19 S. J. Tester, *A History of Western Astrology* (Woodbridge, 1987), pp. 196–202; as well as J. Thiebault, 'Jeremiah in the Village: Prophecy, Preaching, Pamphlets, and Penance in the Thirty Years' War', *Central European History*, xxvii/4 (1994), pp. 441–60.

20 F. Oberholzner, 'From an Act of God to an Insurable Risk: The Change in the Perception of Hailstorms and Thunderstorms since the Early Modern Period', *Environment and History*, xvii/1 (February 2011), pp. 133–52.

8 ON BIRDS, LIVERS AND SACRIFICES

1 Plato, *Timaeus*, 72b.

2 Homer, *Iliad*, 69–70.

3 Homer, *Odyssey*, 15.493–597.

4 See E. L. Hicks, *The Collection of Ancient Greek Inscriptions in the British Museum* (Oxford, 1896), vol. iii, no. 678.

5 Xenophon, *Anabasis*, 6.1.20.

6 See M. Jastrow, 'The Liver as the Seat of the Soul', in *Studies in the History of Religions*, ed. David Gordon Lyon and George Foot Moore (New York, 1912), p. 143; as well as Mary R. Bachvarova, 'The Transmission of Liver Divination from East to West', *Studi Micenei ed Egeo-Anatolica*, liv (2012), pp. 143–64.

7 Philostratus, *Life of Apolonius*, 8.7.15.

8 Pausanias, *Description of Greece*, 6.2.4; Juvenal, *Satires*, 3.44.

9 W. Burkert, *The Orientalizing Revolution: Near Eastern Influence on Greek Culture in the Early Archaic Age*, trans. M. E. Pinder and W. Burkert (Cambridge, ma, 1992), p. 50.

10 I have used the translation in D. Collins, 'Mapping the Entrails: The Practice of Greek Hepatoscopy', *American Journal of Philology*, CXXIX/3 (September 2008), p. 335.

11 Suetonius, *Caesar*, 81; Plutarch, *Caesar*, 63.5–6.

12 Cicero, *On Divination*, 1.38.82–3.

13 Ammianus Marcelinus, 6.16.

14 Jon G. Abbink, 'Reading the Entrails: Analysis of an African Divination Discourse', *Man*, XXVIII/4 (December 1993), pp. 705–26.

15 Gallup News, 16 June 2005, news.gallup.com, accessed 28 March 2019.

9 THE MAGIC OF NUMBERS

1 See on this entire topic R. C. Archibald, 'Mathematics before the Greeks', *Science*, n. ser., LXXI/1831 (January 1930), pp. 109–21.

2 See Christopher Dunn, *Lost Technologies of Ancient Egypt* (Kindle edition, 2010).

3 On Pythagoras and his followers, see www.storyofmathematics.com, accessed 28 March 2019.

4 English translation in T. Tobias, *Number: The Language of Science* (London, 1930), p. 42.

5 According to D. Grewal, 'People See Odd Numbers as Male, Even as Female', *Scientific American*, 31 August 2011.

6 For a list of the passages in question, see 'Philo Judaeus' at www.newworldencyclopedia.org, accessed 23 June 2019.

7 See W. T. Stace, *A Critical History of Greek Philosophy* [1920] (Kindle edition, 2010), loc. 2348.

8 Plato, *Republic*, 537b–d.

9 Plato, *The Laws*, 5.737–38.

10 See '42 (Number)', at https://en.wikipedia.org, accessed 23 June 2019.

11 Benjamin Jowett in the introduction to his translation of Plato, *The Laws* (Oxford, 1892).

12 See A. F. Stewart, 'The Canon of Polykleitos: A Question of Evidence', *Journal of Hellenic Studies,* XCVII (November 1978), pp. 122–31.

13 Vitruvius, *On Architecture*, 3.1.

14 See for example Piotr Sorokowski and B. Pawlowski, 'Adaptive Preferences for Leg Length in a Potential Partner', *Evolution and Human Behavior*, XXIX/2 (March 2008), pp. 86–91.

15 See, for a description of a few of the things in question, I. Stewart, *The Beauty of Numbers in Nature* (Cambridge, MA, 2017).

16 E. Finn, *What Algorithms Want: Imagination in the Age of Computers* (Kindle edition, 2017), loc. 235.

17 L. Fanthorpe and P. Fanthorpe, *Mysteries and Secrets of Numerology* (Toronto, 2013), p. 28.

18 G. M. Browne, 'The Composition of the *Sortes Astrampsychi*', *Bulletin of the Institute of Classical Studies*, XVII/1 (December 1970), pp. 95–100.

19 See, for a more detailed explanation, https://digitalambler.wordpress.com, accessed 28 March 2019.

20 See, on the Greek origins of Jewish numerology and kabbalah, K. Barry, *The Greek Kabbalah: Alphabetical Mysticism and Numerology in the Ancient World* (York Beach, ME, 1999).

21 N. Bland, 'On the Muhammedan Science of Tâbír, Or Interpretation of Dreams', *Journal of the Royal Asiatic Society of Great Britain and Ireland*, XVI (1856), pp. 139–40.

22 See on this G. A. Miller, 'The Magical Number Seven, Plus or Minus Two', *Psychological Review*, LXIII/2 (March 1956), pp. 81–97; and R. E. Reynolds, '"At Sixes and Sevens" and Eights and Nines: The Sacred Mathematics of Sacred Orders in the Early Middle Ages', *Speculum: Journal of Medieval Studies*, LIV/4 (October 1979), pp. 669–84.

23 See A. Cusimano, 'Importance of Medieval Numerology and the Effects upon Meaning in the Works of the Gawain Poet', MA thesis, University of New Orleans, 2010.

24 'Medieval Numerology: A Brief Guide', https://web.cn.edu, accessed 28 March 2019; C. A. Patrides, 'The Numerological Approach to Cosmic Order during the English Renaissance', *Isis*, XLIX/4 (December 1958), pp. 391–7.

25 R. A. Peck, 'Number as Cosmic Language', in *Essays in the Numerical Criticism of Medieval Literature*, ed. C. D. Eckhardt (London, 1979), p. 17.

26 See J. Edge, 'Licit Medicine or "Pythagorean Necromancy"? The "Sphere of Life and Death" in Late Medieval England', *Historical Research*, LXXXVII/238 (November 2014), pp. 611–32.

27 Lecture to the Institute of Civil Engineers, 3 May 1883, in *Popular Lectures and Addresses* (London, 1889), p. 72.

28 L. D. Balliett, *The Day of Wisdom According to Number Vibration* (Atlantic City, NJ, 1917), pp. 30, 32, 39.

29 J. Williams, *Numerology* (Kindle edition, 2016), passim.

30 'Find Your Master Number', at www.numerology.com, accessed 23 June 2019.

31 D. Sharp, *Simple Numerology* (San Francisco, CA, 2001), back cover.

32 See 'Numerology as Sacred Language and Numbers' Deeper Meanings', www.kasamba.com, accessed 28 March 2019.

33 L. Thomas, 'Numerology', www.leethomas.co.za, accessed 23 June 2019.

34 C. Covell, *Ecstasy: Shamanism in Korea* (Elizabeth, NJ, 1983), pp. 54–5.

35 A. D. Berkowitz, 'Biblical Numerology Predicts Trump Will Usher in Messiah', www.breakingisraelnews.com, 16 May 2016. See also 'The Gematria of Hillary Clinton and Donald Trump', https://mosaicmagazine.com, 25 May 2016.

36 https://en.wikipedia.org/wiki/Yosef_Hayyim, accessed 23 June 2019.

37 D. Haber, 'Foretelling the Future by the Numbers: An Introduction to Arithmancy', www.beyondhogwarts.com, accessed 28 March 2019.

38 Axel Munthe, *The Story of San Michele* (New York, 1929), p. 110.

10 DECODING THE BIBLE

1 See H. J. James, 'From Calabria Cometh the Law', *Mediterranean Historical Review*, xx/2 (December 2005), p. 188.

2 See on this M. Reeves, *The Influence of Prophecy in the Later Middle Ages* (Oxford, 1969), pp. 360–61.

3 See for example 'The Number 666 According to Muslims', https://heavenawaits.wordpress.com, accessed 28 March 2019.

4 See, on Lupton and his successors, D. Brady, '1666: The Year of the Beast', *Bulletin of the John Rylands Library*, LXI/2 (1979), pp. 314–15.

5 For more on the mystical character of seven, see the subcategories under 'Classical World' at https://en.wikipedia.org/wiki/7, and https://en.wikipedia.org/wiki/777, accessed 23 June 2019.

6 L. Linthicum, 'It's Now U.S. Route 491, Not U.S. Route 666', *Albuquerque Journal*, 31 July 2003.

7 See, for an easy explanation of Newton's method, Josh Jones, 'In 1704, Isaac Newton Predicts the World Will End in 2060', www.openculture.com, 14 October 2015.

8 Verses 11:2–3 and 12:6.

9 For this kind of calculation see 'Bible Codes: A Day Can Equal a Year', www.bible-codes.org, accessed 29 March 2019.

10 Gregory of Tours, *The History of the Franks*, 4.16.

11 For example, https://dailyverses.net/random-bible-verse, accessed 29 March 2019.

12 M. Laitman, 'The Ties between Letters, Words, and Numbers', www.kabbalah.info, accessed 28 March 2019.

13 See 'Bible Codes Made Simple', www.biblecodedigest.com, accessed 28 March 2019.

14 C. R. Echelbarger, 'Bible Codes', *The Real Truth*, https://rcg.org, accessed 29 March 2019.

15 See 'Bible Code', http://download.cnet.com, accessed 29 March 2019.

16 On the alleged feats of these two gentlemen, see 'Nathan Jacobi, PhD: Interview – Pt I' and 'Directory of Moshe Aharon Shak's Articles', www.biblecodedigest.com, both accessed 29 March 2019.

17 See on these methods G. Scholem, *Major Trends in Jewish Mysticism* (New York, 1961), p. 100.

18 M. Drosnin, *The Bible Code* (New York, 1997).

19 A. E. Berkowitz, 'North Korea's Nuclear Tests May Set Off Apocalyptic War of Angels, Warns Bible Codes', www.breakingisraelnews.com, 20 March 2017.

20 Ibid.

21 See, for a comparison of the various programs on offer, R. A. Rheinhold, 'Bible Code Software Comparsions,' Prophecy Truths, 1 March 2007, at http://ad2004.com.

22 See, for a short summary of the debate, the subsection 'WRR Authors' of the page 'Bible Code', at https://en.wikipedia.org, accessed 23 June 2019.

11 FROM PATTERNS TO CYCLES

1 G. Santayana, *Reason in Common Sense* (New York, 1905), p. 284.

2 Thucydides, *The Peloponnesian War*, 1.22.

3 See A. H. Bernstein, 'Thucydides and the Teaching of Strategy', *Joint Force Quarterly*, XIV (1996–7), pp. 126–7.

4 J. Needham, *Time and Eastern Man* (London, 1965), Occasional paper No. 21, pp. 8–9; M. F. Lindemans, 'Ragnarok', *Encyclopedia Mythica*, 1997, www.pantheon.org; N. M. Farris, 'Remembering the Future, Anticipating the Past: History, Time, and Cosmology among the Maya of Yucatan', *Comparative Studies in Society and History*, XXIX/3 (July 1987), pp. 566–93.

5 See M. Eliade, *The Myth of the Eternal Return*, trans. Willard R. Trask (Princeton, NJ, 1965), pp. 3–11, 155.

6 L. N. Vodolazhskaya, 'Reconstruction of Vertical and L-shaped Ancient Sundials and Methods for Measuring Time', *Archaeology and Ancient Technologies*, II/2 (August 2014), pp. 1–18.

7 Livy, *History of Rome*, Preface, 4.

8 Marcus Aurelius, *Meditations*, 5.13.

9 See, for a discussion of ancient authors who expressed this view, A. W. Lintott, 'Imperial Expansion and Moral Decline in the Roman Republic', *Historia*, xxi/4 (fourth quarter, 1972), pp. 626–38.

10 William Shakespeare, *Henry v*, iii.6; *King Lear*, ii.2 and iv.7; *As You Like It*, i.2.

11 Quoted in E. Garin, *Astrology in the Renaissance* (London, 1976), p. 99.

12 Aṅguttara-Nikǎya, quoted in R. Hooper, *End of Days: Predictions of the End from Ancient Sources* (Sedona, az, 2011), p. 156.

13 P. Crone, *The Nativist Prophecies of Early Islam* (Cambridge, 2014), pp. 245–7; 'Kalpa (aeon)', https://en.wikipedia.org, accessed 23 June 2019; and Eliade, *Myth of the Eternal Return*, pp. 113–14.

14 Polybius, *The Histories*, 36.17.5–7.

15 Ibid., 5.15.

16 Petronius, *Satyricon*, 116.

17 Julius Caesar, *Commentarii de bello gallico*, 7.13.1.

18 K. van Lommel, 'The Recognition of Roman Soldiers' Mental Impairment', *Acta Classica*, lvi (2013), pp. 155–84.

19 Charles de Montesquieu, *The Spirit of the Laws* (1748), 11.6.

20 Ibid.

21 Charles de Montesquieu, *Considerations on the Causes of the Greatness of the Romans and their Decline* (Ithaca, ny, 1968), introduction.

22 See F. Orestano, 'Picturesque Reconsidered – and Preserved', in *Britain and Italy in the Long Eighteenth Century*, ed. R. Loretelli and F. O'Gorman (Newcastle, 2010), pp. 16–30; and, for Nazi Germany, A. Speer, *Inside the Third Reich*, trans. R. and C. Winston (New York, 1970), pp. 56, 154.

23 See, for the American colonies, S. Persons, 'The Cyclical Theory of History in Eighteenth-century America', *American Quarterly*, vi/2 (Summer 1954), pp. 147–63.

24 T. Barnard, *A Sermon, Delivered on the Day of National Thanksgiving, February 19, 1795* (Salem, ma, 1795), pp. 21–2.

25 See, for the details, S. Zitto, 'Lessons from the Center of the World', *Washington Examiner*, 24 September 2017.

26 See T. Snyder, *The Road to Unfreedom* (Kindle edition, 2018), locs 991, 1002, 1306, 1433.

27 'Second Day after Easter' (1827), http://spenserians.cath.vt.edu, accessed 29 March 2019.

28 William H. McNeill, *Arnold J. Toynbee: A Life* (Oxford, 1989), p. 287.

29 See R. Harris, 'Does Rome's Fate Await the U.S.?', *Mail on Sunday*, 12 October 2003.

30 www.globalfirepower.com, accessed 23 June 2019.

31 Vilfredo Pareto, 'The Circulation of Elites' [1916], in *Theories of Society: Foundations of Modern Sociological Theory*, ed. T. Parsons et al. (Glencoe, IL, 1961), vol. II, pp. 551–7.

32 See, on the way it was done in the early days in particular, W. A. Friedman, *Fortune Tellers: The Story of America's First Economic Forecasters* (Kindle edition, 2014), locs 114–25, 215–319.

33 J. C. Ott, *When Wall Street Met Main Street* (Cambridge, MA, 2011), p. 2.

34 D. Izraeli, 'The Three Wheels of Retailing', *European Journal of Marketing*, VII/1 (1973), pp. 70–74.

35 See on this problem D. Coyle, *GDP: A Brief but Affectionate History* (Kindle edition, 2014), passim.

36 I. Petev, L. Pistaferri and I. S. Eksten, 'Consumption and the Great Recession', Stanford, CA, 2011, www.tau.ac.il, accessed 29 March 2019.

37 M. Gorbanev, 'Sunspots, Unemployment, and Recessions', *MPRA*, 2012, https://mpra.ub.uni-muenchen.de.

38 See for example P. Schwartz, *The Long Boom: The Coming Age of Prosperity* (New York, 1999), as well as H. Kahn, *The Coming Boom: Economic, Political, and Social* (New York, 1982).

12 WITH HEGEL ON THE BRAIN

1 For the Jewish invention of linear history see G. J. Whitrow, *Time in History: Views of Time from Prehistory to the Present Day* (Oxford, 1988), pp. 51–2, 55. Also, in more popular form, T. Cahill, *The Gifts of the Jews: How a Tribe of Desert Nomads Changed the Way Everyone Thinks and Feels* (New York, 1999).

2 Quoted in Whitrow, *Time in History*, p. 47, n. 15.

3 See, for the evidence, D. N. McCloskey, *Bourgeois Equality: How Ideas, Not Capital or Institutions, Enriched the World* (Kindle edition, 2017), locs 735–2185.

4 D. S. Landes, *Revolution in Time* (Cambridge, 1983), p. 231.

5 See on this G. S. Stent, *Paradoxes of Progress* (San Francisco, CA, 1979), pp. 28, 31–2.

6 H. G. Wells, *An Experiment in Autobiography* (London, 1934), vol. II, p. 645.

7 J.M.F., 'What Are Bellwether Counties and Can They Actually Predict Elections?', *The Economist*, 6 November 2016, www.economist.com.

8 See on this particular disputation D. E. Luscombe, *Peter Abelard's Ethics* (Oxford, 1971), pp. 55–7.

9 See, for a good explanation of Hegel's system, N. G. Limnatis, *The Dimensions of Hegel's Dialectics* (London, 2010).

10 A. Woods and T. Grant, *Reason in Revolt: Marxist Philosophy and Modern Science* [1995] (Kindle edition, 2015), loc. 2102.

11 On *Aufhebung* see W. Kaufman, *Hegel: A Reinterpretation* (New York, 1966), p. 144.

12 G.W.F. Hegel, *The Philosophy of History* [1837] (Kindle edition, 2010), loc. 1520.

13 See on this P. Paolucci, *Marx's Scientific Dialectics: A Methodological Treatise for a New Century* (Leiden, 2007), esp. pp. 69–206.

14 K. Marx, *Capital* [1867] (London, 2016), p. 19.

15 Karl Marx, 'Estranged Labor', *Economic and Philosophical Manuscripts of 1844*, www.marxists.org, accessed 29 March 2019.

16 V. I. Lenin, 'Prophetic Words' [29 June 1918], www.marxists.org, accessed 29 March 2019.

17 Francis Fukuyama, 'The End of History?', *National Interest*, xvi (Summer 1989), pp. 1–18.

18 R. Lydall, 'Revealed: How the Average Speed of Traffic in London Has Plummeted to Just 7.8 Miles per Hour', *Evening Standard*, 9 December 2016, www.standard.co.uk.

19 See for example M. K. Dodo, 'My Theory on the Trump Phenomenon', *Journal of Alternative Perspectives in the Social Sciences*, vii/4 (2016), pp. 593–661.

20 Karl Marx, 'The Eighteenth Brumaire of Louis Napoleon' [1852], www.marxists.org, accessed 29 March 2019, p. 1.

13 ASK, AND YOU'LL BE ANSWERED

1 D. Slider, 'Party-Sponsored Public Opinion Research in the Soviet Union', *Journal of Politics*, xlvii/1 (February 1985), pp. 209–27.

2 'What the Future of Online Surveys Looks Like', www.surveypolice.com, 7 October 2016.

3 N. Silver, 'Google or Gallup? Changes in Voters' Habits Reshape Polling World', *New York Times*, 11 November 2012, www.nytimes.com.

4 See E. Siegel, 'The Science of Error: How Polling Botched the 2016 Election', *Forbes*, 9 November 2016, www.forbes.com.

5 See P. Squire, 'Why the 1936 Literary Digest Poll Failed', *Public Opinion Quarterly*, LII/1 (Spring 1988), pp. 125–33.

6 R. Poynter, 'No Surveys in Twenty Years?', http://thefutureplace. typepad.com, 24 March 2010.

7 See B. Clark, 'Facebook and Cambridge Analytica', https://thenextweb. com, 21 March 2018.

8 See, on the way it is done, J. Landeta, 'Current Validity of the Delphi Method in Social Sciences', *Technological Forecasting and Social Change*, LXXIII/5 (June 2006), pp. 467–82.

9 B. Schwarz et al., *Methods in Future Studies* (Boulder, CO, 1982), pp. 12–14.

10 Y. Dror, *The Prediction of Political Feasibility* (Santa Monica, CA, 1969), passim. Also, in much greater detail, G. J. Skulmoski, F. T. Hartman and J. Krahn, 'The Delphi Method for Graduate Research', *Journal of Information Technology Education*, VI (2007), pp. 1–21.

11 R. Lewinsohn, *Science, Prophecy and Prediction* (New York, 1961), pp. 137–8.

12 See P. E. Tetlock and D. Gardner, *Superforecasting: The Art and Science of Prediction* (Portland, OR, 2013).

13 See J. Achenbach, 'Analysis: Obama Makes Decisions Slowly, and with Head, Not Gut', *Washington Post*, 25 November 2009.

14 See R. Haskins and R. Margolis, *Show Me the Evidence: Obama's Fight for Rigor and Results* (Washington, DC, 2014).

14 THE MOST POWERFUL TOOLS

1 See B. Frier, 'Roman Life Expectancy: Ulpian's Evidence', *Harvard Studies in Classical Philology*, LXXXVI (1982), pp. 213–51.

2 C. Klosterman, *But What If We're Wrong? Thinking about the Present As If It Were the Past* (Kindle edition, 2016), loc. 1389.

3 Muhammad Imdad Ullah, 'The Word Statistics was First Used by a German Scholar, Gotfried Achenwall: Introduction to Statistics', http://itfeature.com, 26 February 2012.

4 H. T. Buckle, 'History and the Operation of Universal Laws' [1856], in *Theories of History*, ed. P. L. Gardiner (New York, 1959), pp. 114–16.

5 L. H. Tribe, 'Mathematics: Precision and Ritual in the Legal Process', *Harvard Law Review*, LXXXIV/6 (April 1971), pp. 1329–93.

6 See on this M. Campbell-Kelly and M. Croaken, eds, *The History of Mathematical Tables: From Sumer to Spreadsheets* (Oxford, 2003), p. 10.

7 See, for a description of MONIAC, K. Vela Vilupillai, 'Introduction to the Phillips Machine and the Analogue Computing Tradition in Economics', Department of Economics, University of Trento, discussion paper, December 2010, at https://core.ac.uk/reader/6610489.

8 C. McKenzie, 'Has Computer Programming Really Changed Much Since Lovelace's Time?', www.theserverside.com, January 2012.

15 WAR GAMES HERE, WAR GAMES THERE

1 See, on much of what follows, M. van Creveld, *Wargames: From Gladiators to Gigabytes* (Cambridge, 2013).

2 See, for the nature of strategy, the classic discussion in E. N. Luttwak, *Strategy: The Logic of War and Peace* (Cambridge, MA, 1987), pp. 3–68.

3 See, for anthropologists' descriptions of such games, R. M. Berndt, 'Warfare in the New Guinea Highlands', *American Anthropologist*, new ser., LXIV/4:2 (August 1964), p. 183; W. Lloyd Warner, *A Black Civilization: A Social Study of an Australian Tribe* (New York, 1937), pp. 174–6; and K. F. Otterbein, 'Higi Armed Combat', *Southwestern Journal of Anthropology*, XXIV/2 (Summer 1968), pp. 202–3.

4 Juvenal, *Satires*, 10.81.

5 See, for the political uses of the games, O. Hekster, *Commodus: An Emperor at the Crossroads* (Amsterdam, 2002), pp. 128–9, 138–50.

6 Tacitus, *Annals*, 13.25.

7 Jean le Bel, *Chronique* [1904], ed. J. Viard and E. Déprez (Adamant, 2005), vol. II, p. 35.

8 See, for the German manoeuvres of 1937, F. Halder, 'Warum Manöver?', *Die Wehrmacht*, 28 September 1937; and, for the American ones of 1940–41, P. Lauterborn, 'Louisiana Maneuvers (1940–1941)', www.historynet.com, 25 November 2008.

9 See S. B. Patrick, 'The History of Wargaming', in *Wargame Design*, ed. staff of the *Strategy and Tactics* magazine (New York, 1983), pp. 30–44; also N. Palmer, *The Comprehensive Guide to Wargaming* (New York, 1977), pp. 13–17.

10 See, for an English translation of the original instructions for the game, by von Reisswitz, *Kriegsspiel: Instructions for the Representation of Military Maneuvers with the Kriegsspiel Apparatus*', trans. Bill Leeson, [1824] (Hemel Hempstead, 1983).

11 Matthew Handrahan, 'Wargaming Looks toward $200 Billion Industry Revenue', www.gamesindustry.biz, 25 September 2013.

12 T. Zuber, *Inventing the Schlieffen Plan: German War Planning, 1871–1914* (Oxford, 2002), pp. 145–9.

13 See the account of the 1894 game in particular as printed in Generalstab des Heeres, ed., *Die Grossen Generalstabsreisen – Ost – aus den Jahren 1891–1905* (Berlin, 1938), pp. 1–50.

14 See, on war gaming the invasion of the USSR, R. Hofmann, *German Army War Games* (Carlisle Barracks, PA, 1983), pp. 37–66; and B. I. Fugate, *Operation Barbarossa: Strategy and Tactics on the Eastern Front, 1941* (Novato, CA, 1984), p. 73.

15 See, on the war games held before Pearl Harbor, R. Wohlstetter, *Pearl Harbor: Warning and Decision* (Stanford, CA, 1962), pp. 355–7, 377, and on those that preceded Midway, A. P. Tully, *Shattered Sword: The Untold Story of the Battle of Midway* (Washington, DC, 2005), pp. 61–2, 67, 410.

16 See, for what one war gaming firm claims it can offer, John E. Treat, G. E. Thibault and A. Asin, 'Dynamic Competitive Simulation: Wargaming as a Strategic Tool', *Strategy + Business*, 3 (second quarter, 1996), at www.strategy-business.com, 1 April 1996.

17 On this method and the way it was (and is) done, see William M. Jones, *On Free-form Gaming* (Santa Monica, CA, 1985), passim, at www.rc.rand.org, accessed 31 March 2019; S. Ghamari-Tabrizi, 'Simulating the Unthinkable: Gaming Future War in the 1950s and 1960s', *Social Studies of Science*, xxx/2 (April 2000), pp. 172–6; and S. F. Griffin, *The Crisis Game* (Garden City, NY, 1965), pp. 71–86.

18 T. B. Allen, *War Games* (New York, 1987), pp. 196–7.

19 See, for the details, R. Todd, 'War Games in '99 Predicted Iraq Problems', www.cbsnews.com, 5 November 2006.

16 LOOKING BACKWARDS

1 Reuters, 'Former Greek Statistics Chief Found Guilty of Breach of Duty', www.reuters.com, 1 August 2017.

2 See M. Heyd, *'Be Sober and Reasonable': The Critique of Enthusiasm in the Seventeenth and Early Eighteenth Centuries* (Leiden, 1995).

3 See B. S. Turner, ed., *From Max Weber: Essays in Sociology* [1921] (Oxford, 1958), pp. 196–245.

4 Tertullian, *De Carne Christi*, 5.

5 P. Marinova, 'These Execs Say Psychics are Helping Them Make a Fortune', www.fortune.com, 21 September 2015; N. Squires, 'Boom Time for Fortune-tellers and Tarot Card Readers in Italy as Economic Crisis Bites', *The Telegraph*, 2 October 2017, www.telegraph.co.uk.

6 T. Segev, *David Ben Gurion: A State at All Costs* [in Hebrew] (Tel Aviv, 2018), p. 635.

7 See, on the way the models are applied as well as some of the social effects, C. O'Neil, *Weapons of Math Destruction: How Big Data Increases Inequality and Threatens Democracy* (London, 2016), passim.

8 A. R. Wallace, *Miracles and Modern Spiritualism* (London, 1881), p. 1.

17 WHY IS PREDICTION SO DIFFICULT?

1 See N. N. Taleb, *The Black Swan: The Impact of the Highly Improbable* (New York, 2010).

2 L. Ragnhild Sjursen, 'Studying Shooting Stars to Improve Weather Prediction', http://sciencenordic.com, 29 October 2014.

3 See, above all, R. J. Geller et al., 'Earthquakes Cannot Be Predicted', *Science*, CCLXXV/5306 (14 March 1997), p. 1616.

4 J. Locke, *An Essay Concerning Human Understanding* [1689] (London, 1998), 2.1.

5 F. Nietzsche, *The Gay Science* [1882] (New York, 1974), sec. 92.

6 See R. Sapolsky, *Behave: The Biology of Humans at Our Best and Worst* (Kindle edition, 2018), locs 518, 22, 531–41, 2159–362.

7 See D. Kahneman, *Thinking Fast, Thinking Slow* (New York, 2013), pp. 79–88.

8 N. Byrnes, 'As Goldman Sachs Embraces Automation, Even the Masters of the Universe Are Threatened', www.technologyreview.com, 7 February 2017.

9 J. Folger, 'Automated Trading Systems: The Pros and Cons', www.investopedia.com, 12 May 2019.

10 G. Cespa and X. Vives, 'High Frequency Trading and Fragility', *European Central Bank Working Paper Series 2020*, www.ecb.europa.eu, February 2017.

11 B. Russell, *Our Knowledge of the External World* [1914] (London, 1993), pp. 159–89.

12 See on this debate R. Lucas, *The Future: An Essay on God, Temporality and Truth* (Oxford, 1989), pp. 1–4.

13 G. W. von Goethe, *Faust*, 1.1112.

14 P.-S. Laplace, *A Philosophical Essay on Probabilities* [1825], trans. F. W. Truscott (New York, 1902), p. 4.

15 See 'The Uncertainty Principle', *Stanford Encyclopedia of Philosophy*, https://plato.stanford.edu, 12 July 2016; Weizmann Institute of

Science, 'Quantum Theory Demonstrated: Observation Affects Reality', www.sciencedaily.com, 27 February 1998; and C. Wendt, 'What Are the New Implications of Chaos for Unpredictability?', *British Journal for the Philosophy of Science*, LX/1 (2009), pp. 195–220.

16 See, for a popular explanation of the idea, G. Musser, 'Is the Cosmos Random?', *Scientific American*, CCCXIII/3 (September 2015), pp. 88–93.

17 'Tiny Particles Have Outsize Impact on Storm Clouds and Precipitation', www.sciencedaily.com, 25 January 2018.

18 See, on this lack of success, Sapolsky, *Behave*, locs 9365, 9423–9, 9438–99, 9646.

19 See, for what follows, P. E. Tetlock and D. Gardner, *Superforecasting: The Art and Science of Prediction* (Portland, OR, 2013), passim.

20 Nietzsche, *The Gay Science*, sec. 285 and 341; *Repetition and Notes on the Eternal Recurrence*, in *The Complete Works of Friedrich Nietzsche* [1915], ed. O. Levy (n.p., 2017), vol. XVI.

21 F. Nietzsche, *The Gay Science* [1882], book 4, section 341, available at https://theanarchistlibrary.org, accessed 18 December 2019.

22 See, for a partial list of such visions, 'List of Predictions of the End of the Word', https://rationalwiki.org, accessed 25 June 2019.

23 R. Luxemburg, *The Accumulation of Capital* [1913], trans. A. Schwarzschild (London, 1951), pp. 364–5.

24 A. Wood and T. Grant, *Reason in Revolt: Marxist Philosophy and Modern Science* (Kindle edition, 2015), loc. 363.

25 *Bulletin of the Atomic Scientists*, 2017, https://thebulletin.org/doomsday-dashboard.

26 Herodian, *Roman History*, 4.12–14.

27 See A. G. Greenwald et al., 'Increasing Voting Behavior by Asking People if they Expect to Vote', *Journal of Applied Psychology*, LXXII/2 (May 1987), pp. 315–18.

28 See C. Holtz-Bacha and J. Strömbäck, eds, *Opinion Polls and the Media* (London, 2012), esp. pp. 225–81.

29 F. Lugo and others, 'Herding Behavior and Rating Convergence among Credit Rating Agencies: Evidence from the Subprime Crisis', *Review of Finance*, XIX/4 (July 2015), pp. 1703–31.

30 H. E. Kimmel, *Admiral Kimmel's Story* (Washington, DC, 1955).

18 IS OUR GAME IMPROVING?

1 See for example H. Rosa, 'Social Acceleration', *Constellations*, X/1 (April 2003), pp. 3–33.

2 Plutarch, *Crassus*, 7.3.
3 Herodotus, *The Histories*, 7.27–9.

19 A WORLD WITHOUT UNCERTAINTY?

1 J. R. Elton, *Return to Essentials: Some Reflections on the Present State of Historical Study* (Cambridge, 1991), p. 8.
2 See, for a good overview of the idea, 'Course in General Linguistics', at https://en.wikipedia.org, accessed 26 June 2019.

FURTHER READING

Blenkinsop, Joseph, *A History of Prophecy in Israel* (London, 1996)

Eliade, Mircea, *Shamanism: Archaic Techniques of Ecstasy* [1951], trans. Willard R. Trask (Princeton, NJ, 1972)

——, *The Myth of the Eternal Return*, trans. Willard R. Trask (Princeton, NJ, 1965)

Friedman, Walter A., *Fortune Tellers: The Story of America's First Economic Forecasters* (Princeton, NJ, 2016)

Garin, Eugenio, *Astrology in the Renaissance: The Zodiac of Life* (London, 1976)

Gerson, Stéphane, *Nostradamus: How an Obscure Renaissance Astrologer Became the Modern Prophet of Doom* (London, 2012)

Lenzi, Alan, and Jonathan Stökl, eds, *Divination, Politics and Ancient Near-Eastern Empires* (Atlanta, GA, 2014)

Lewinsohn, Richard, *Science, Prophecy and Prediction* (New York, 1961)

Miller, Patricia C., *Dreams in Late Antiquity* (Princeton, NJ, 1998)

Ogden, Daniel, *Greek and Roman Necromancy* (Princeton, NJ, 2001)

Reeves, Marjorie, *The Influence of Prophecy in the Later Middle Ages: A Study in Joachimism* (Oxford, 1969)

Taleb, Nassim N., *The Black Swan: The Impact of the Highly Improbable* (New York, 2010)

Tester, S. J., *A History of Western Astrology* (Woodbridge, 1987)

Tetlock, Philip E., and Dan Gardner, *Superforecasting: The Art and Science of Prediction* (Portland, OR, 2013)

Whitrow, Gerald James, *Time in History* (Oxford, 1988)

ACKNOWLEDGEMENTS

I wish to express my thanks to those who, wittingly or unwittingly, helped me with the present enquiry, the most difficult one I have ever undertaken. The immediate members of my family apart from the most important ones are Mr Thorsten Bruckner, Colonel (ret.) Dr Moshe Ben-David, Mr Larry Kummer, Mr Moritz Schwarz, General (ret.) Erich Vad and Prof. Avihu Zakai. All are fine intellectuals in their own right. And all, thank goodness, are always ready to listen to my ramblings, however confused they may be. Another is Ms Luise Vad, who gave me my first opportunity to present my ideas to a small but very select audience; still another, Drora Levanon, an old, old friend who kept asking pertinent questions.

What shall I say? Bless you all.

INDEX